Cold Cold Heart

A Heart and Soul Story

JOHN LEO ORGAN

 FriesenPress

Suite 300 - 990 Fort St
Victoria, BC, V8V 3K2
Canada

www.friesenpress.com

Copyright © 2020 by John Leo Organ
First Edition — 2020

All names have been changed to protect the innocent.

ISBN
978-1-5255-7314-9 (Hardcover)
978-1-5255-7315-6 (Paperback)
978-1-5255-7316-3 (eBook)

1. BIOGRAPHY & AUTOBIOGRAPHY, ENTERTAINMENT & PERFORMING ARTS

Distributed to the trade by The Ingram Book Company

This book is dedicated to everyone in it.

Table of Contents

Disclaimer:

Some names and identifying details have been changed to protect the privacy of individuals.

I have tried to recreate events, locales and conversations from my memories of them. In order to maintain their anonymity in some instances I have changed the names of individuals and places, I may have changed some identifying characteristics and details such as physical properties, occupations, and places of residence.

This book is based on actual events. However, some of the characters, incidents portrayed and names are fictitious and any similarity of such to the name, character, or history of any actual person is entirely coincidental and unintentional.

Note To All et You;

Visit me on my web page (use the top browser) at:
Go to Youtube, and in the top bar type in: john-organ. rocks, and click. When the next page comes up, scroll down until you come to: John Organ- Topic, and click on it, to find my songs. I have recorded another couple hundred songs that I will post for Your enjoyment when I am finished this tablet in e-stone. I wrote them with Everybody in Mind. Enjoy! John

Forward

July is when Tourists flock to the Lake. Short, cold days in winter conjures images of hibernating shadows, curling up around fires until the next day, which will be about a minute longer of light and life. Deep down, we know that it's not how many minutes you have, as much as what you do with them. It's simply a sin to waste a day in a time-monitored existence like life! I do my best to complete each day effectuated and fulfilled. I trade my minutes for gratifications that make life worthy. We all do, in our own ways.

The Lake is Life, and it is a giving entity. Every time I visit the aqueous glass surface, I take down a soul in need of replenishment, and leave with a new song, or two. This July morning was no different; I borrowed from Her waves and floated in Her currents. Sunning off on the dock, dripping in the silent warmth, I suddenly heard the calamity of a stone hammer colliding with a steel pipe, banging over and over.

The gentleness that had washed my clogged mind clean was suddenly replaced with the rhythmic beat of mechanical noises, pushing away the peace on the shore, and in my eyes. I thought of prison gangs on hot summer mornings, breaking rocks with their sledge hammers. Or perhaps the banging on a singular, rusty chain; for one that escaped on his way to a fascinating, yet frightening freedom. Maybe this banging was in time with a hydraulic punch in a car factory, waiting to discharge its poisons into Lake Michigan. I mused out loud, but to no one in particular, "What a ton of noise!" On this dreamy Lake I decided it sounded more like a Ton of Pain, and on cue, my fingers scribbled;

A Ton of Pain

Two thousand pounds; just insane,
Two thousand pounds, a ton of pain.
Weight on my shoulders; slidin' in the rain
Sweat and mud; and a ton of pain.
Chorus:
Temples splittin' my head feels broke
Make it a double and a med-weed toke.
Sky's fallin' to which I was chained;
Two thousand pounds and a ton of pain!

I jumped in the canoe and worked out the melody, with the paddles keeping time. I finished the words, and looked up to witness that I was closer to the distant shore than was near home, so I kept paddling northerly. I began to build up an honest Artist's sweat. I dispelled rowing, and just floated toward the alien shore. It was promising to be a 'hot one', and no one was lying. I sat back, thinking how I had left abruptly, and now I had nothing to drink. It was only noon, but I was day-dreaming of a cold Moosehead frosty.

Luckily for me, the Lake was in a giving mood, and she warbled me with surrounding cant-illative chants of the heat bugs, out basking in the sun. They were frying in full frolic, and I began to scratch, scrawl, and squiggle words to one of our favorite and soothing sounds of summer. Sounds that remind us we are mere amusement to the Gods of Heat. I floated along the shoreline, between satire and sadness, composing my feelings, but with nothing to drink in the hot noon hour sun. I mused that even a cool breeze would help my ease, and then substantiated that in my ballad, which I baptised, 'Lookin' for a Cool Breeze'…

Gazin' out the window (listening)
To cicada's serenading tease,
Diamond Back squints in the sun

Lookin' for a Cool Breeze!
Hydro wires singin' sweetly
Wavy lines on the horizon,
Rays goin' all the way
Night time brings on compromisin'.

Moppin' off my brow
Like I got no immunity,
Like an afternoon on Venice
Fraternity of lunacy!
I can't leave my shady nook
Birds can't leave their trees,
Chillin' out hangin' back
Lookin' for a cool breeze.

Chorus:
Empty sails are thirsty,
Silent chimes frozen still,
Abandoned kites lie stranded;
No moans from tired windmills.
Let the Wind Dancers out!
Have the Rain Dancers appease,
Make it whistle 'tween my teeth;
Lookin' for a cool breeze!

I continued scribbling my songs as I drifted past a Tourist who was stretched out in a lawn chair, looking nonchalant on his dock, while bobbing up and down with the waves. He inquired as I glided by,
"What cha writin?"

I confessed that I had just drafted two songs on the way across the Lake. He asked me if they were any good. Always ready to barter with day-trippers, I said, "Ya wanna hear them?"

3

He grinned absently and said "Ok."

I noticed he was drinking a Heineken, so I told him it might cost him a beer. He obliged, and I did my part, and sang about my 'Ton of Pain'. His wife, and another couple, came over and they expressed their 'satisfaction' with my ballad. I told them I had another, and they hustled up another cold Heine for my brooding thirst. When I was finished they applauded. It made my day. That's what us Starving Artists live on; approbation, endorsement, and the odd cold beer!

I now paddled back to the south side of the Lake, with two new songs, an alleviated pallet, and an idea! For years, when I shared my latest escapades, I have been prompted and prodded to write them in a memoir. I meandered up to the cabin, guzzled a cold Moosehead, sat down, and wrote the first chapter of what I suddenly realized was my diary, or journal, or maybe just my confession. I put it away until October, when it leapt out at me one day as I was looking up a song to rehearse. I sat down and continued writing it, daily, until it was completed, on the first of January, 2020. As I now read my ramblings, some of these adventures still have me howling at gripping and engrossing memories. I'm satisfied and spirited to share them with you; the Unknown and Unsuspecting. I hope yo'all have as much fun reading these stories, as I did remembering and regurgitating them. Enjoy!

Chapter 1
Jack

I was born John Leo Organ @ 1:43 a.m., December 31rst, still being the year of 1956. Fifty six happens to be my favorite number. But the Powers that Be wrote on my Birth Certificate that I was born at 10:30 pm, on the thirtieth. Apparently that was when the Doctor in Charge had signed out and gone home, as my birth was not yet imminent, in his opinion. This was the First Day of my labyrinthine and constantly convoluted existence. That same evening, every potato in my Fathers cold steel storage barn froze. Life smiled, and offered me Its Cold, Cold Heart.

My first real recollections of 'Me' were mainly with the family pooch, sitting under the kitchen table. We had enough space down under there to sort out, and share, the common rights and understandings of our *Existence Together.* Our first agreement, in our laissez faire *existence,* was that *nothing* that fell on the floor during the next meal was for the Cats. Anyways, there were always too many Felines around for a fair, two sided, conversation with one carnivorous Canine.

I've always admired the way Dogs stake their claim on the turf, and will fight for it, down to the last kibble. But at their best, Cats just do that e*lastic stretch* thing, on the edge of any surface, in a seductive prowess, while conning everybody to be their slave, and forfeit our valuable territories to them. And they get away with it, even though in some Arabian countries, they're looked upon as mere long haired rats! Even worse, they carry the aura of being, 'One of Those', that are not to be contended with without an appointment. I mean, other than posing, what did they contribute to the society that we had constructed, safely hidden under the kitchen table? Still, they lazily lounged about, with no conviction of their pussy-dogmas and pseudo sensualities that anyways are more befitting Royalty, than mere mousers.

My *under-the-table* best buddy was named Jack. Meanwhile, below the 49th parallel, John Fitzgerald Kennedy was President at the time, and my dad, Bud, called me Jack. As I aforementioned, we Jacks had an understanding; a partnership, a bond between us. We were like mates who have gone through an incredible a*dventure* together, or a hardship, like that dude, Robert Falcon Scott, who wandered off into the snow on his troop's journey to the South Pole, as to not hold things up.

Or perhaps it was more like the fellowship forged in a war! Or perchance, when you and your beguiled mates endured the same horrific Science Teacher together, for a semester of *true hell and high water* experiences! Such gruesome and grisly tales that are best left for dusky corners at selective cocktail parties, thirty years later, when the scars are worn for fashion rather than first reactions. These ancient, ghastly narratives are now muttered in a contemporary point of view, where space and time are just waiting to repeat themselves, anyways. A dark place, where you don't have the fears, or tears, left in your soul, because it's true; Time heals all, unless of course you're Richard Nixon.

All of this aside, Jack was my first Ally; my first Confident. My first Friend! But Jack was forced to sleep outside at night. I don't mean the only friend I ever had that slept outside, I mean, he was my first Friend, and he slept outside. I somehow couldn't work out a deal for him to sleep in my room, even though I knew all the *Big Wigs* on my warm side of the door. They simply would not listen to me, or take me serious, that a 'mutt' would sleep inside. They deduced he should be outside roaming the cold darkness, protecting us against what, the night? Against the Cats I guess.

It seemed, to me at least, something like a great injustice was being portrayed against a Great Dog Artist. I saw the look in his frozen eyes each morning when he came in to thaw out. He would have that far-away stare of a *hard core survivor;* like Leadbelly, or Robert Johnson, who were caboose-riding in die-heart times of dust and cold, huddling from winds with fatigued, red eyes. And no shoes, because somebody 'borrowed' them on that last B&O run, when nobody was lookin', and time seemed forever.

I came down for breakfast one suspicious September morn, and found myself about to start grade one at Flamborough Center School, two miles away. This was just after Labour Day weekend, in 1961; a date that will go down as, "a day which will live in infamy." And Mrs. Sleeve was to be my Teacher! She was expected to teach me, and twenty-five other infantile students, to read, add, subtract, reason, judge right from wrong, recite the alphabet, to distinguish good from bad, to hold our heads high, to learn to respect the future carefully, and to try and understand decisions that we didn't necessarily agree with. She was trusted to design us to embrace the *coming year,* and to prepare us to manifest the life we desired, divinely. She filled many roles, and holes, from the psyches of our everyday lives. Today, she would probably be considered *politically incorrect,* or *whatever.* Her immediate goal was just to get us to 1962.

Mrs. Sleeve also used to cut my hair, 'Opie Taylor style', in the kitchen of her house in the small town of Flamborough Center. She was my mother's chosen 'babysitter' for me and my almost twin sister, Marilyn. My mother, Regina, was now working full time in the Butcher Shop that Bud had just opened on his farm. They both had become slaves to making it work, which meant long hours, and new perspectives. But that's how successful businesses are started. Accordingly, they were slaves to the Butcher Business for twenty-five years. My father didn't mind. It got him out of the house. He cut his black crop of hair into a brush-cut, for the rest of his life.

He also jumped right into a never ending daily routine of buying cattle, planting fields, and feeding and caring for his herd until they were eventually taken to the Slaughter House. He then cut up the carcasses, packaged them, and delivered these customized orders of beef to customers who did not want to trust their shopping to supermarkets in the city. Now this was the early Sixties, and certain factions in Society had started revealing facts about poisons and additives in our everyday foods. They were also ahead of their time, warning about the environmental distresses on the land. Anyways, who could you trust more than Bud Organ?

Meanwhile, down south, an Irish Jack Kennedy was in the White House, and we were living in Camelot because of this! I never told my parents, but Mrs. Sleeve used to keep her horse in the kitchen. It would mosey in and out as I was eating, or getting a haircut. Now this was something that you wouldn't even see on TV, like on the Andy Griffiths show in Mayberry RFD, South Carolina. Southern characters like Gomer and Goober often left us suspiciously wondering where their strange antics would have led them in life, if they weren't coddled by such a loveable community, with a Sheriff that was one part Southerner, two parts Guru and three parts Humanitarian.

These Mayberrians lived in simpler times that seemed more similar to 1861 than 1961. But the influence of good people, all around them, protected and guided them in their everyday lives. This was what Mrs. Sleeve's kitchen was like for me. But this also was a simpler time, so it was no one's business what she kept in her kitchen. Just like the way no one worried about what ol' Gome & Goob did in their spare times after closing their garage. When the orange sky slid into darkness, we all went to sleep, and did not dream of another day until it was upon us. It was God's will. We were living the good life. We were truly embracing our *manifest journeys* divinely.

One busy morning I came downstairs to the kitchen, for another ominous breakfast. There was a feeling in the air that made me realize something was *ajar*. My Irish eyes weren't smiling as they darted right to left, left to right, and then cross-eyed. I didn't see Jack, and I had things to discuss with him. And stuff to put in his Stash! Seeing my inquisitive eyes, Regina informed me *he* wasn't there, and then slid into the pantry to prepare breakfasts and lunches for five sleepy, hungry kids; in God's Country. I had to ask my older sister, Mary, where Jack was. She informed me that he was ejected from the kitchen, and my life, for leaving a deposit beneath the table, that no one expected, or appreciated. To me, there was no rationale for this. But my parents had acted according to their beliefs. Apparently there were no missed or misguiding facts, nor any contributing circumstances that were overlooked in their time of reckoning.

I was reasoning like Perry Mason in my astonished and appalled mind. Why, Jack had no priors to date! There had to be a reason for this astute atrocity under the table. Maybe Jack's lack of an opposing thumb left him unable to open the door. Maybe he was over fed? Perhaps he was sick. Maybe he knew something we didn't… Maybe it was the Cats! Yea, all of them! I'll back Jack up… they were always plotting against him! They were always giving him that *sinister stare* out of the corners of their eyes, day and night. Anyway, who would I now feed underneath the table? And who would I discuss my *daily strategies* with? Or debate crummy house rules with? So who would now sleep outside? And who could I plot against the Cats with? So who would I now be Friends with? I told my mother that Mrs. Sleeve let her horse live in the kitchen, and I reasoned that horse poops were much more of a *ta-doo* than Jack's small mistake. It was explained to me that Jack was taken to the Dog Pound, and *he* wouldn't be coming back.

I waited ten years before Steinbeck gave me some insight on what had happened on this cold morning, when I read,

"Cane rose up his against his brother Able and slew him. And Cane went away and dwelt in the land of Nod on the east of Eden. Now why don't you go away someplace?"

I was going to Nod to meet Jack there!

Sasha

At Flamborough Center School, Sasha Heartly always seemed to put a twinkle in my eyes. The only thing I could compare it to was when I stayed too long behind the big glass plates that were erected for the cold *Winter Trots* at Woodbine and Greenwood Horse Racing Tracks. The Woodbine Track was in Toronto, for the betting man. Greenwood was out in the sticks, for the farmers who had used horses to plough the fields in their younger days of vigor and vinegar, veracity and virginity, and vivid vulgarity after a few hoisted at the Kirk House Hotel. I remember I would be floating on a cloud of second hand smoke for a few races, as my eyes would suddenly see pink streams, then crimson blood-red spots, and finally blinding black blotches against the sky, until there was only darkness.

I would then pass out from the thick streams of burnt second-hand, yellow nicotine, trapped behind the dripping glass. Clouds of noxious smoke all headed up my nostrils and down my throat, and into my liver, which would trigger a premature urge for a beer and maybe some chewing tobacco.

But my jaunts of juvenile jollies I got when seeing Sasha, early in my life, revealed to me that she had an aura of *Eloquent Enlightenment* about her. The kind you only feel at certain times of your existence, and never forget. The Heartlys were a Scottish family that lived in the distant town of Waterdown. Her father was a confident, *in-your-face* jovial entrepreneur, who had just put a new pool table in the new gala rec-room he had built himself. It was a room for Sasha to teach me to play pool, and some other things. Bud didn't like Sasha's dad, Slim, or his jovial brashness. Neither, did it seem, his ability for making bucks that were there to make; for the brave (and strong and free).

The way I saw it, Slim was busy raising his family to carry on the Scottish tradition of learning enough from life, to not end up being a Potato Farmer. My black haired, English speaking Father of Dublin decent, and my red haired, thin, passionate Mother of Belfast history, were the biggest mix up that you had ever seen (to borrow from the Irish Rovers). Regina thought Sasha's mother was a gossip, and Bud thought her father owned one too many pool tables. I guess in the tradition of living behind the Center Road Swamp, at the end of the Seventh Concession, my parents would have dropped them off at the Pound, if they could of. It was no big deal however to Sasha or I as she lived fifteen kilometers away. And to farmers like us Organs, it might as well have been all the way to Killarney. Sasha and I carried out our Shakespearian Tragedy at school. I can't remember a single neighbour my father ever like... except the Wagners.

The Wagners were a Canadian born family of German decent, on Mr. Wagner's side. They bought the tiny strip of land that ran along the CN railway track, on one side, and Bud's field on the other. It was this strip of land, however, that kept our three consecutive Organ Farms from owning all the land to the tracks, on the east side of the Seventh Concession. Bud was supposed to have bought it, but one of those eleven o'clock real estate deals surprisingly squelched that notion.

Now, one might think this would have been more than an adequate reason for a rivalry of sorts with the new neighbours, but my father seemed to actually respect, even admire the hard working Huns, and their children. I always thought that this was a strange brew, because their eldest son, Hunter, aka Killer, worked on his race car all day, and then squealed it down the dark concessions late at night. Killer, it seemed to me, was in search for somebody like himself; a loner with fast wheels, coupled with a need for territory. A *Steel-Chromed-Wolf!*

Their second son, Peter, was a sports stud. He was a cool teen, with a swagger like Fonzy from Happy Days. And then there was Ernst. Ernst was a bit of a smaller Deutschland model. He made me wonder sometimes where he was coming from. But I guess Ernst eventually showed that he was watching and listening, as he proved to be a skilled Architect, just like his dad, Hans. Hans himself was a large man, muscled, with sea of mid drift. His wife, Iris, aka Mrs. W, was from the local 'Fifth' family. The Fifths were one of those broods that seemed to be around *forever,* with a *'Century Farm'* sign in their front lawn, and from who all the best stories were about, in the 'good ol' days'.

But this was 1961. Nobody was telling good ol' stories' about the war anymore, or tales about the Fifths. Kids were starting to tell stories about themselves. Or who Killer was racing that night! Or who was on the Top 30 Radio Charts! 1962 was a-comin', and there was something in the air... something that felt new. Something like America hadn't felt in a long, long time. That is, since two long wars, a depression, eight years of Ike, and then our tiny Canadian spot in time, when Diefenbaker cancelled our technically advanced Avro Arrow Jets.

A forlorn conformity had swept the continent in the Fifties, with Government sold beer, the man in the white suit, and strangely professed *Bible Belts* across America. In 1961 there were some new ideals in society, and a new leader in Washington who made us all look up and take notice. There was now an Irish Catholic President who empowered my family to proudly grow potatoes, and stubbornly be practicing Catholics in Wasp country. And that's when my dad started calling me Jack.

Julia was the only girl child in the blossoming Wagner brood. She was a shining brunette who was knew she was beautiful. She was confident, and well protected by her four Ostdeutschland brothers. And then there was Dean.

Dean was the youngest of the Wagner family. He was born in 1955. As you know, I was born in 1956. He was smart, charming, hip, informed, charismatic, cunning, good-looking, well liked, and confident with that smile of a winner. And Mrs. W. adored him! Dean's father was, besides an Architect, a hunter, somewhat mysterious, and a leading figure at the Rod & Gun Club, where he made his own bullets. Mr. Wagner added an extension to his small house beside the railway tracks, with his *Mehr al sein Sohn,* who dug out the basement with shovels and pick axes. Hans then framed the new extension, installed the electrics, dry walled, and painted up a new bedroom for Julia. They also built a TV room, complete with a huge steel, modern (at that time) antennae, attached outside to the burgeoning building. This new antennae brought in strange stations I hadn't even heard of before. It changed my life, culturally.

Dean was my first influence on our side of the railway tracks, after Jack's under-the-table disappearance trick. He had the trust of his Parents. They were obviously trained by Doctor Spock. Both of them gave him the respect and freedoms to grow up true, north, strong and free-o. Simple freedoms, like owning a bicycle. He could explore other concessions, and have *cherishing childhood stories* to tell Iris when he got home. And she would listen to his every word!

I was not allowed to own a bicycle until I was fourteen, and even then it took my school teacher to sway them. Apparently, she had told Bud and Regina that she believed I was academically astute, and they should indulge me, and grant autonomies allotted to such bright young boys, like *moi*. So, I got my first bicycle in June 1969. By December I was experimenting with LSD, and had left home. By June 1971 I was living on Britannia Beach, in Ottawa, with Rave Rushie and Raoul Raggae. I was secretly afraid of Alice Cooper.

Dean was my first *Musical Mentor*. He introduced me to Buddy Holly. His elder brothers had acquired Holly albums at the Towers Mall Record Store, in Aldershot. This store offered all the music it took for me to make it through my childhood and early teenage-hood years. One grand day, while playing road hockey in his laneway, Dean told me about this British group that was going to be on the next Ed Sullivan show. That was on Sunday evening, February ninth, 1964. The only instruction was, "be there or be square!"

'Ed', was on one of the only channels we got at the farmhouse in 1964. My family, like millions of other viewers, never missed Ed Sullivan. What can I say? It was John, Paul, George and Ringo! The Beatles! As I wrote in one of my songs years later, "My mother scraped my brain off the living room floor!"

Now it's true what's been said about there being divisions in life, and the next day, one became; 'life before the Beatles, and life after the Beatles'. It didn't take long to witness this truism. The very next day at school, kids had their hair combed forwards into bangs. And they sported a black Beatle boot on each foot! During Ed Sullivan's show the night before, the whole world gasped, and then took a step back in awe. Parents wondered how to control the over flow…the mess… the carnage surely to ensue! No one could be unaffected, somehow, after that night of *the next thing* finally happening. Everybody was reborn into a generation of hugs, hysteria, hyperbole, and pop music.

This suddenly gave us, the Youth of the World, our own perspective. On everything! And with this sudden empowerment, we immediately learned to judge; everything and everybody! We now knew never to trust anybody over thirty again, until we turned thirty ourselves. But by that time you couldn't trust the Young Punks.

We suddenly had all the answers! We considered conspiracies! Camelot had crumbled, and The Great Society meant a suspicious Brave New World! It was a new world exposing old vestiges, and offering new vantages to examine. We suddenly had our own perspectives on J. Edgar Hoover! Viet Nam! Hoola Hoops! Ken Kesey! Guitars! Zen! Our own Canadian flag! Camaros! California! A New Age! Anticipations of newness! Everything anybody had ever done before was now *fragile and antiqued.* We wanted new information. We craved honesty and integrity. Schools were in our aim. God help those Teachers! God help those doting Parents! God help God! We had been set free! And we intended to rejoice. Thanks Dean!

This *newly found freedom* was not the mind numbing event to read about in the newspaper the day afterwards. It was definitely not to browse back about in Rolling Stone Magazine in 1978. It was all about being here and now! You just had to be there to understand!

Dean kept me in time and tune for the rest of the decade. But by then we listened to different drummers; me to a beat of a Culture replaced by a Counter Culture, an unwanted war that wouldn't go away, a Society that was choking itself to grasp new conditions, expectations, experimentations, successes, failures, resources, alternatives, ultimatums, inner spaces, explorations, outer spaces, new consciences, learning curves, changes, heroes, zeroes, questions, answers, loves, hates, and the feeling we had lived fifty years in a micro second that could not be tracked, or traced, by the ancient guarded realm of antiquated Time and Space, or Reality and Disillusionment, but by passing the next Acid Test with flying colours!

Chapter 2
Ormie

1955 was a year of infamy for the Organ clan. This was the year my grandfather, Ormie (Ormond?) Organ, sold his fifty acre potato farm to his son, my father, Bud. My dad's real name, that is the one on his Baptismal Certificate, was Leo Organ. I don't know if he had a middle name, but regardless, his first name became his middle name to all that knew him, and his first name became an unchristian 'Bud'. As in *Bud the Spud*. Or a potato bud; a sprout, a shoot, a flowerlet, floret, plumule, or a burgeon. Just definitely not a marijuana bud! Anyway, what could a lad who had earned the nickname 'Bud,' which he wrote on his cheques, and all legal documents for his entire ninety two years going to do? Not buy the potato plantation?

Things were just looser back then. If everyone thought you should be called Bud, then it just was so, apparently. That's what his letters in the mailbox were all addressed to. In his entire life, I never heard him called anything else but Bud. He never legally changed it. I can imagine some *old-school* towns, like Flamborough Center, throughout Canada a hundred years ago, where people just felt uninhibited enough to call themselves whatever they liked. It was certainly a good advertisement for his occupational life choice. I guess it was kind of like when there were two Canadian 'Rough Rider' football teams, in the same League, and nobody seemed to notice, or care.

Incidentally, Ottawa had the first team of RRs in 1898, in the Canadian Rugby Union. Saskatchewan changed their name, from the 'Regina Rugby Club', to 'Rough Riders', in 1924. Ottawa had just dropped the name in favour of 'Senators', and like Bud, they changed it back to Rough Riders again, when it felt right. And then they changed it to the 'Red Blacks', but that's another millennium… I myself changed my name, officially, but not legally, to *Moon Dog* early in my teens. People to this day know me by that handle. Like father, like son?

My mother, Regina, (which she always told me meant Queen of Heaven…ok…) and Bud were living with Ormie's family on his farm, until 1955, when his wife, my Grandmother Shannon, died. Regina had hated them both. She was pregnant with my sister, Mary, before she and Bud were married, so when they moved into the crispy, virgin, white Catholic farmhouse, they were instructed to sleep in separate rooms. This *heavenly potato farm* was a shamrock shade of stoic Catholicism. My mother, according to Shannon, was a, "Blighted bloody whore of Orange decent", that had taken Oedipus, or rather Bud, away from her. She would get some sweet Irish revenge, and made Regina's life cursed in *her* house.

Bud could never bring himself to break the surly bonds of Mother and Son, no matter how Regina felt in the room next to his. Just another true love and hate story. There was nothing Shakespearian about this tragedy. No Romeo and Juliet. There were no divisions. Simply nobody ever supported Regina. She forfeited any chance of peace, or sanity, from day one of meeting Bud. At seventeen, Regina had been expelled by her Father from his farm, for cussing him out after he whipped a horse's eyes when it wouldn't hook up to the plough. There was an Orange Glow out on his grange, from sunup to sundown. Life was hard.

Suddenly, Grandma Organ's death freed Regina, so to speak. Ormie sold the farm to Bud, and moved in with his only daughter, Gertrude, and her husband George in Toronto. This seemed manifest, as Ormie had weekly commitments at the corner of Church and Carlton, to oversee his greatest investment he ever made, in my humble opinion.

In 1931, Ormie stunned his Black Smith buddies and befuddled family, when he bought a season-ticket pass to watch the Toronto Maple Leafs at the newly assembled *Maple Leaf Gardens*. Before televised games! Incredulous! This made him my Hockey God, from my birth on it seemed. At a certain age, I could finally view games with him at M.L.G! I altered watching games with my brother Paul, and my Uncle George. Man that was something special! Dean Wagner never went to games at Maple Leaf Gardens, yet this Irish potato farmer's sons did multiple times a year! What could be better? I lived, ate, and breathed hockey as a kid.

Dean and I used to walk in freezing weather and through waist deep snow down old abandoned country gravel roads, which took us to lonely fields of nothing but rocks, wind, and snow, to play pond hockey. This was before the term 'Global Warming'. And also before nice, sleek and warm *ski-doo suits* were on the market. Dean and I just grimaced as we froze our hands and feet, while walking a couple miles to the Pond with our heavy duffle bags full of equipment. We also carried our sticks and skates which we slung over our already padded shoulders. We forged through fields forgotten by all but wicked and wonderful winter. We trudged and cursed the cold. Maybe Dean reacted out loud more than I did. I just mumbled and grumbled about frost bite, and bitter mid-Sixties cold.

When we would finally arrive at Tommy Swamp, we would silently rejoice. But *'Tommy'* was always covered in one, two, or even three feet of snow. Oh, did I mention we each also carried a shovel to clear the ice? Of course we did! The first thing was to get our gloves and boots off, with totally frozen fingers and toes, and then somehow get our skates on. Dean would always get his on first. He then helped me, as my fingers and toes always seemed to be more frozen stiff than his.

Once I had my skates on, I felt like I was ready to die. By the time I sssstood up, Dean would already be gliding along on his blades, which he had sharpened the night before. This enabled him to remove snow at a nippy rate. He would always encourage me to get up and start to thaw out by grabbing my shovel, and pushing the snow, which would become the 'boards' in our ensuing game.

I would fight slicing winds and the insane cold, and start shoveling. The first five minutes, it was all I could do to skate with my frozen toes and numb fingers. My face frosted bright red from whipping pond breezes. The second five minutes, I would skate a little straighter, a little quicker, and more fluently. Then by the third five minute session around the pond, I would finally start to warm up. Soon I would begin to crack a sweat, and then... Poof!...Our biggest winter jackets would come off! I skated and skated until... Bam! ... Our second layer of coats came off! By the time we had the pond surface cleared, we would both be down to only one sweater. We would then grab a puck and start to stick-handle articulately through snow lumps and pieces of clothing, strategically positioned on the surface of the frozen water.

Soon, Davey Keon, Frank Mohovlich and Tim Horton would be skating against Jean Beliveau, Maurice Richard and Doug Harvey. These characters, in our minds, were driven by our pulsing legs, and generated by our sucking frozen pond air into our mouths. The Toronto players, on Dean's side, would fake and deke every one of my poor Habitants out of position, and zero in on goalie Jacques Plante. Jacques would be guarding the goal net, which was represented by two rubber boots. And he would usually score, as I was also Jacques. Well, the Maple Leafs had taken the Stanley Cup that year, their third in a row, so I could be forgiven for them being better than me and my *Habitants*. After an hour or so, *other players* would start appearing at 'our swamp'. Always, it seemed, in warm cars with cold glares.

They would show up in jerseys with insignias of the hated Boston Bruins, and dreaded Detroit Red Wings. Chicago had, and has, the best jerseys. Their stoic painted Indian Faces, smiling on the crest, were adorned with brightly coloured Head Feathers, and wise eyes guarding tight lips. Dean, of course, would be donned in his blue and whites, and cat-called anyone else that didn't. Especially my traitorous colours; bleu, blanc et rouge. Nobody ever wore New York Rangers jerseys. They were lame.

We always played all morning-2-afternoon, until it got too dark to see the small black puck. Then, if everyone with a warm car had already left, which happened more often than not, Dean and I would change out of our skates and uniforms, grab our sticks, shovels, and coats, shove everything we could into our duffle bags, and head home. But it never mattered that we were tired. We were there again the next day. We wouldn't miss weekend games. It was what we did.

As John Denver would sing ten years later, "life on the farm *was* kinda laid back." I would return home from Tommy Swamp to a warm supper, and then watch the hockey game on T.V. In 1964, *Hockey Night in Canada* started broadcasting the games at the end of the second period, for some strange reason… I guess they figured Canadians didn't have the attention spans to make it through the full game.

So I had to be satisfied with one period of professional hockey a week … That is, unless it was my magical turn to join Ormie at the Gardens! In this case I would gladly miss our sacred *Saturday Swamp Game*. Saturday night games at MLG meant staying over Friday nights at my Auntie Gert's and Uncle Georges at 42 Wanless Ave, in residential Toronto. I would try to not be too hyper, thinking about the game the following evening. I think I drove Ormie nuts, but he took me anyway. My older brother, Paul, was such a better choice of company. He was kind of a younger *spitting image* of Ormie; thick and muscularly built, and he never whined.

I'll never forget the Leaf games at M.L.G. Or stop marvelling at the patience Ormie showed, putting up with me chatting constantly on the bus ride to the Gardens. We always had two hot dogs and coca colas at the end of the first period; standing in that long, long line up. But it was worth it. It was Heaven! And I owed it all to my grand Grandfather Ormie. Thanks Ormie!

But my so-called *gratitude* was put to the test one morning, back at the Farm, during one of our sugar-dusted breakfast bowls of Quaker Oats. Ormie often stayed-over with us at the Farm, I guess to give Auntie Gert and Uncle George some time to themselves. They were both working Professionals, and Ormie was like a big kid. This is what happens to adults when they are not in control anymore. When he visited the Farm, Ormie slept in the first bedroom at the top of the stairs. The two old flights of stairs winded down into the kitchen, where I was eating my breakfast, waiting for the familiar sounds of feet forging down steps.

I figured I knew what was coming on this Dark Day of Doom and Misadventure. I was anxious, and beyond that, I didn't know what to think. On this particular morning I was treading on *new territory,* and I was waiting for things to unfold, as they soon would. Ormie finally appeared down the stairs, and he immediately stood over me, as I was eating diligently at the table, waiting. And here it was! Ormie grunted, and then proceeded to start militaristically questioning me, point blank, while obviously doing his best imitation of Major Conn Smythe. Smythe had been in both World Wars and was awarded the Military Cross as a Hun killing Leaf Boss. Ormie soon got right to the point. I'll never forget his choice of words; kind of Don Cherry-ish, as in a booming voice he urged me to explain to him how I could, "In a good English speaking family like ours, suddenly become a fan of the Montreal Canadiens?"

There was something that we called *'the Equalizer'* back in the days before *'political correctness'*. This was still before Prime Minister Pierre Elliot Trudeau made it Law, in Canada, that all students had to learn the French language in schools of Ontario (and supposedly other provinces, but that never happened with the dirge and discipline like it did here in Lower Canada). This was before civil rights were passed, before Canada had its own flag, before the Canadian currency dipped to less value than that of American currency; back when every Canadian dollar printed was matched by gold weight in the vaults of the Old World.

This *'Equalizer'* was also known as 'a good back-hand', usually given across the unsuspecting victim's head. Ah yes, the good ol' days! But I knew this particular *'Equalizer'* was coming. I mean, all I had to do was remember those games he took me to as a loyal, moral, respectable Blue and White Leaf fan! All that patience he conjured to deal with my hyper energy on the way to the Gardens... All those bus rides we took to Church Street together! All those hot dogs we ate between loving smiles! But I was getting the sense that I needed to answer his question before this latest version of the *'Equalizer'* was delivered, post gratis.

Maybe I answered just for the drama. Maybe it was to *bend time* before the 'blow' was delivered. But it was my Last Chance. My Stay of Execution, as it might be. So I looked up and ventured to Ormie, the God of hockey tickets and wholesome entertainment, ever so meekly, "Because I like Jean Beliveau!" There was only silence! Nothing but a *void of sound* and *vacuum of space*! There was only time, fear, agony, and the anticipation of the still looming *'Equalizer'*. Ormie looked at me, still keeping silent, still threatening, levitating and looming on the same spot. He replied raucously, "OK".

And that was it! That became the *'Equalizer'* of the conversation. This signified the end of angst and agony for me. It was suddenly a New Age in which I was allowed to voice my own opinion, no matter how timidly! I was allowed to venture beyond the safety net of *'right answers'* that were not my own.

Chapter 3
People that Laugh
Too Much

Before school, Jack was my only friend. But as realities go, that reality was short lived. However, school auspiciously loomed ahead for me. I had seen it happen to my sister Marilyn; disappearing one morning, and returning full of stories that night. But I was warned: I was next!

It just didn't seem right. At least there was the calming reality that Mrs. Sleeve would be my grade one teacher at Flamborough Centre School, which was where I indeed would be going. The town of Flamborough Centre was a small dot on the horizon, but it was the closest gathering of people to us farmers, out on stony no exit roads, where we tended our livestock and grew crops. It was where my older brother Paul played baseball every summer. It was also home of one of my earliest landmarks away from the Seventh Concession; Carey's General Store. Carey's was located a mere stone's throw from the school that my mind was promised to.

So in 1961, Mrs. Sleeve would not only be cutting my hair, but she would also be teaching me in grade one. She would still be babysitting my sister and myself, and letting me ride her horse, when it wasn't in her kitchen.

Grade one was the longest experience I ever went through. It seemed to go on forever. Another reality that crept into my new existence, in school, was that being born on the last day of the year, technically this made me five years old in grade one. This was the start of my always being the youngest of every grouping I was placed in. This truly had an effect on my maturing, perhaps a little later than most. Throughout life I always hung with people older than me. At fifteen years of age I was living with my friend Mike, who was nineteen. I don't think I ever caught up.

Meanwhile, reality affected our whole family in 1964. Regina had been pregnant during my grade four experience. I believe she must have gotten pregnant every time she had sex... six children... do the math. Their separate bedrooms turned into separate beds. She would tell us children years later, how she would beg my father to not have sex, as to avoid the inevitable... of being an uncovered Catholic. Soon after she bore Michael, the youngest of this round of the Organ clan, she had a nervous breakdown and stayed on the couch for an extended period of time... off and on till '67. But life went on regardless. My older sisters took care of Michael, born on November 4th, 1964.

We begged Regina, throughout her whole pregnancy, to name the baby Ringo... I mean we really did. We had a Paul, I was a natural John, and there was our Uncle George. I needed a Ringo! But my parents would have no part of it. The handle 'Ringo' was too rangy for Carlisle, Ontario in 1964. Besides, Regina thought this would be sacrilegious, somehow. She was born Protestant in Bellville, Ontario, as her family immigrated from the cold and rainy *North of the Green Line*. Bud's forefathers blossomed out of the sunny South; staunch Catholics who worked hard, drank CC for stamina, and paid on the collection plate when passed at Catholic services. Bud never missed the sacred offerings basket, even if we went without.

Naturally, my mother had to change religions to be allowed to marry Bud. And especially to be allowed to live in Ormie's farmhouse! My Grandmother referred to Regina as, "That Protestant Bitch." After her heart attack in '55, Regina bore me in '56. She claimed I looked like her father (who had kicked her out of his house at the tender age of seventeen), and would draw other similarities between myself and this heartless-sounding man. Cold, Cold Heart indeed! It made me shudder. But at least I was able to go to school now, and put our dysfunctional family behind me, at least for a few hours each week day.

Mrs. Sleeve was now and forever in my rear view mirror. So was Sasha Heartly. I was stretching out, and school allowed me to evolve. But I was constantly in trouble from day one. I was the only student in grade one to ever be put out the door, to stand in the hallway. Et tu Mrs. Sleeve? By grade six I was hitting my stride, as I was in a constant battle of wits with my German teacher, Mr. Gaul. He was sure I was the anti-Christ, and finally at one point, he moved my desk, with me in it, out in the hallway. For four months! This passed my record of three weeks that I accumulated in grade five, when it was decided that the hallway contained the perfect acoustics for my never ending joke telling, and constant laughing. For months, only my empty, echoing epiphanies rolled down the vacant hallway that I shared simply with boots, and small puddles of water.

Before grade five, I had already sealed my fate before the school year even started. The summer before, during a neighbourhood *War Game of Slingshots* that we were conducting out on the lonely Concession road, I was bored. I hadn't struck anything new with my *elastically weapon* in too long a time. Suddenly an unfamiliar white convertible passed us by. But not before I carefully lined up the car, and fired my *stretchy ammo*. The car stopped abruptly, and the livid driver got out. He got right to the point, and introduced the lady in the passenger seat as the new grade-five Teacher at Flamborough Center School. She was blonde, and very good looking. Her first words to me were;

"What grade are you going into this fall?"

I could barely get the word, "Five" out, when she retorted,

"Good Luck!" Obviously I would need it, as she did not seem to share my sense of *alienated Irish* country bumpkin humour. Maybe she would forget that any of this happened by September...

Certain people, that others think laugh too much, are always scrutinized. I think this is out of an inbred fear. We, the 'Laughers', make 'Laughees' feel like they are not in control, which is their greatest power. Losing control to a gap toothed Hyena, in front of a classroom full of potential Hyenas, is considered dangerous. It always has been. But in grade six, four months was a huge chunk of the year to be banished from the classroom. Mr. Gaul distastefully dropped off an assignment, each morning on my desk, with expectations expressed in ink. This assignment would then be examined, and marked, and documented upon each night, by a band of Pseudo Psychiatrist Teachers. Their jobs, apparently, were to mark my progress and profile, for whoever cared.

I would write the same tests and exams as the rest of the class, when the time came. And I always barely passed these tests, though some other students did not. This increased his disregard and disrespect for me. But this disgust for me soon became time monitored.

The original building of Flamborough Center School consisted of three ancient levels; one ground level with class rooms, one upper-level for grades six, seven and eight, and a split basement that contained washrooms, and a cement room on each side. These two cement rooms were known as the 'Girl's Side', and the 'Boys Side'. This was a WASP school, so I guess it couldn't be a mortal sin, but it was a big deal for a male student to enter the female concrete capacity. Creaky old wooden steps connected each level.

My *hallway isolationism* was on the top level, perched at the peak of the groaning stairs. There was a long wooden hand railing that I learned to ride down, or shall I say, 'glide down', without ever falling off. I could then scamper out the door, and then down to Carey's General Store. There I would stock my system with sugar treats until I was out of money. Feeling *victorious,* and now sugar hyper, I would return to the school and creep slowly and gingerly up the wooden stairs, to my desk, where I would never have time to finish my assignments.

Now the thoughts of my failing the sixth grade must have made Mr. Gaul think... If he failed me, wouldn't I repeat my next year with him again? It would be as much a failure for him as me; a whole summer of preparing to lock horns with each other for another year of mirth and mayhem. That was my guess anyway, because on June 25th, when we got our report cards, I passed with a 59.6 percent!

Great changes were happening in Society in 1967, and that included Flamborough Center School! That summer the school was torn down, and an ultra-modern, brand new Institution was erected in its place. Marilyn and I were sent to our first Catholic Separate School, St. Thomas, for grades seven and eight.

Well I hated the idea of being *separated* from my old school chums. I hated the idea of suddenly going on two different bus rides to this new school (ironically I swapped buses outside the new Flamborough Center School). I hated the notion of schooling with a bunch of Catholics. I also hated not really being accepted on the F.C. baseball team anymore, since I was the only team member who didn't school at F.C. District. I hated being so hauntingly close to the R.C Church. I hated that the girls all wore the same uniform (until I was older at St. Mary's, where I learned to appreciate their rosy, frosty legs)! I hated having to fit in at a *new school* all over again, this time without Mrs. Sleeve. I guess I just hated change.

I sure hated little smiling Nuns telling me what to do, in the name of God.

A few minutes later I saw Camille Earl, of course with a cigarette perched tween his chapped lips, and his bother Rip, who despite being only a grade older, was in a different universe. He had an English-accented maturity beyond those his age. He had the hair, the smokes, the smile and some English Charm. Girls liked him. And his basement bedroom beside Taurus's, at the Earls, offered such freedoms. He could smoke down there, and all that Rhythm and Blues!

Beyond the Earls, I noticed Patrick Schiller and his older sister Marie. The Schrillers used to live on the Forth Concession. My sister used to date Duster, the oldest lad in the Schriller brood. Duster would come over and visit her frequently, and usually brought Patrick with him, to keep me out of their hair. But unlike Hans Wagner, Patrick's father, Thomas Schiller, enjoyed a drink or two, and was a *'hard knocks'* kind of fellow. He was the type that worked all the time, and while he was away some of us kids played strip poker and spin-the-bottle in his shed. We once dug an extensive underground fort in the field behind their house. It was equipped with tunnels and below surface rooms that we *country kids* would 'neck' in. We were always playing *spin the bottle*, despite our rural innocence. One day Mrs. Schiller phoned a taxi and moved out, with the kids, to a house in Malstone. And three years later, here was my reunion with Patrick.

Life can be hard for children who just want to grow up. And leave certain things behind. Cover the scars and move on. Some evolve through a soft-core Punk phase, living for the day. Author Starship was the biggest and toughest person in grade seven... the most feared guy in this classroom. That is, except for our new Teacher, Mrs. Griffiths.

Mrs. Griffiths was put on earth to guide *me*. To help me change, evolve, and transform into a better student, and a nobler human being. We started off, typically for me, on bad terms. Within my first week she marched me down to the Office to have my hands (and soul) strapped. And here was this tiny, angry nun who was a feared, jeered, yet righteously steered School Principle named Sister Margarita. She was a Sister with a *heavy eye brow!*

Mrs. Griffiths was an intellectual. But she was far beyond what passed for most teachers. She read all the Artists and Authors of the Lost Generation. She was familiar with Jack Kerouac and William Burroughs. She signed our School up with the 'Bookmobile', which would come by our school once a month. Every student *had* to buy at least one book, and write a review of it before this *'library on wheels'* returned the next month. She was a liberal thinking woman of the Sixties. She had us studying lyrics of Bob Dylan and such. She once had the class write an essay on the Simon & Garfunkle song, 'Save the Life of My Child Cried the Innocent Mother'. She was different. And she shepherded me!

Mrs. Griffiths asked us exciting questions. She deliberately made us think outside the boxes we came trapped in. She had the crow-bar to open our minds! But she had expectations from us all! She fought a battle for a fallen Camelot-like culture to pass on knowledge to her students. She introduced us to current events as to heighten our interests while broadening our outlooks. She was more Beat Generation than a hippie. She admired consciousness and comprehension. And she disliked stupidity. And there was lots of the latter in schools of the 60s.

This was back when kids with Dyslexia were just considered 'slow'. Those with ADHD or ADD were just 'left back'. Hypertension was just 'youthful exuberance'. Dyscalculia? Well it was known that most girls were weak in math… boys just needed a 'kick in the pants and they'll be ok'… Processing Deficits characters would surly improve with maturity and time… The Autistic were 'wild kids' and there was one in every classroom!

Those with Behavioural Disorders were considered 'trouble makers'... Brain Injuries were happening on unsupervised play grounds across the country... Cerebral Palsy, malnutrition, and chronic severe stresses... all out there for the next five generations to diagnose and treat.

Mrs. Griffiths was a Prophet for the New Age. And yet she could be brutal on those that did not measure up. Author Starship was a Troglodyte in her eyes. As were others she did not like, or give much hope for. And there I was, getting on her bad side in the first few days of our relationship. Damn!

She continued to scowl at my new face throughout the day. At one point she warned me that she had researched my past academia at Flamborough Center School. She confided in me that she knew what an absolute trouble maker I was there. She also warned me, that I would not spend almost half the year in her hallway! I would simply be expelled from the entire Wentworth County of Schools, which meant I'd only be allowed to attend schools out near Toronto. Furthermore, she growled, there was the first major test coming up the next day, in science. She warned me that if I failed it, she would recommend such an expulsion, because she had the rest of the tattered Great Society to deal with. I assuredly would not be Her Problem for the next two years, until I was some High Schools Problem...

So out of the kettle and into the fire was I! At home that night, I tried to study with some of the techniques she had taught the class that day. The next day, I trudged to my desk with the weight of the world on my twelve year old shoulders. Pass this test! Sink or swim! As the question papers were passed out I glanced at Mrs. Griffiths, but she was not showing any cards. My deal had been dealt. So I wrote the test, the bell went, and I was off for possibly my last lunch in a Wentworth County School. Ouch.

We all came in from lunch break an hour later, to an irritated, unreceptive Mrs. Griffiths. She immediately handed back the marked assessments. She was livid. Maybe even a little crazy! She was screaming at us, and threatened us with the Apocalypse, and worse! She said that these were the worst results of any tests she had given in her academic career. She screamed and yelled, then cast us all off the cliffs of decency and morality, to the fires of a hell designed specifically for each one of us! As her raving went on, she exclaimed that she was embarrassed by the *lot of us*. Furthermore, she encouraged all students to look at my exam.

Wow! I wondered how much worse than everyone else's mine could be?! I was wondering what I was going to say to my Parents. Maybe I would have to move in with Auntie Gert, Uncle George and Ormie! Man, I suddenly remembered that Aunt Gertrude, a teacher herself, was out of the vane of Mrs. Griffiths; someone who had the pride of Knowledge within her, and weak people were indeed an embarrassment to her as well.

My mind was wandering. And wondering! So much that I almost missed Mrs. Griffith telling the class that, "Everybody had failed the exam. Everybody!...with the exception of John Organ." Well I was the only student named John Organ, so was it possible she meant me? She carried on. She wanted everybody to view my papers. I had obtained a mark of 99 percent!

My life was never the same. I rarely wrote a test in the next two years that I achieved under ninety-nine percent. She truly turned me into at least *her* version of an Intellect. Throughout the year she endeared herself to me. She had transformed me into what I became, and am to this very day… a human being with knowledge, confidence, awareness, insight, cognition, expertise, competencies, abilities, a life-long pupil of pride, one of comprehension and compassion, a man of mastery, a blooming flower of fluency, a person of utter understanding, a Wizard of Wisdom, and mostly; a Creature with a newly formed desire to learn. If this specific event had never taken place, I would not be writing this today.

Chapter 4
Truman

Truman Capote was more than just a successful writer. He was a Statement. He had a dazzling personality, with demeanor. He was credited for the invention of non-fictional writing in 1965, with the release of his book entitled, 'In Cold Blood'. It was his peak, and his down fall. It broke him for years, until his releases of 'Thanksgiving Visitor' in 1967, in McCalls Magazine, and he then released it as a book in 1968. Other books and publications after, 'In Cold Blood' include; 'The Dogs Bark' in 1973, 'Wenn die Hunde Bellen, Stories und Portraits' also in 1973, and 'Children on their Birthdays' in 1976, 'Music for Chameleons' in 1980 'Miriam' in 1982, and 'Cercueils sur Mesure' in 1982. Books after his death, in 1984, included; 'I remember Grandpa' in 1985, 'Answered Prayers' in 1986, 'Jug of Silver' in 1986, 'Una Navidad' in 1989, 'One Christmas/ un Noel: The Christmas Visitor/L'Invitee de Jour' in 1991, 'Complete Stories of Truman Capote' in 1993, 'The Early Stories of Truman Capote', A House on the Height' in 2001,'Summer Crossing' in 2005, and 'The Portraits and Observations: Essays of Truman Capote' in 2007.

Truman's *Live Publications* and books came out as early as 1945 with, 'My Side of the Matter', 'Other Voices Other Rooms' in 1948, A Tree of Night and Other Stories' in 1949, 'Local Color' in 1950, 'The Grass Harp' in 1951, 'A Christmas Memory' in 1956, also 'The Muses are Heard' in 1956, 'Observations' in 1959, also 'Brooklyn Heights Memoir' in 1959, and 'Heights Memoir (with the lost Attie pictures)'.

The book people associate immediately with Capote is indeed 'In Cold Blood'. This was his accurate, tell-tale account of the grizzly murders that happened in 1959 on Herbert Clutter's Farm, in Holcomb Kansas. It is, to this day, the second best-selling *true crime books* ever written. It featured a *triple narrative* describing the lives of murderers Richard (Dick) Hickock and Perry Smith, the four innocent victims, and the effects this had on the people in the Community. Due to his cultural status, as opposed to his raging charm, many of Holcomb's residents took Truman into their homes to tell him their versions of how it had affected them.

But now, I want to say that the book Truman wrote that stimulated me, and remains one of my first Artistic memories and influences in my life, was 'Breakfast at Tiffany's'. Capote wrote this in 1951 as a short novel, and three stories. In 1956, he sold the novella to Harper's Bazaar, with expectations that it would be accompanied with photos by David Attie. However, Harper's editor Carmel Snow was fired, and conflicts with Hearst Publishers surfaced when they asked for changes in sharp language. Next they limited Attie's photos to just one. An angry Capote resold the novella to Esquire, where fantastic reviews made Norman Mailer claim that Truman Capote was, "The most Perfect Writer of my generation." Well move over Hemmingway! The novella was loosely adapted for the 1961 movie, 'Breakfast at Tiffany's'.

I've expressed already that my time under the kitchen table spent with Jack, was my first memory as a child. But at the age of five, I was on my own all day. The rest of my Family was out working or going to school. On a lone stone road, the television was my baby-sitter and information center. Late at night I would come downstairs, claiming I could not sleep. I came downstairs at the same time every night ironically; when Jack Parr's, 'The Tonight Show' came on. He was different, and I realized this early in my career as a TV Critic.

One night Jack kept referring to 'Holly Golightly'. I was amused by the words, and I finally asked my mother, "What does 'Holly Golightly' mean?" Regina explained Holly was a character in a new movie that apparently came from writings of Truman Capote. More fun words to say; Truman Capote! Sometime later, I was watching the Sacred Tube, and it was announced that, 'Breakfast at Tiffany's' was on later that night. My parents said they intended to watch it.

Bud watched the movie in ode to Jack Parr, whom most considered a genius. Well, I couldn't sleep that night either, so down I came to witness a memory burned into my brain to this day.

I related to this woman, Holly Golightly. She went to parties, and led a life out of her New York apartment. She had a Cat with no name, and some guy lived in an apartment below hers. I was confused that Audrey Hepburn was so young, as I had seen Catherine Hepburn in movies by 1962. But like most other things at that age, I mixed them up. Capote had wanted Marilyn Munroe for the part, to no avail.

The movie's theme song, *'Moon River'* romanced and captivated me at such an early age. The Beatles hadn't hit the charts yet, and neither had Dylan. This movie represented an aura of expressionism for me at that time. It matured me past the juvenile, 'Mary Poppins' when it appeared on the movie screen years later. Nothing affected me like this again, screen wise, until I saw, 'Those Days of Wine and Roses' the next year, and then, 'Hard Day's Night' the following year again.

My mother would see me relating to these movies that commented on Society, in what was still, *'the Old Days'*. She told me I was growing up *too fast*. Funny, watching Holly Golightly made me *want* to grow up faster, and join this sect of people in a *heightened age* that made everything else in this concrete world seem so slow. Life seemed like an iceberg; grinding over ignorant and prejudiced pebbles of sins. But these sins seemed different than the ones that were discussed in Church, or by my Parents. While I watched the movie, I grasped at things that I wasn't sure I really understood in 1962. But with Jack Kennedy in the White House, and Grade One now stalking me, combined my feeling of being alone all of the time, I was ready for something new. Luckily, looming ahead was the Sixties!

Searchin';

I've looked for Truth. I've searched for stashes. I've inquired about the obvious. I have postulated my poignancy. I've pursued past sorrows. I've chased the vanities. I've examined the extremities. I've scrutinized the infallible. I've voiced my veracities. I've researched my concepts and nominated my notions. I've explored the unknowns of the universe with my soul. I've hunted for clues to the *next thing*. I have aligned my beliefs with authenticity. I've revealed the N*aked Truth* and disregarded the nitty-gritty. I've lost and I've found. I've gained then lost ground.

I've looked, followed, and chased different realities throughout my life. But I think what I always searched for the most, in my youth, was a Father Figure. After being blamed for everything in Bud's unlucky cosmos, from the potatoes freezing at my parturition, to *global warming*, Bud was never the *Begetter Image* I fancied or imagined. It was something like a theme of '*neither one of us could win'. It reminded me of* the moral in the movie, "The Man who shot Liberty Valance," where the winner didn't always win. Of course, on the other hand, Bud was no John Wayne, and I sure as hell wasn't any hero that was gonna take over the town of Shinbone!

To me, Bud seemed to be missing *something* in his life. Perhaps it was his Mother, who died from cancer mid-stream. She had controlled his every whim. Maybe it was his having a child with a *product* of an Orange ancestral, WASP heritage, who was probably the first woman he had intimately romanced. Then there was the moving of his new, delicate and pregnant wife, into his Parent's Farm where she would be discriminated upon daily. Maybe he was missing *taking a stand* against those he silently disagreed with in Society. Bud was a teen-ager during the '*Dirty Thirties*', and a farmer during WW2. So he never saw any action, at home or abroad, so to speak.

Bud's only advice to me, in the fourteen years we lived together, was to agree with the Authorities, and just do whatever I was told. But how could I take his advice when I could never remember him looking happy, or satisfied? He was living out the existence of a *Hollow Man*. Maybe he was Dorothy's *Tin Man*. Something inside was missing. Was it that the excitement escaped when he married for honour? For Bud, to spend a single day off working on his farm was unheard of.

He never took an airplane trip in his life. He never went further than Kentucky, where he went once to see a horse race. This must have been cool, actually. To drive south and witness the Derby, first hand, must have been a bit of an *adventure*. But that was about the only *adventure* I ever heard about. Maybe Bud was one of those stoic figures you see in a National Geographic, with his spear, his tattoos and paints, and children by his side, waiting for the next slaughtered calf. Meanwhile, we would all smiling for the camera.

So, *according to Garp,* Bud was living out the existence he preached, and professed, to his Flock; "Be a loyal Sheep, and watch out for Wolves." This is what he did himself, and was the life he led. So why was he always so unhappy? Unfulfilled? Perhaps it came from being unchallenged in his youth? Out in the country, he didn't play baseball as a kid, or even go to school past grade two. He was just always on the Farm. And I was always on the Road. So he considered me a bum. Not a *Wandering Profit* by any means. Bud was just unable to see any point of view that presented risk, danger, or anything that might seem unpopular to his fellow Droogs.

A good, or rather bad example of this occurred on many Sundays, while driving to the Catholic Church we attended to talk to God. Ten minutes into the drive, on cue, Regina would point at a twenty acre field that was going for peanuts, located on the busy Center Road. She had heard from Charlie Chump, a Municipal Worker, that the Town was seriously considering re-zoning this area, so they could build a series of surveys for the Next Generation that was already here. We listened to her beg Bud, every Sunday, to listen to her. Or at least to Charlie, and make this *relatively* small investment to obtain an early retirement. "This was just the kind of investment someone like Slim Heartly would take advantage of", Regina would rage.

But Bud would not listen. Soon, the land was bought, and the new owner applied successfully to have it re-zoned, *residential*. Every Sunday we would drive by, and say a prayer for Bud, as houses and surveys kept springing out of the ground on the site. It took a while for Regina to look like she was over her indignity, but of course, she never really did. It was simply one of God's Truths that someone else, with the same advanced information that Regina had, was the Town's new millionaire. And not us!

I believe, ironically as it seems and sounds, that I got my taste of music from Bud. He used to walk around singing Petula Clark's hit-song, 'Down Town' all through the mid-Sixties. He liked Lois Armstrong, the Irish Rovers, and eventually supplemented 'Down Town' with Harry Nilsson's classic 'Everybody's Talking at Me' from the 'Midnight Cowboy' movie. His favorite, ironically, was the sadly uplifting, 'Raindrops keep falling on My Head' from the Paul Newman movie, 'Butch Cassidy and the Sun Dance Kid'. He didn't listen to Frank and the Rat Pack, and he never was interested in Rock and Roll, or the Blues. He would sing along to Maria Muldar, or Ronnie Hawkins, and would serenade along with, 'The Night they Tore Old Dixie Down' every time it came on the radio. These were early memories, but golden ones! All my favorite notes on Bud were musical.

Bud was a *Worker Bee*. Not a drone that would spend the day satisfying the *Queen Bee*. He would have my brother Paul working like an ox, until he began to look like one. Paul was strong and muscular as a bull in a China Shop...well, that is, Bud's butcher shop. Paul was an exceptional student until grade nine, when he started attending Waterdown High School. He then, for some reason, proceeded to fail grade nine, and ten, before he quit his academic life forever. He was out of school by 1968 and by 1969 he worked in Bud's Butcher Shop full time. In 1967, at sixteen years of age, Paul travelled to Montreal, by himself, to attend the Centennial 'Expo; Man and His World' expose. Paul always had something on his mind, or somewhere to go. He was like *Joe Buck, the Midnight Cowboy;* loose on the streets of New York City, but always dreaming of different horizons.

Paul would hire me to work for him, once he started his own Company that installed aluminum siding and eves troughs. He helped me out as a young Teen, but he was not the Father Figure I alluded to needing. Regina would see me bored, and with no one to hang with after grade six, as I was taken away from my Flamborough Center companions. Especially Dean Wagner, even though he still lived next door. Going to a different school suddenly meant I was not included in F.C. baseball teams, or football games, or anything!

George Lennon worked at his dad's Gas Station, and Camille was busy on his own turf with his Malstone Dudes and Droogs, who together were always on the search for *no good*. With nothing to do, and no one to do it with, Regina would demand to Paul that he do something with me. With our six year age difference seemingly at its height, this left us to always to play catch, with the leather baseball glove that I never used anymore. I would get truly excited, and we would throw the ball for ten minutes. On cue, Paul would stop and be gone to Town. He never once lasted more than ten minutes! I'd beg him for another ten minutes, but never to any avail. Paul, in time, in another time, became my best friend. But to me, he could never be a Father Figure'.

On Christmas Eve in 1969, Regina's alcoholic brother, Jim, was in his stalled car on a Railway Crossing, in her hometown of Bellville, Ontario. He kept cranking the starter, but to no avail. The train hit his vehicle and killed him. The following day, Christmas, her Father died. His health had been poor for years, and Christ's Birthday became his Death Day. Six days later, on New Year's Eve, her Mother died. Everybody said it was from a broken heart. I was not allowed to attend any of the funerals.

Paul went to say goodbye to the Buried Breathless, but standing by those bereft of life, suddenly Paul had a revelation! The three remaining Sisters decided to sell the whole farm, with house, barns, and milking parlor et al, for ten thousand dollars! The Real Estate salesmen advised them that if they sold it this cheap, it would sell quickly. He reasoned for them, that they could then put these unfortunate events behind them. Bud earnestly tried to expose him to the Sisters, that it was too low a price, and that the salesman probably intended to buy it himself and then resell it.

Whether it was grief, or insanity, the Sisters decided to let the salesman sell the property the way he saw fit. Once again she opted to, 'trust the Professional', as Bud had taught her, and us kids. The Sisters all reasoned, "That's what he did for a living, so he must know what he's doing!"

Paul had been working a year now, and had two thousand dollars in the bank. He told Regina and her Sisters that he would buy it, and they could happily keep the farm in the Family. Bud could then co-sign for the eight thousand dollar balance. What could be better? Unbelievably, they turned down Paul's offer, and the farm they all grew up on was sold to Strangers the next day.

Paul went *bezerk*! How could they do this to him? It was a steal of a deal, but for a Stranger? We all knew Bud was just too paranoid to go to the bank and co-sign against his farm. Just like the field he refused to buy, he was afraid to even *think* of using his blessed farm for even a nickel of collateral.

Paul changed that day. He left home, and led the life of a playboy until all his money was gone. He kept drinking and partying until he was suddenly fifty thousand dollars in debt. This tragedy went on until the end of the Seventies, when Paul's Company paid it all off. This was an incredible relief to Bud! Years earlier, he had to co-sign against Paul's last thirty thousand he still owed, to keep him out of jail. Bud could have co-signed for only eight-thousand, and Paul would have never have gone through these nightmares. But in the end, they were Bud's nightmares, not Paul's. Paul died the next year in a car crash; debt free.

Still Searching;

I remember, at every summers end, Duke First would combine Bud's twenty acres of grain, and thirty acres of oats and barley. In 1967, with Paul at Expo, I tailed along behind Bud all one dusty August summer day, to help keep an eye on things, don't you know? Through the afternoon, Bud took off to Town in the truck. I remember constantly looking for him, and asking everybody where he was.

This was the last of my *age of innocence*. I was distressed throughout the day as Bud did not return until late. I was concerned; that the grains needed to be properly delivered to the waiting silos, and the augers needed to be monitored for stones, and wood pieces that might clog the whirling steel rotating helical screw blade, called a *flighting*. I was flustered that all this was all going on, and Bud wasn't there. It was the last time I remember thinking, "Where's Daddy?"

It was my last memory of being a *Child*. Two years or so later I was running away from home, doing LSD, and starting to never really having a relationship with Bud again. From Baby to Boomer, in just two years!

The Earls, who I was close to, never offered a family image, or a Father Figure. They were too English, and I was an Irish potato farmer. I hadn't read James Joyce or Hemmingway yet. Besides, the Earls had a brood of their own to attempt to tame. Mary's husband Richard was too young, and too much of a *Swinger* to counterfeit himself as a Father Figure to me. They never had children of their own. Both their own families were Scary Entities (including myself), and they were not interested in duplicating anything that resembled a family like the ones they came from. Half the kids in the Organ Family never had kids of their own. The Horror! The Horror!

Father O'Riley from Church was a 'Father', but not one for my ideals. He had the Children of the World to worry about in his role as a 'Father' Image. By that time I was sleeping in unlocked cars at night, and attending school in the day time. Most fathers in 1969, '70, '71, were battling a Generation of *no-goodnicks* of their own. What a Generation we were... our parents were distraught by absolutely everything we did, and the cops just wanted fresh faces to beat. Add Viet Nam to the mix and it was a *Party with no Boundaries*. Many were looking for *Justice*. I was still searching for guidance and protection. I was still fourteen!

Leaping ahead, fourteen led to fifteen, and one spring day I found myself attending one of my 'Theatre Arts' classes at high school, in 1972. I never went to classes anymore, but shit happens… On stage, Vladimir had just asked,

"Shall we go?"

To which Estragon replied, "Yes, let's go."

This ended the play, and I made the next line mine. I confronted the Estragon actor, named Mike, when he disbanded the stage, and informed him that this bit of theater had touched something new and deep within my mind. He surmised to me that maybe this was Beckett's intention. Mike was four years my senior. He seemed to be polite, but doffed me off quickly. An hour later I met Serge, Mike's younger brother, by one year. A week later, the three of us were living together in an apartment, at suite 609, Camelot Towers Apartments, in Hamilton.

Mike was a Father Figure to Serge, but Serge never picked up on it. Mike, in a maternal moment, rented the apartment so Serge could continue going to school, and so he had a roof over his head. But days later Serge was on his way to Vancouver, and I was left to observe this *more of a man than a boy like me* character, Mike. Because of Mike I could continue High School in a different culture. I suddenly had a place to sleep that wasn't a Toyota's or Chevrolet's back seat, and I could spend my time with someone who worked full-time, and had concepts of life that, before this, I never conceived of!

Mike had a car which he lent to Manshika's brother, Philip. Manshika lived in B.C. and Phil was still attending St. Mary's. He would use Mike's car to travel safely out west with. Mike travelled mostly by bicycle anyway. He would travel endlessly on his bike, from town to town, hundreds of miles in a single day. This amazed me! How could anybody be in such physical shape, and accomplish such feats?

The first thing I did, when I returned from my west coast
Dead Head Trip that summer, was buy a ten-speed bicycle. I
started travelling from town to town by pedaling instead of hitch-
hiking. One morning I awoke and rode my bicycle, in the rain
for a large distance, and eventually in snow, for ninety miles from
Hamilton to London. When I got there, Philip, Cecil and some
Girls from Quebec, and I, drank and partied until dawn.

When I finished my last beer, about 8 am, I hopped on my
bicycle and pedalled back to Hamilton. I had a flat tire along the
way, so it was just getting dark when I returned to *Clappison Cut*,
where I drank some shitty wine with a buddy. I was flying half-
mast, and I thought I would phone and see if Paul could give me
a quick ride into the City. Bud answered my call, telling me that
Paul was out. I told him that I'd pedalled about two hundred
miles in the last thirty hours; through rain and snow, etcetera…
and if Paul wasn't there, could he give me, and my bicycle, a ride
home because I didn't have a light on my bike. Bud said if I had
travelled two hundred miles already, another few miles wouldn't
kill me, and I was on my own.

I pedalled my way back to the apartment where Mike was. I
told him of my trip to London and back, and I laughed when I
told him my dad wouldn't spring for a lift when I told him I had
no light on my cycle. Mike was concerned, and he told me to
phone him for a ride next time. Philip hadn't left with his Toyota
yet, and I was grateful just for his offer. I was touched by his
generosity, actually.

I've never told Mike this, but I was enthralled that I suddenly
knew someone who would actually 'be there for me'. Was this
a Friend, or that Father Figure I was craving at such a young
age? I figured this was somebody that offered something, with
no expectations, other than my safety. Was Mike someone that
could accept me as the *legal liability* that I was at a fragile age
of fifteen years? He was someone I could learn from certainly.

Someone I wanted to show respect to, despite our age difference, not because of.

Mike was very well respected by our Clique. His nick-name was *Mr. Natural*. At nineteen, he had an apartment, a job, a car, a beautiful girl-friend, and a career. There was something going down here in my life. Maybe it was called Direction. There was definitely Trust. There were other good Influences around suddenly. Through Mike I met Trent Haliday, whom I soon travelled to the West Coast with. Mike was one of my first Good Influences. Serge was a Crazy Influence. But I needed some of both; the Ying and the Yang.

From the books Mike read, to the opinions and perspectives he conveyed, this was the Father Figure my mind and soul starved for. I suppose, on certain levels, I was like one of the juveniles delinquents he worked with; I had been homeless, not communicating with my parents, but in my case, I was at least still one step ahead of trouble. Was Mike really a Father Figure for me at such an influential age, or was this just Mr. Natural, truckin' with his chips cashed in?

Chapter 5
Behind the Music

Elvis was Enormous! But it all began for *me* listening to Bob Dylan. Many successful Rock Icons said their inspirations came from Elvis. But that's because that's all there was way back then, before the Wheel... Little Richard was on his *own trip,* and Chuck Berry had already gone to prison. Buddy Holly, Ritchie Vales and the Big Bopper were dead in some American Nightmare that came in the form of Burning Wings. Ringo hadn't signed with the Beatles yet, and the most that many white people read into music was just wondering, "How much that doggie in the window" was.

I remember the first time I heard Bob Dylan. Bud was driving us in the *family car* down the long and winding road to Bellville, to visit Regina's Parents at their dairy farm. That's a long time ago, but it was after the invention of the Wheel, of course. I was a lad too young to have any direction, or reason, when I suddenly heard, 'Blowin' in the Wind' over the *ride's radio.* I'll never forget it. I wanted to stand up and salute! I wanted to understand. I wanted to sing along. I wanted to scream. I wanted to cry. It touched me so deeply! Like no sound in my life had ever touched me before... not a human or a toy, not an audio image or the sun, nor the rain, or a promise of a day off school, or Robert Kennedy smiling; nothing!

"How many roads must a man walk down
Before you can call him a man?"

And I was hooked!

"Yes 'n' how many years can a mountain exist
Before it is washed to the sea?"

Yes I thought... nothin' really exists. It's all an illusion! We're all here to die...nothing's for sure except that...So I'll stop taking things for granted. There's a world out there! It's scary and it's incomplete, but I want to be part of it! It made me wanna ask questions! I wanted answers! And I wanted them Now (then)!

"Yes 'n' how many times can a man turn his head
And pretend that he just doesn't see?"

I saw Black People on TV attacked by White Police with night sticks, and blown away with fire hoses. Cassius Clay had just become Heavy Weight Champion of the World! Yet he was treated like some *Second Class Creature* because he was Black skinned! It was the first time I really thought along those lines of reason.

The hypocrisy! The prejudice! Who could I ever believe again? All the lies! All the pain of man! The indignity! I had heard about the Ku Klux Klan. Kennedy seemed to want to help. I thought about how Lincoln had a Secretary named Kennedy and Kennedy's Secretary was named Lincoln. What did it all mean? Who was behind all this?

Didn't anybody ever notice there wasn't a single Black Man, Woman or Child in Carlisle, or Flamborough Center, or in Waterdown? There was not a single Negro in any school, or soda shop, in this whole area! But there were some Chinese living in these towns. And some French people who didn't speak English. I wondered how they existed here. My next door neighbours were German and the Fatherland was responsible for the deaths of seventy million people! Why were things the way they were? Didn't anybody else care besides me and Bob Dylan? I felt betrayed. What was Society feeding me? I wanted to puke!

"Yes 'n' how many ears must one man have
Before he can hear people cry?"

I had never felt this way before. He was singing to me! He could hear my tears! He could feel me sigh! He had no answers, but his telling me that it was, "blowin' in the wind" alarmed me! It made me want to be Real! I wanted to tell the world! And for the first time in my life, I felt like there were people out there that might truly listen!

Well, that was the first time I ever heard Bob Dylan. 'With God on Our Side' was my favorite Dylan song. I loved Him singing it with Joan Baez! 'Mr. Tambourine Man' was my favorite ballad. 'Bringing it all Back Home' was my favorite album'. And a couple years later it all changed. He went to England and told himself, "Don't Look Back!" I heard from the press Bob had gone crazy and was doing his pensive, chilling ballads to wild rockabilly beats, with a Band, no less, called the Band!

What's more, I heard he was booed at every concert he performed for the Queen's People! All I could think was, well sure, bloody Brits will do anything to make the Beatles number one! And I swore I would buy his new album called, 'Blonde on Blonde'. I knew George Lennon would understand. As would Camille, Taurus and Rip, nestled in their Basement Lounge where they were no longer waiting for the *Change*. It was here, baby!

So I bought this double album. It pretty much cleaned me out most of my soil offering berry picking money. I listened to and marvelled at it. I couldn't believe people actually booed these songs. They were so driving, and deep, yet upbeat. The only song The Hawks (soon to be The Band) played on the album was, '(Sooner or Later) One of Us Must Know'. But they played many Dylan songs behind him on stage in England, masterfully. And Britain booed this?

The Beatles now sounded so childish. It was known that Lennon was writing, what the other Beatles called, "ala Bob", but he could never match the roots or the *'Dirt under the Fingernails Sound'*. The voice of a Raga-Muffin! His beat was completely *different*. I was at a crossroads. To hear more of this new, true sound, I started listening more to the *Hawks*, when they backed up Rockin' Ronnie Hawkins raucous sound. I suddenly understood. These guys were Soulfully Rockin'! Bob merely couldn't help himself!

With the influx of folk music, and Human Rights happening in the Streets, I started listening to Buffy St. Marie instead of Joan Baez, and Peter Lafarge, who sang 'Ira Hayes' and 'I Ride an Old Paint'. Yet I felt there was something missing. These Artists were not picked up by radio stations, apparently because they sang about the White injustices done to the Indian Human Beings. They were told by the Stations that they didn't play their songs because people wanted to listen to music to feel happy, not guilty. Feeble!!

There was a Native Human Being who Bud hired, off and on, in the early to mid-sixties, to do jobs on the roof, and anywhere else that Bud did not feel safe. As he was eating one day, I asked this Human Being if he had heard of *Link Wray*. He looked at me like he had seen an Eagle being attacked by a flock of small birds… like it didn't make sense. He said, "How do you know about Link Wray?" I almost felt like I had done something wrong. I told Him I had heard 'Rumble' on the radio, and I thought it was the Greatest Guitar Rift in history! He suddenly decided that maybe I was worth telling something to, something that he knew that I was already dying to hear.

He said, "Did you know Link Wray was an Indian?"

I said "Yea I did."

He asked me if I listened to other Indian Artists. I told him I had never heard 'Indians' on the Top 30 Chart. He grunted and said,

"You ever heard of Robbie Robertson?"

I perked up and said, "Oh yea, he's in the Hawks. He's played behind Dylan," feeling proud and informed.

He said "He's an Indian". I was shocked. Dylan was playing with Indians?! Nobody was commonly saying 'Far out' yet, so I just grinned about this fact. He then said, "Ever hear of Buffy St. Marie?"

And once again I boasted my tiny bit of knowledge, and reassured him, "I know she's a folk singer down in the Village, but I haven't heard much of her music."

He affirmed, "She's an Indian." I was stunned. He then said, "Ever heard of Peter La Farge?"

I gushed that I knew Johnny Cash recorded an album of his songs, called 'Bitter Tears: Ballads of the American Indian', that my brother Paul owned. This time we both chanted together, "He's an Indian'!?!" I was aware of La Farge because of Cash singing, 'Ballad of Ira Hayes', which Pete wrote and had recorded himself.

I remember seeing Johnny on TV, onstage, introducing a Peter La Farge song he was about to sing. I remember Cash saying that he personally had "No Indian in his Blood, but plenty in his Heart", or something to that effect. The times they were a-changing!

The Human Being next told me to go to the Library and look up *Indian Artists*. When I said I would, he taunted me, "Don't waste your time." He then said the only thing I'd find there were pictures of Iroquois Braves being wiped out, for the good of the White Nation.

As a young Irish rebel who was feeling change in the air, I went over to Camille's house. I knew Taurus would know about *Indian Artists*. He knew everything about music! And he was my Mentor, about all music *non-Beatles* and pop. Taurus did not become my direct musical Mentor until the Seventies, as Camille played Taurus' and Rip's albums for me in their basement, cause Taurus was much older than I was at first, but he's younger than that now.

Taurus had a stack of Native Indian Artist's LPs that included all the music the Human Being had discussed with me. When we took the conversation upstairs, Mrs. Earl expressed to me that in England, "Indians of America were considered Elite Artists". The only 'Indian' music I could remember hearing wasn't music by Native Indian Artists at all. Only gumbo mungo beats, by White Studio Musicians on TV movies, where John Wayne shot them between Cowboy songs.

When I went to St. Thomas School the next year, one day Mrs. Griffiths directed our class to open one of our texts that discussed Canadian Artists like Bruce Cockburn and Robbie Robertson. I expressed my interest in Native Musicians, like Robertson, and she directed me towards some books that were right there in the classroom, which included, 'House Made of Dawn' by Scot Momaday. Who knew? The *secret* of Elite Indian Artists was getting out. It was only natural. One day recently, I felt particularly wounded for Native Drummer, Randy Castillo. I felt abused and nonplussed in my soul for Randy, so I burned some sage and spoke to his Sabotaged Spirits in my song…

Wounded Knee…

Wounded Knee
Wounded eyes

54

Wounded hearts
Wounded minds.
Wounded Nation
Wounded Shrine
Wounded Universe
Wounded Time.

Wounded Spirit
Wounded Brew
Wounded Me
Wounded You.
Wounded Charlie Patton
Wounded Link Wray
Wounded Night
Wounded Day.

Wounded Circles
Wounded Zeroes
Wounded Feathers
Wounded Heroes.
Wounded Past
Wounded Present
Wounded Intentions
Wounded Lament.

Wounded Eagle
Wounded Streams
Wounded Dancers
Wounded Dreams.
Wounded Redbone
Wounded Pride
Wounded Jimmy
Wounded Inside.

Wounded Rocks
Wounded Trees
Wounded Sinners
Wounded Graffiti.
Wounded Jessie Ed Davis
Wounded Attitude
Wounded Robbie
Wounded Accrued.

Wounded Peace
Wounded Wars
Wounded Skies
Wounded Doors.
Wounded Buffy
Wounded Cultures
Wounded Clouds
Wounded Vultures.

Wounded Rainbows
Wounded Riel
Wounded Manitou
Wounded Hell
Wounded Bows
Wounded Arrows
Wounded Papoose
Wounded Sorrows.

Wounded Mildred Bailey
Wounded Rainbows
Wounded Beats
Wounded Meadows.
Wounded Days
Wounded Nights .

Wounded Beliefs
Wounded Rights.

Wounded Language
Wounded Fears
Wounded Crows
Wounded Tears.
Wounded Wigwams
Wounded Teepees
Wounded Reservations
Wounded Deeply.

Wounded Lone Wolf
Wounded Red Cloud
Wounded Crazy Horse
Wounded Out Loud.
Wounded Sitting Bill
Wounded John Trudell
Wounded Catherine Tekakwitha
Wounded Struggle.

Wounded Tecumseh
Wounded Nancy Ward
Wounded Pontiac
Wounded and Ignored.
Wounded Wilma Mankiller
Wounded Big Bear
Wounded Worriers
Wounded and Aware.

Wounded drums
Wounded Buffalo
Wounded Randy Castillo
Wounded Geronimo.
Wounded Chiefs

Wounded Dan George
Wounded Handsome Lake
Wounded Ben Nighthorse.

Wounded Cornplanter
Wounded Black Kettle
Wounded Delaware Prophet
Wounded Petal.
Wounded Lac La Croix
Wounded Mary Two Ax Earley
Wounded Before Dawn
Wounded Prematurely.

Wounded First Nation
Wounded Second Chance
Wounded Billy Mills
Wounded Rain Dance.
Wounded Birds
Wounded Harold Cardinal
Wounded Red Jack
Wounded Incontrovertible.

Wounded Wakan Tanka
Wounded Ponies
Wounded Rituals
Wounded Cronies.
Wounded Again
Wounded Banshee
Wounded Forever!
At wounded Knee.

Jimbo

When I was a kid, in my life, there was only music. I worked diligently at local farms so I could buy albums. Most people don't own hard copies of their own music today, so Millenniums can't dig what a record, tape, or CD collection was all about. Sadly, this leaves them void to one my Youth's greatest loves; my Music Collection.

Whether it was picking back-breaking beans at Olson's farm, or raspberries at Newman's berry patch, my employers all raved to my parents that I was out-picking all the other workers by leaps and bounds. The fact was, I had just been turned on to the new band *Cream*, with Ginger Baker, Jack Bruce and Eric Clapton. I desperately wanted to buy their first album, 'Fresh Cream' and also their latest, 'Disraeli Gears'. To my ears, they had left the Beatles so far behind musically, and artistically, that I realized it was a *New Age*, all over again.

Hadn't that just happened with Dylan only a couple years before? And then again with the *Fabs* on Ed Sullivan! They started the first British Invasion. And all along, there was Motown! I began to understand that throughout life, People, Fads, Artists and Musicians had to be constantly *'reinventing'* themselves, just to remain alive. Artists and bands needed to keep abreast of the avant-garde, to keep being truly cool, to groove with the Times, and to Make it Happen!.

In 1966, Cream changed the whole *chemical process*. I absolutely had to own these albums, and I picked berries like a psychotic monkey grabbing bananas for the hottest She-Ape in the Jungle! Clapton, and Cream, were another part of the *Social Change* that was happening everywhere in the Sixties. They were part of the change back to guitar. It was a global change. These albums changed the way I thought. Then the culture changed back to the Beatles again, when the 'Sergeant Peppers Lonely

Hearts Club Band' album was released on June first, 1967, in America on Capitol. I didn't hear the album until July. Thank again George Lennon!

In the meantime, I was picking berries and groovin' to Jeff Beck, greatest guitarist in history. Man, I was picking a hundred pints a day compared to everyone else's fifteen to thirty. I could hear those albums with every berry I picked. As I toiled, I thought about Ginger Baker's style of drumming… as being much more… almost jazzy… compared to Ringo's pounding, or Keith Moon's insane bashings until his kit was dishevelled upon the stage… you know… My Generation … literally!

I thought Clapton's *Gibson Les Paul* guitar riffs, and Vox *Wah-Wah Pedal, was* more for the Soul Searchers than Beatle George's *Fender Stratocaster*. But keep in mind I hadn't heard Georg's electric licks on the 'Sergeant Peppers' intro cut yet. That was on the *other side* of what was being created. So was George's surprisingly creative Sitar on his cut called 'Within You Without You'. Dazzling! Paul McCartney's bass truly *speaks to Time* itself as truly one of the best. And the only Creature I ever saw that was in any way comparable to John, was Kurt Cobain.

Yea, then the second English Invasion transpired! And man, I was there! Nothing suddenly could compare to Pete Townsend's windmill guitar licks and song writing! With all these sounds in my mind one day, as I was taking my hand basket of freshly picked raspberries around the cement silo, on my way to the shade of the cool garage, *Wham!* It all changed again!

Step after step I kept hearing the most interesting, subtle, poetical, self-examining, prophetic, masculine, different, never-before-never-again moment of clarity! I suddenly heard the words of the New Mantra of the just discovered Universe. And it was saying;

"You know that it would be untrue.
You know that I would be a liar.

If I was to say to you
Girl we couldn't get much higher.
Come on baby light my fire!"

There was something so absolutely stranger, darker, and out of body experiencing to these words. And they were sung to the sounds of a Beat Generational eloquence and ominousness; of Kerouactisity, with no bass. Talk about re-inventing the Galaxy that we once thought had boundaries! God, we needed trans dental meditation, gurus, mantras, mind expanding agents, Ravi Shankar, Allen Ginsburg, Hunter Thompson, Woodstock, Mothers Little Helpers and trips to the Moon after hearing Morrison *Light the World on Fire!* Jim came on like a Vampire in Leather. He was the newest, darkest, *Neon Californian Man!* Other west-coast groups like *The Byrds* had started a new buzz, but Jim kicked the Doors of rock and blues Wide Open. He was a seething *Self-Destructive Madman* that would start a riot on a bored whim, and then sing fragilely, and beautifully, to the Spirits of Indian braves who were still wandering the bi-ways and *desert paths* of their Limbos in Time.

Buying the new Cream albums suddenly, within a micro-cosmic second, seemed as antiquated a notion, to me, as buying a Beatle album was the week before. Not that I'm trying to portray myself as Tom Wolfe, in his novel, 'The Painted Word'; criticizing or chastising anybody for their work, or breaking a butterfly upon a wheel. This is simply one of the conditions of *Changing with the Times*, then *Changing to Create the Times.* The new Mick Jagger? Ha, indeed! Mick hadn't yet created 'Sympathy for the Devil', which in doing so, he and Keith created a whole new Rhythm and Blues space and sound. So, his time had not even come yet. Jim's time had come!

I had truly never related to another kind of music like the Doors before. Or since! Mind you, Jim gave his soul for his music and words. The Devil never had a Poster Boy like this One, who was already drunk when they met at the Cross Roads. The earth was echoing Jim's harmonies against a crimson sky of things to come. He reflected the mood of narcs busting our asses, Viet Nam protesters, James Dean, and Altamont! He was a Painted Poet and a Marked Man. A life well used, as well as abused. A narcissist with wings, and fangs!

The Earls and the Irish Potato Farmers

The Earls were an English family that lived in Malstone, out in the Sticks. In the 1960s, they would appear for an occasional visit at Bud's farm. Their family would suddenly drive up my parent's laneway, every so often, with the car stacked full of a gentle, grinning English Brood. Mr. Earl had come over to Canada as an Engineer in 1955, to work on the Avro Canada CF-105 Arrow; a Delta Winged Interceptor, built by Avro Canada. He brought his wife Tanya, and his sons Taurus and Rip. Tanya was a well-read, intelligent woman, who was somewhat pseudo refined, and a nature I can only describe as intriguing, yet somewhat overpowering. She felt she needed to be, as their three boys were *Poster Children* of the Sixties.

The Earl's third son, Camille, was born in an airplane flying over the Atlantic. He was stocky, like Tanya, and likewise very well read, like Tanya. I recognized right away, the first time we spoke, that Camille was different; he was keen. Cool. They all spoke their entire lives with English accents. They acted out their lives in English fashion. Like a lot of English Lots, they believed, after Britain conquered and tamed the Globe for centuries, that they are the reason that there is any *rhyme or reason* in the world today. They carried an aura of an attractive arrogance beneath their breaths, and were only too kind to admit it, if pressed.

Tanya was this way, and Camille was aware he was advanced, intellectually and culturally, past many of the *out-back* kids that he attended school with. He read full time. He could recite Ginsberg's 'Howl" while the rest of us were barely reading *Mad Magazine.* Of course, Camille read *Mad* also. His brothers, Taurus and Rip, had fantastic bedroom *lounges* down in the basement, with a *boss stereo,* and tons of music that would change my life. They had every album I had never heard. Taurus, like Dean Wagner, became my *Second Musical Guru.*

He introduced me to R&B things like '30 Days in the Hole' by Humble Pie, as well as masterpieces by; Johnny Winter, John Mayall, Joe Cocker, the Hollies, Traffic, early Fleetwood Mac with Peter Greene, the Stone's new R&B sound on Beggar's Banquet, Muddy Waters, Alexis Korner, jazzman Chris Barber, Blues Incorporated, Long John Baldry, Graham Bond, the Bluesbreakers, Jack Bruce, Ginger Baker, Peter Green, Mic Taylor, Jeff Beck (most resourceful guitarist ever), Bo Diddley, Yardbirds, George Fame, Zoot Money, the Spencer Davis Group, Steve Windwood, Small Faces, Ray Davies, Eric Burdon, Van Morrison, The Creation, the Action, the Who, Clapton, Ian Anderson, Cream, Davy Graham (who played with Alexis Korner), Alvin Lee and Ten Years After, Savoy Brown, Free, guitarist Paul Kossoff, Jethro Tull, Zepplin, Black Sabbath, Deep Purple, etcetera... I mean, I had heard scraps of this music on our Amplitude Modulation Radio two miles north east on Bud's Farm, but Taurus owned ALL these albums, and knew everything there was to know about Rhythm and Blues. Pop groups, like the Beatles, were not appreciated in this space. I had to grow.

Camille and I would gobble some LSD at St. Mary's, and then hop on the school bus, or hitch a ride over to his parents place. There we would cruise down-stairs, to Trip on this Music that tasted distorted, and wasn't at all about Penny Lane or Herman's Hermits. We would Peak, then get Weak, then inevitably seek permission for me to stay overnight... then Peak again in Camille's room at midnight, and come down long enough to maybe slog off for an hour. We would rise to the new sun, go to school, get more LSD, and start another day.

From fourteen years old to seventeen I invested in about five hundred trips of LSD, along with mushrooms, MDA, peyote, ecstasy, cocaine, mescaline, MDMA, methamphetamine, PCP angel dust, and to keep the buzz going, I smoked China, sucked off cylinders of Laughing Gas, and dabbled in stimulants when necessary. Between 1969 and 1973, none of the kids I went to School with had any time for *academics,* or the *curriculum* offered at St. Mary's. But we wouldn't miss school for the world!

Camille made it at St. Mary's until early 1972. By then I was preparing for my first trip to the West Coast, after our Irish Roman Catholic Principle was sent to Jamaica to dry out from too much rum, cigarettes, and innocent *cosmic involvement* with us, his self admittedly insane students. It was all a scheme to get rid of Father Rafferty O'Riley. So the second-in-command, Sister Mary Elephant, took her stab at Power and Control. In Father O'Riley's absence to protect us, Sister Elephant kicked all the Dead Heads out before Rafferty was able to return. Thanks Sister Mary Elephant!

All I needed was a little push in the Right Direction! But I'm getting ahead of myself. First, St. Mary's had much to teach me!

Chapter 6
St. Mary's

While attending St. Mary's High School, located in Hamilton on the grounds of the massive stone-erected Catholic Basilica Church, I had much to learn. The Church was perched on the Highway 403 ramp that exited freeway drivers, and hitcher-hikers, towards Toronto. As I mused, St. Mary's had a lot to teach me, in just the right amount of time. Things like; charm, stamina, bravery, sex, hiding, love, partying, politics, chess, movies, strategies, cliques, expectations, disappointments, victories, modesty, music, bragging rights, Richard Nixon, conscientiousness, reading, hockey, art, religion, war, Waiting for Godot, motorcycles, writing, hitch hiking, rings, jewelry, smoking, drinking, chillin', deals, meals, navy seals, chemistry, colours, images, land lords, blue grass, the Byrds, traveling, surviving, giving, taking, pain, sorrow, losses, gains, basketball, Baltimore Orioles, Peter Max, Gerry Garcia, trigonometry, cheap wines, police, sidewalks, Jim Morrison, triple beam balance scales, trust, The God Father part one, Jack Nicolson, Ken Kesey, West Coast Swing, San Francisco, curries, highways, bi-ways, Gordon Lightfoot, Ravi Shankar, risk, strangeness, Dr. Strange Love, astrology, fun, Bangladesh, God, idols, statues, hashish, mantras, sincerity, lies, meditating, LSD, stone roads, rocks, Muscle Shoals, the desert, the Joshua Tree, loading, reloading, rolling joints, saying yes, being brave, Detroit, night clubs, Freak Brothers, Woodstock, Viet Nam, bombs, fire, H2O, trying, Texas, fear, obscurity, cities, Lao Tzu, equality, inequality, rainbows, rain, museums, Vancouver, mountains, running away, sleeping in cars, James Dean, rebels, revolutions, painters, rent, tapestries, Danish beer, mesculine, mushrooms, melodramas, bongos, spoons, singing, chalk boards, skinny dippin, weekend trippin, picture frames, spark plugs, geometry, Spain, Kareem Abdul Jabbar, Q & A, T & A, rushes, brushes, Fry Boots, harmonicas, cafeterias, churches, vestibules, rules, money, rip offs, England, David Geffen, Neil, stars, cars, bars, truckin, cops, couches, pizza, turn tables, maps, the big picture, inner space, back alleys, bent bumpers, Elia Kazan, turning the cheek, tractors, Terry Molloy, Brian Jones, orgies, Marilyn, Twiggy, Janice, Cher, the Ponies, Egypt, dictionaries, clouds, fields, ravens, hawks, doves, cowards, liars, cheats, clean sheets, Taj Mahal, Gas Town, Broad Shoulders, promises, peep shows, cutting grass, dreaming, teachers, assassinations, lost chances, Court and Spark, the Hurricane, Jimmy, Seattle, Glendale, Willie, crows, Merle, Pig Pen, trains, sculptures, circles, answers, chances, casting couches, Tarantino, Jeff Beck, believing, forgiving, translating, Bobby Orr, Candelabras, Caesar salad, getting over it, foot in cold water, have nots, Dean Moriarty, Steely Dan, squares, diamonds, tooth paste, dandruff, keepers, Chief Dan George, the past, mosquitoes, do's, don'ts, entertaining, screaming, whispering, wishing, denying, surprising, guessing, Black Sabbath, bus transfers, brown sugar, counting, running, memorizing, Quick Silver Messenger Service, whores, subways, collateral, granny glasses, dirt, mud, cement, and math.

For sure, there was a bit of math. It's all relative.

In its stately splendor, St. Mary's High was a large Roman Basilica building, built with the donations from the collection plates in Roman Catholic Churches from loyal Dioceses, over the years, across Southern Ontario. Who knows, maybe there was grease on the fire all the way from Rome. But there it was; for the sake of Heaven and Earth, bought and paid for. And for our convenience!

We were termed a 'Separate School', and were taught by R.C. Priests, Nuns, and Teachers who were either Catholic, or Italian, or both. This made sense because of the eight hundred St. Mary's students the first year, seven hundred and fifty were of Italian or Portuguese decent. And then there were *us;* fifty white dudes with attitudes! We were Dudes and Dudettes who came from the Sticks. Country kids, whose Catholic parents battled for years to keep them in Catholic schools, for their entire academic careers.

But that did not include this *hick* from out in the potato fields of Carlisle. Bud's farm was in some different County, and we were not in any Catholic jurisdictions, apparently. And this drove my very Catholic Mother very crazy. She had changed to this Catholic religion, in a WASP community, and we never missed Mass. My brother Paul was an Altar-Boy in the Church, and in time he rebuilt many facets of the Chantry.

But times were changing by the end of the Sixties, and with the Basilica Church suddenly sponsoring the new St. Mary's High School, we were in the *daunted door.* Regina's prayers were answered! My first blow-job was in this church, while the organ wailed something uplifting.

To get to St. Mary's from Carlisle, I had to get up at six in the morning and transfer on three different buses, at three different Schools, across Wentworth County to get into Hamilton. Almost two hours later, I would get off my third bus on the Hunt Street Bridge, dump off my books at my locker, head out to the top of the massive stone steps in front of the Church, and smoke my first joint of the day. This would be about 8:30.

We would puff, and compare what new drugs we scored at the Dundas Pool Hall the night before. Then we'd discuss what scores we were going to make, as soon as we ventured down onto the highway ramp that took us to Rochdale College. You could score any drug imaginable from the Draft Dodging Dealers that our

Prime Minister, Pierre Elliot Trudeau, had just given amnesty to, so they could legally hide out here in Canada. Thanks Pierre! All the best drug dealers from every city, in every State, crossed the forty-ninth line of latitude, and made a trek straight to the coolest spot in Canada; Rochdale College.

Who was that Unmasked Man?

I was standing in the brand new, circular constructed, *Christ the King* school building. It was erected beside St. Mary's. We used the third and top floor of the huge building for classes. The third floor was an open concept, where no walls separated classes, but distance provided concealment and privacy. I attended my *World Religions* class up there three times each week. I had an *acid* hang-over that morning, as I was standing vacantly, waiting for everyone to show up.

George Lennon and I usually sat together at the back of the Class, making funny sounds (funny to us), while we were creating and documenting a new language. This new style of speech was something we had started at the back of French Class, which we only attended sporadically, when we felt inspired to continue our private lexicon. I realized a few years later, that the full notebook, or glossary, was full of gibberish and phrases that were very similar to the Jamaican language.

I worked with a group of Jamaicans in 1974, and one day, in comical frustration, I called one of then, named 'Dart', a "Rosshole mon." Apparently that was a swear word on the Island. They asked how I knew such a dirty word. When I told them I made it up, they stared at me strangely. I dipped back a few years to other semantics from the back of my French Class, like, "Bumbaclot." They screamed and howled, as apparently I had hit the jack pot again. Every other 'created' word I expressed, apparently, was a form of Jamaican colloquy. And

68

almost always, they were profane or obscene words of some form of indecent impropriety.

Dart was always begging me for some pot. When I brought him some hash one day, he was disgusted. He promised me that some day when I visited him on the Island, he would get me some real good buds. So finally I got Dart some *dangerous buds,* and he reaffirmed that upon my arrival to his homeland, he would get me three foot long buds. I grinned, and told Dart I would look him up for sure. But the visit never materialized, as Dart ended up *wooing* the Bosses' wife, and moved into his house as the Bossman moved out. The next time I saw Dart, I called him a 'bumbalapussylarossholeclotmon'. That too, it was revealed to me, was a serious Jamaican swear word that they obviously borrowed from George's and my 'Book of Unknown Obscenities'. Who knew?

By this time, George had stopped attending Classes at St. Mary's, which explained my waiting alone for whoever, or whatever, was happening next in the top of this round building. I was lost for a time without George. The Beatles had broken up and that also left me unfound. I wasn't ready for Black Sabbath quite yet.

George told me the day the *Fabs* broke up was the saddest day of his life. It was much worse for me, as already so many of my heroes were dying, or dead... Buddy Holly, JFK, Malcom X, Martin Luther King Jr., Otis Redding, Bobby, Cesar Chavez, Gandhi, the suicide of Ernest Hemingway, Albert Camus, Marilyn Monroe, Patsy Cline, Sam Cooke, Bobby Fuller (4), Lenny Bruce, Jayne Mansfield, Frankie Lymon, Brian Jones, Sharon Tate; to name a few... I thought the World was Dead.

When a friend or a family member dies, a piece of your heart dies with them. But when a Hero dies, it takes with it so many dimensions; of Your Idealism, Your Freedom, Your Inspiration,

Your Philosophy, Your Bravery, a piece of Your Mind; a piece of Your Soul… Ed Sullivan turned me on to the Fab Four (thanks Dean Wagner!), but it was George who understood who they really were. George was a truly gifted genius, not an Intellectual per say, but an Entity of Knowledge and Understanding. Classmates were aware of his *potential*. George and I shared writing and reading books, poetry, philosophy, time, space, and we were in tune together with John Lennon. In High School, George really looked like Lennon off the Abbey Road album. We agreed that was the Band's greatest moment of talent and expression. To this day it is my favorite piece of music.

And now they were gone. And so was George. Stairways seemed empty, and halls were just filled with inaccessible faces. Life was bitter sweet, and the sky was distant and vacant. The Future seemed desolate and devoid. Life became a song no one listened to, like an army without a cause, a revolution with no direction, a heart without love. Flowers without water die. Life with no sun is demur. Motherless Children cry when no one listens. Old soldiers never die, just fade away. It's was a predictable syndrome; the *Cult of the fallen Fabs* were now a huge Planetary Tribe, with collective holes in their souls and psyches, for which an alternate sect of Psychiatrists and Mental Therapists would make their fortunes upon. We would simply waste away until we had children to fill our time with, instead of being twentieth century Disciples of peace, art and love. Like discarded toys that were out dated, Beatle People walked the streets in the rain. Rainbows now struggled to be seen amid day-glow neon flashes. We helplessly became a generation of freaks, not so innocent anymore, waiting for Kent State.

What was to done with us? We were dazed and confused fourteen year old kids, with burnt out fantasies, and fashions that didn't matter anymore. This was a collective time for many of us who had lived with our parents in the Sixties, and now found ourselves out on our own. Some of us were still sleeping in unlocked cars! It created a sense of unrest, and mistrust, after Charlie Manson did his dirge for Satan in hippie hair and harems... no one trusted a Freak at that point. We weren't cute anymore. Beatle haircuts and boots just got ya stomped out on the road. Tarantino got it right once upon a time...

Money stopped flowing, and a new generation of *poverty* was forced upon America. Frisco was like poison. The needles and rip offs were now just part of its own sub culture. It was part of growing up. They warned us... never trust anyone over thirty, don't get in cars when the driver's drooling, and Nixon sucked.

I suppose all this was flowing in and out of my mind, when suddenly this tall, skinny, smiling, presumptuous and presiding Freak with a massive afro down to his waist came bounding and leaping up to me. He coyly put three albums in my hands, as if to say, "It's gonna be alright!" He smiled, ear to ear, and then bounded off again. In just a moment I was left with these albums in my hands, and the question left on my lips of; "Who was that unmasked man?"

I had seen him from a distance around St. Mary's, and all I knew of him was that he bounded when he walked, and he smiled a lot. I had never spoken to him before, and I guess I still hadn't. But that's the kinda stuff that happened all the time in the *Magic Years*. There was a generational trust between us. And strange shit happened. Impressions were made, and Legends were born. I then glimpsed, for the first time, at the album covers. I recognized the *Grateful Dead* from a song I had heard on the CHUM FM radio station out of Toronto, called 'The Golden Road to Unlimited Devotion'. I didn't dig that song, but the album (their first) was incredible. These particular albums were called, 'Working Man's Dead' and 'American Beauty'. There was another album by the group, 'The New Riders of the Purple Sage'.

The songs on *American Beauty*, coincidentally, reflected the two and three part harmonies of the Beatles, or 'Crosby, Stills & Nash', with sweet voices calling sweeter ears to listen. There was a song called 'Truckin' that was the audible equivalency of an *R. Crumb* comic; a song serenading the history of the Dead and the Cosmic Culture, at that time.

When I heard the first song called 'Box of Rain', I acknowledged this was something really different; a real flowing beat to the sound of laid back country-rock ballads. It was kind of *Country Rock* in the sense that there was nothing to compare it to back then. Next, 'Friend of the Devil' was as classic a gem as 'Momma Tried' by Merle or 'Ring of Fire' by the Man in Black. Getting turned on to the Grateful Dead and the New Riders at the same time is perfect, now, or back then. I saw them gig together at around twenty, twenty-five concerts in the Seventies.

They were like Dylan and the Band; a hell of a one-two punch. But that's what the Dead did! They were chosen minstrels by Owsley from their first Acid Test at Babs' cabin, to their appearances at the Fillmores East & West, the Avalon Ballrooms, Woodstock's three days of Peace and Music, European Tours, Egypt and eventually Mars! It was always as much, or more, about the Cosmic Beat than the literal Sound. We were a Cosmic Tribe. We would recognize each other immediately. Like war veterans, or athletes on the same sports team, we were the same portion of the same problem, and result. We loved it and lived it.

My life was saved by this unmasked man! I told him the next day, after playing the albums all night long, to take them back because I was probably sleeping in an unlocked car that night. We grinned. We knew. All my heroes weren't dead all the sudden, because of the *Dead!* This was the cue for my marching on, just to a new beat. I told him that in one night's appreciation, I was now a Dead Head.

My life soon revolved and evolved around their concert tours. I guess Oak was a Dead Dog. Every fiend, woman, animal, musician, prophet, or biker that I ever knew, from that moment on, were Dead Heads. We WERE the Counter Culture. Naturally, everything I did in life from that moment was in conjunction with the new *Fab Five*. I knew I was wearing my post-Beatle-pose perfectly, but I never expected this to happen. I was now one of Gerry's Problem Children.

Chapter 7
Canadian Gray Hound
verses American
Grey Hound

As the bus was pulling out of the Gray Hound Station in dank, winter gray Hamilton, I could hear from the bent background Don McLean singing, 'American Pie', from a gray speaker up on a frozen gray garter. He was saying 'goodbye' and so was I. Don, to the American Dream, and I was movin' on ala Gray Hound. I had just eaten a tab of Green Frog acid, I was broke, and I was headed out on this bus to Detroit, where Gordon Lightfoot was singin' about that Black Day in July. Well this was December, Gord. Frozen Motor City Madness!

It was a day like any other in Dreary December of 1971. I had my breakfast of porridge and smiles from Regina, who was off the couch after a rough couple years due to mental stresses. She reminded Marilyn and I to grab the lunches she had made. "Thanks Regina."

Marilyn was attending high-school at Notre Dame Academy, which was located somewhat in its Gothic glory, on the scenic, windy *Snake Road*. All my sisters attended this Convent for their high schooling. Mary started in grade nine, while Patricia took the Waterdown Public High School detour route. Pat was more advantageous. She enjoyed flirting, and fighting, with *the Rough House Boys* of Wentworth County.

That was until one day, when she was in a *'To the De*ath' water-gun battle with 'Crusher', aka Tim Schiller, and his Droogs of the

Day (as Alex would say in one of his Clockwork moods). Things come and go in cycles; beats cannot be predicted, or ignored. For instance, Yo-Yo's were big in the age of Beaver Cleaver, but they were put on the shelf by the early Sixties. Squirt guns were the Weapons of Destruction that day at Waterdown High, and my older sister, Patricia, was in the Front Lines!

Their juvenile excitement came to a pinnacle as kids were running and screaming through the hallways. The *never-ignored loud speaker* acknowledged their young and *not-so-innocent* frolics, and told them it was time to Stop! The Principal warned that there would be consequences for the next warm pistol not holstered! Now I have to say, of anybody in my Family, Patricia was the only one even close to my level of not liking to be told what to do. She kept her pistol liquidly loaded and ready for *action*, like any good Soldier, I suppose. Lunch hour was coming to an end, and Patricia made one last brave charge to soak 'Crusher' before class started. So when he ducked into the Men's washroom Pat followed, and indiscriminately squirted everybody engaged at the line of urinals. She emptied her pistol at the Enemy and was about to dash to class, when the Principal, who was now finished at his urinal, turned around and shouted, "Organ, get in the Office!" He called our Parents and said Patricia would never return to his blessed Waterdown High. He was right. Patricia was enrolled at the Notre Dame Academy the next day with some cajoling and begging from our Parents. It must have been weird for my rambunctious Sister to suddenly be dealing with the sacrosanct Sisters.

This particularly gray morning, Marilyn and I were waiting at the bottom of the stairs, just inside the outside door. We were waiting for the bus that would take us to our R.C. Separate Asylums. Now Marilyn had some MDA tucked away in a Kleenex, in her purse, for her and Samantha Creed to do that day at School. It was great to *trip off* in those massive Churches, with the giant stain glass windows and the pipe-organ sprawling its evoking sound from up above. The things we did in the Churches on our School Campuses are better left unsaid, in case God ever reads this!

I hadn't figured out my own *high* for that day, but at St. Mary's that was half the Challenge, which is to say half the Fun. I was sitting there in *anticipation* of another day of learning to *protest the obvious,* and decide which drugs go best on gray days, compared to grey days.

Suddenly Bud broke my train of thought! He came down the stairs and announced to me that if I didn't get a haircut that day, to not bother coming home! This was the kind of threat more *zealous parents* used on their fourteen year-old kids in those days. I took this as an invitation to my adventure for this day. "Thanks Bud!"

We soon both boarded the school bus as it pulled up outside the house (first of three buses for both of us). It was always noisy on the First Bus. I was thinking about what Bud had said below the loud chatter. I was thinking about where I would sleep that night. I was wondering what Woody Guthrie would do. I was thinking that a person could actually plan their lives around a text like Woody's book, 'Bound for Glory'. It told of plans and strategies that Woody, and most people of the Thirties, used to deal with tragedies and heartaches of a cruel and destitute time; the Dirty 30s. Mrs. Griffiths had insisted I read it. "Thanks Mrs. Griffiths!"

I was thinking I would get to St. Mary's, get rid of my books, smoke a joint, and ascertain what to do with my sudden day off. It was kinda like Ferris Bueller's Day Off, but without the car, or his attractive girlfriend, and definitely no baseball game that day. I was thinking it was cold out, but was it not cold for

General Brock at Queenston Heights?! The cruel Russian snows fell on Napoleon, yet he was not deterred. Maybe a little obsessed however, since he and forty thousand French Soldiers didn't make it home for Christmas.

As I was thinking about *my next thought,* suddenly Marilyn screamed! She was standing in the aisle with her eyes wide open, and bellowed out, "It's out of the Toilet Paper!" While everyone on the bus looked at each other, all shocked, confused, and bemused, I understood exactly what she meant. She was getting off on the MDA. It had come out of the toilet paper and into her stomach, into her blood system, and was Blowing her Mind! It was only logical!

I got off my Third Bus, finally, at St. Mary's and went looking for my morning joint. Just like a morning coffee and a cigarette, I had a joint and a hit off a cold beer. Stephen Dori, Dave Avon and Rave Rushie each had the same look of adventure in their eyes as I felt in my stomach! We smoked some hash on the church stairs, and then decided to go downtown and bum some money for some LSD. It was a good plan!

It was snowing. Once downtown, we split up to start panhandling. We would meet in half an hour, outside the Running Pump Hotel. It was always better to panhandle alone. Otherwise it looked like we were doing exactly what we were doing… bumming money to get high. An hour later we ate some Frog acid, and counted out three dollars and thirty-five cents that was left over. I grabbed the cash and deposited it into the new Savings Account, in my pocket.

"Why do you get the cash?" Stephen asked.

I said, "Watch this", and they followed me across the street to the Bus Station, on Rebecca Street, in the Gray North End. I walked up to the Ticket Seller and enquired "How far will this take me?" as I plopped down the change.

'You could go one way to Detroit," she replied in a drawl... never particularly expecting me to take her up on it of course.

"I'll take it" I declared, and got on the Bus.

So as *American Pie* was drifting even more into the background, I was on my way to Detroit. Shit was going on down there. I was fourteen. But I was a big kid, and I had false ID saying I was eighteen. I borrowed it the day before from Rick Shyhatt, and I was going to return it, but I just needed to cross the border with it first. I was sure he would understand when he heard that I was on the run! Another juvenile, taking my turn as a Soldier in the War between Generations; fighting never-ending battles of patronizing parents, skirmishes of being Young, the dirge against hypocrisies, politics, Nixon, Viet Nam, The DEA, protesting bullshit, the cops, Trudeau, Teachers, and Authority Figures telling us what to do when they couldn't see beyond what Society told them, a long time ago.

But we were figuring things out by ourselves. The times they were a-changing... I wouldn't be the only Soldier sleeping in an unlocked car that night. I wouldn't be alone looking for New Answers to Old Questions. It was all being played out on TV every day. The lies and hate during the Age of Insanity. When Sesame Street was over, you flipped the channel to watch War.

Cold's ok. So is hurt and pain when you're chasing something you really believe in. Something like running away from a haircut? When you think that you're right, you can feel a New Breath replacing the Old. When you feel sure of your concepts, you find yourself with Fresh Confidence! That's when you're fightin' the good fight. You know the one that makes you feel like an Artist. Like Mohammed Ali or Malcom X. Cold is beyond Cool.

So I got off the bus in the Detroit Greyhound Station on Howard, and immediately started searching out Grey Alleys for a place to sleep that Grey Night. I was counting the blocks from the Bus Station to the alley so I would have some kind of land-mark, or reference point… for what I don't know. At fourteen it's easy to get lost, and the Greyhound Station was the only place in Detroit I knew. It was noonish and I was *cruising*. I had found a flea bitten, hard core alley to sleep in, for later. I ate my lunch Regina had made me, and I was feeling like visiting Motown!

The truth about Detroit in the early Seventies, was that it was hard. MC-5 hard! Wayne Kramer, Iggy Pop and Alice Cooper had *costumes and edge*; Motor City Style! I wandered downtown, but didn't see Artists playing in the streets, or Friendly People gathering in the park like in Hamilton. It was just a bunch of guys laid off from Ford with a bunch of Grey Faces. There were fires burning on street corners. There was smoke coming out of buildings, and the snow began falling harder than before and then, *BOOM!* I got a super rush off the Frog! It was a Gas!

There were dudes all over the place, jivin' like in a Freaks Brothers comic book. I was gettin' down and trippin' round town, and I thought,

"This is important! This is reality up front! This is where it's happening! Too bad that Stephen, Dave and Rush couldn't be here! This is a groove!"

After a couple hours, I had a *Momentary Lapse from Hallucinating,* and decided to go through another park that I had come upon. At least I thought it was a park. It really was more like a *Jungle*. I thought about going through this sub-arctic tropical mess, but then I thought about all the streams, and the bog, and the strange obstructions I would be encountering. Suddenly I started think-ing about wild animals on the lurch, but then I thought, "Forget about it! What the hell… there's plenty of people around… If a gorilla or a leopard attacks me, they would help me!"

Now this 'acid' was only about fifty micrograms, I figured, but it was a still a couple hours before I came down enough to realize my reservation at the *deuced-out alley*, which I had made earlier, was long forfeited to an afternoon of forging through this downtown *Jungle*.

I didn't have a clue where I was. But I did know that I had no money, no more food, no Direction, and no Reason to be here anymore. I went to a phone booth and called my sister Mary, collect. Richard, her husband, and a cool dude, accepted my call. I told him I was having a fine day, and then blubbered out, "Rich, I can't find my alley, so could I stay the night at your place?" Richard tried to respond like he understood, but remained silent. They lived just across the border, in Windsor.

Well Regina and Bud had already phoned Mary, to announce that it was obvious to them that I had left home, as the School had informed them at noon that I hadn't attended classes that day. It was long after when I should have been home, if I was just skipping out. Marilyn was staying at Samantha's parent's house, coming down, but she had recently informed Regina, by telephone, that she didn't know where I was. She apparently reminded them that Bud had told me not to come home if I didn't get a haircut on that Gray Day. So they started phoning around ...

So when Mary took the phone from Richard, she already knew the poop. Mary worked as *Head Nurse* at the Detroit Hospital, and she knew the area well enough to assure me that she could be there within an hour, so just stay where I was, etcetera, etcetera, etcetera... (now echoing). So Mary picked me up and drove me across the border to Rich's and her house, which was cool. But the coolest part was that she didn't tell the parents that I was there. "I've won them over," I thought. "They're hip! They can be trusted. I was doing ok as a Soldier. I had converted the Masses of Two to My Side!"

Richard ran an *Elks Men's Store* in Windsor, and he hired me to work there. There was a crew of young guys and a Gal working there, and they made me *their project*. Lisa would talk to me real close, and Rich warned me she would probably even get closer. Rich ran the *joint,* with four Salesmen, and Lisa (I don't know what she did exactly), who treated me like a Gerent. I wished I had some more acid!

After a week, Mary asked me if I thought that maybe it was time to go back home, and deal with Bud, knowing now that she and Rich were in my corner. I said "Sure". They offered to drive me, but I took a bus instead... less bother the better... When I got off the bus back in Hamilton, I hitch hiked over to Camille's parent's house in Malstone, figuring I'd spend the night there.

I knocked on the door and Camille answered it. He grinned and greeted me like a Returning Soldier, or a Prodigal Son, or something. He said everybody was aware I had taken flight to the Motor City, so I was sort of gaining points as a 'Corporal in the Ranks of the Freaks Regiment of the Cosmic Conflict'. I was recounting my Adventures and Encounters of the Jungle when Tanya came round the corner, and with a dubious smile from ear to ear said, "Oh there you are!"

She immediately phoned Reg and Bud. So... an unexpected swift counter-move by the Enemy! It was a strategic victory on their part, as I was immediately whisked home. But you have to remember to respect your Enemies, or you then become like them, and then what was this war even for?

Chapter 8
Pride and Prejudice

The Sixties are remembered for the Beatles, hippies, LSD, free love, free sex, rock and roll, Landing on the Moon, Timothy Leary, Ken Kesey, the Camaro, the British invasions part 1 & 2, Peter Max, psychedelia, Twiggy, Thomas Wolfe, JFK, RFK, inter-related cultural and political trends around the globe, Sonny and Cher, and Woodstock; an Aquarian Exposition. If you were white that is. If you weren't, it was a decade of catch up. Images more real that would come to mind for minorities included the assassinations of Malcom X and Martin Luther King Jr., fighting for civil rights, fighting for a right to vote, fighting the cops, a thirty percent chance greater of fighting in Viet Nam, losing the Kennedy's support, fighting to be accepted in institutions of learning, fighting poverty, fighting in the streets, fighting in urban riots and massive rallies, fighting off cops at peaceful sit-ins, fighting for a front seat on a bus, fighting discrimination and prejudice, fighting for food, fighting for breath, and fighting so their children wouldn't have to fight as hard for scraps that fell off the plate of a Dominant White Society.

I know this because I saw it on TV. I saw the KKK in White Hoods, a slight figure lighting himself on fire in the Streets of Saigon, and yes, we did see half of the President's head fly off. As well as Martin Luther King getting gunned down on a balcony at the Lorraine Motel, which was part of the complex of the National Civil Rights Museum, in Memphis Tennessee.

But I was born white. Not a WASP, but I ate well, and attended my schools mostly unmolested. I had money for albums, and a donated (by Bud) brand new suit to attend Church in. I lived on a respectable and profitable farm, not the Bronx. Anybody not born White would say I was spoiled. I guess I was, even though we struggled, like our White Neighbours.

Bud had a habit of categorizing people; Indians were Drunks (maybe not as drunk as me and my buddies), he called Englishmen 'Chirpers', Italians 'Wops', Frenchmen 'Frogs', and he called Mary's German husband, Richard, *'Krout'*. He called Richard this from the time he met him in 1966, until the last time I saw Bud in 1997. I did not see him for the last twelve years of his life. I thought this was better, for both of us.

The truth is Bud was not prejudice. He just grew up in an environment where everybody used those racial *nick names*. Hell, he lived in a country where the Aboriginal Peoples were only allowed to vote in 1960. This was how he was raised, in WASP controlled Southern Ontario, from the early Twentieth Century up until the Sixties. At that point, my sisters started a losing, life-long-battle to make Bud seem less offensive every time he lapsed back into semantics of the Thirties, when indoor toilets were a luxury.

But he never changed. There was no need to. These were the same White Neighbours he spent a majority of his life living beside, and everybody, Bud figured, knew that he was not Prejudice. He was just blissfully ignorant. Interestingly enough, you would not hear such slurs out of Regina. She had enough problems of her own. She had converted from being a WASP to a Catholic, so she could marry the Man she had created an Embryo with, before taking marriage vows to defend his racial slurs, and be subservient to his hostile Mother. Being white, with all its perks, and not being happy or fruitfully fulfilled in life, seemed strange to me.

What else was strange was that until I was fifteen and off the farm, and out of Flamborough Center, and through with St. Mary's, I never knew a Black person.

I was living with my chums in East Hamilton before my land-lord was the first Black Person I ever really knew. When I moved to Vancouver a couple years later, I was friends with many cool Black People, simply through exposure. Especially in Kitsilano, where I would get my ass kicked playing hoops at Kits Beach. Was this all Bud was missing? Exposure to the world outside the Farm that he was born on and never left? Perhaps...

I'll never get a handle on his nick-naming Richard 'Krout' for a life time hook. He was a product of his time, indirectly affected by both World Wars, as he was born in 1919. He knew about soldiers that never came home from across the Pond, causing hardships, grief, and sorrow for many. But he did not know any of them personally. And he did not participate in WW2, person-ally. As a farmer he sort of had a *Pass*, like the White Students in America did for Viet Nam. And being born at the end of the First World War, he was too young to know victims, or any of the unpaid, dishonoured Canadian soldiers. The Allies won both wars, and perhaps Bud, like many, was unforgiving for Germany being so brutal, ruthless, and down-right criminally insane with Hitler and his Henchmen at the helm.

He was lucky. Never missed a meal, and didn't get a scratch. But he called Richard, his daughter's *life choice*, and a nice guy at that, 'Krout' till the day he died. As rebellious Irish kids, we were trying to tame the shrew, or rather, Bud.

I guess it was aligned, for some reason, with how Archie Bunker called Mike Meathead. We would ask Bud, "If the wars had made such a dent on his psyche, why didn't he go over and fight for Victory?" I searched for an answer. Were these the actions of the dastardly? Did this require another look?

They had won the wars on the battlefields of the world, but Bud's generation's greatest enemies came from their own loins. We, their own children, questioned their attitudes and latitudes as Victors. We battled them about loosening up, and letting it go!

Our Generation then had to defend ourselves for not acting like pompous ass Victors, instead of chartered members of the New Frontier we strived to be. Our opinions were victimized for not wanting young men to go to Viet Nam to fight and die. We actually had to explain to them that Nixon WAS a crook. He stole America's Youth and its Honour, and also that dog back when!

Bud and Regina were just part of a generation that saw war, then poverty, and then war again. They were part of the Crowd that was told to keep quiet, mind your own business, and not ask questions. And that was ok to them. And they tried to impose this *fear* upon us. So we battled each other at the supper table, during the commercials on TV, while they were helpfully and lovingly driving us to where we needed to be, and before and after Regina would sit alone at night, saying Catholic rosary after rosary, while looking for forgiveness for all of us.

Every single morning as I was walking out to catch my first bus, Regina would say in her best pleading voice, "John, please be good today!" What she didn't, couldn't, wouldn't understand, was that I did not try to reason with God about things out of my control. I did not pray, or beg, or plead to God about my antiquated Irish parents. I just smoked a joint as soon as I got to school and forgave them. That is until suppertime, and then the knives of criticism would be launched at Bud's first statement about this Chirper, or Frog... etcetera... it never ended, and we never missed a show!

I was truly in the front lines, unlike my sisters and bro Paul. In fairness, Bud was Webster's pictured definition of a Redneck, and I was the Cambridge definition of an enlightened, educated, Pseudo Intellectual. Bud was truly disappointed by me. At fourteen/fifteen I was in grade nine with a ninety-two percent, and I was advanced into some grade ten classes when Father O'Riley recognized my boredom. But before the last of winter's white curse had disappeared, I was gone! I had permission from Bud to take a powder and go off searching for Jungles, and a proper barber. Thanks for my ticket to ride. But unlike Ozzy's beautiful ballad, I never went home again. I found solace exploring new frontiers that fostered new attitudes and adjustments that were never considered down on the farm.

The space between Bud and I was called *sanity,* for both of us. At fourteen years old I knew it was time to leave. I had such an appetite for destruction!

I was in a world of James Wolfe or Churchill, in as much as expanding after defending myself from Life. We were all searching for something, even if we weren't always really sure what it was.

They say that in our DNA, there are often opposite genes working from Generation to Generation. So is life an adventure or a constant battle? Is there a proper answer? Is everything right or wrong? Is there a Heaven? Are we in Hell? Does it all work out in the End? Does everything that happens have a Reason? Does the Caste System ever stop sub-dividing itself?

Well, if there is a trickle of justice upon this Earth, and karma means anything, sign me up a 'Yes' for every question in Life. Those who search for the right answer, all their lives, sometimes just eventually forget the question. In the end, we all see that Light that draws us towards Itself. The same Light… The same questions… The same answers…

The Flying Club;

At St. Mary's we Freaks had a haggardly assembled, dishevelled group for our High School Hop days, called the 'Flying Club'. I played spoons and wash board, and shook maracas while as many as a couple dozen others would recite lines ala Kerouac, and chant mantras to a befuddled world off the stage. We were like the passengers on Ken Kesey's Bus; stoned, each on our Own

Trip, searching for the right beat, and Furthermore Unafraid. Each time the Entertainment Committee asked us to perform on the stage of the Cafeteria (which was actually the basement of the Basilica Church), we would load up on drugs at Rochdale to keep us in time and tune.

We did some gigs round the School for a couple years, until eventually they insidiously implied that we were all too high, and somehow this was not in their agenda. We were totally intrigued that *the powers that be* had us up there in the first place. Our appearance was zombie-like, and we sounded sort of like the Warlocks at an Acid Test on November 27th, 1965, in Santa Cruz at Babb's house... before Owsley splurged and bought them some amps.

But we were busted here in the Cafeteria, with cops searching us and our lockers, and hauling us over to Father O'Riley's Office. But he was not there, you might remember. He was still in Jamaica drying out on the sand, so they hauled us into what was now Sister Mary Elephant's Office, and she stood there watching the cops strip-search us. I had some more blotter acid in my pocket, but they just threw it on the floor, like the garbage it truly is If Not Eaten! So we all stood there naked *!@ FLASH! Peaking one moment and trying not to ^-(ZOOM! *Grin*, as she grunted and nodded and tried to compare us, in her head, to the last band of males she had the willing police strip-search. It was only a few years before '*streaking*', but I guess she couldn't wait!

But school really was a Gas, and it gave us a reason to see that, as Belushi had said when he was asked why he was leaving SNL, "It had been four years and it was Time for a Change." Time to Move On! Not to movies in Hollywood, like J.B. Just new movies on the backs of our eyelids! Our Futures were calling! The Past was now behind us... This four year commercial for Morality and the Silent Majority was over. It had been a Long Strange Trip... and it was time for a New Groove.

Chapter 9
Waiting for Mike

I think I was always waiting for Godot without knowing it. But I recognized It, or Him, or whatever form Godot was taking that day we met. It was a high school day like any other… more high than school. But I actually went to Theater Arts Class that day because I was lecturing on a project I had prepared for my World Religions Class called, 'The Religious Life of the Beatles'. Now this was a subject I was only too willing to discuss, at any time or place. So this would do.

I was taking this World Religions Class three days a week, and I was inspired by our Ventures into the Beliefs, Rituals and Traditions of Buddhism, Islamic scriptures, Judaism, Christianity, Hinduism, Sikhism, Taoism, Confucianism, Bahia, Shinto, Jainism, and Zoroastrianism.

For my assignment, I would be playing many Fab songs from different periods of 'Beatle Experiences'. After each song, I would be offering and acting out my thoughts of the 'who's, how's, where's, what's and 'why-on-Earths' of their Discoveries and Transformations. I was in a group of four students for this assignment, but I prepared it all myself, feeling quite Spiritual throughout. Nobody cared, but I was enticed and enthralled enough after my presentation to attend two classes in a row! The next Class I attended was the Theatre Arts Class.

Our Group were all sitting around a table in the Theatre Arts classroom, watching the various other groups acting out their skits and plays, for our interests and pleasures. Some were better than others, but they were all good distractions from thinking about our own ensuing assignments. This was my first Theatre

Arts Class I had attended in a couple months, so I was just watching groups that were actually prepared. Suddenly, an older 'young man' appeared on Stage.

With the words, "Nothing can be done", I suddenly entered a world Samuel Beckett scripted for those of us who realized all along that, "Nothing Happens; Twice". There was suddenly nothing interesting going on the in the world for me, outside of this play. I had studied the possibilities and realms of Nothingness before, in World Religions class, as well as in conversations with Roma Dash, on nights where there was just enough Nothingness to go around. I decided I had to speak to this character, Estragon, aka Mike Chase. I didn't know Serge yet, but Mike was his older brother. He was still four years older than I was, and that still made no difference. I needed to speak to him, but after he ended the play he seemed intent on shaking me. He simply and intently moved on.

He was in grade thirteen, I in eleven. Besides this age difference was a vastly disparate world which he existed in. He slightly resembled being Oriental, and was hugely interesting on many levels. Mike was hip, yet cheeky; an intellectual that made fun of intellectuals. He was the eldest of his eight brothers and sisters, he worked professionally with delinquent children, played basketball, religiously bicycled, hiked, climbed mountains, and was the Calm and Wise One of the *group*. And yet was just as excitable and vocal as the youngest. At this particular time he was living in his Toyota car. His father, Fast Eddie, had kicked him out of the huge new house that he was almost finished building. But Mike was nineteen years old, so he was game.

I met Serge at St. Mary's for the first time, later that day. I smoked him up for his first time, and he immediately wanted an ounce of hash. I told him we needed to go to Rochdale College in Toronto, and did he know anyone who had a car, or else we would hitch hike there. Serge said that his older brother, Mike, had a Toyota, and he would ask him to drive us.

I said, "Oh, so you're Estragon's brother?"

His eyes twinkled and he said, "Johnny... Sounds like you've been into Samuel Beckett!"

I told him I had just watched his brother Mike, and my cousin, Rob Hunter, act out their personal searches for Godot earlier that day.

Mike obliged Serge's request, and drove us to Rochdale. Serge and I went in while Mike waited at home, in the Corolla. We came in contact with the *not-so-hard* to recognize plain-clothed policemen, who contacted my Resident Dorm Dweller, in room 605. He went by the name of Jim Morrison. I would eventually get the keys to this apartment in 1975, where I would have access to until they closed the place, and threw us all in a *heap* out on the sidewalks of Bloor Street. Jim Morrison's real name was Grant Foster, whose father was a police detective. Grant was a spoiled yippee. I took Serge down the hallway of the sixth floor. Most doors were ajar, a foot or so, so when you passed them, they would casually let you know that,

"A thousand lot... ten thousand lots of White Lightning Acid were going at a nickel a pop". Then the next room would croon at us with,

"Twenty pound-lots of Black Paki Hash, going cheap"...

Next, "Hundred pound lots of good Mexican pot going fast"...

"Mescaline batches,"

"Peyote here", cocaine there... It went on and on. Serge's eyes were as wide as my grin!

Eventually we came to a room where a young lady was bathing in an old cast iron tub, the kind with the clawed steel legs. Hot water was made available by plastic tubes running from the sink to the tub, which was set up in the living room. She squealed for us to come on in, as her roommate was coming back with cheap pounds of hash, and she would be happy to arrange an ounce for us. This seemed a better proposition than the other Dorms, since we didn't know the tenants, except Jim, who had no hash. Anyways, who would you rather trust... Strangers in a Strange Land, or a Strange Girl nakedly inviting us into her Dorm, and promising us just what we needed!

So we did the deed, and returned to St. Mary's, aka the Basilica. With Mike already out of his parent's new house, Serge was told he had a week to find a place, and hit the road also. My parents were just as anxious to get rid of me. Father O'Riley, my Principle and Friend, advised me there was nothing positive in my continuing living down on the farm. He took a special interest in me, as he did with other students who had difficulties and challenges in life, which seemed out of their hands.

Father O'Riley was always ready to lend an ear, show some soul, and offer his heart. His own nephews, Craig and Brad, attended St. Mary's. Brad lived with his Aunt, as their Father had died a few years earlier. Craig lived in the street; Gage Park to be more specific, aka Needle Park. Craig had been a speed freak for two years, from late '68 to '71. Hamilton, back then, had a large Methamphetamine Population. It was enormous actually. About the same time Yorkville was broken up, the Needle Freaks that didn't end up in Rochdale just drifted on down the Highway, to God-knows-where, and better if ya don't anyway! Father O'Riley had compassion, as an Irish Priest should. But he understood the Untamed Urges and Psyches and Fears and Addictions and Afflictions that a Young Life in 1971 conjured. He himself, it was soon revealed, was a chronic alcoholic. This merely explained some of this, and nothing of that. It was just a time of experimentation gone wild. Gone wrong! Craig was one of the confetti flakes that needed to be swept up at the end of the Sixties, and the beginning of a new decade that started with 'Kent State' and ended with 'Apocalypse Now'.

Mike, in perhaps a regretful moment, decided the right thing to do was rent an apartment so Serge, who was still in school, would have a roof over his head. Mike's job actually paid him to sleep there, to monitor the young Juvenile Delinquents 24/7. He said he rather liked living in his car, being the advent guard character he was. But he got an apartment within walking distance of St. Mary's, and for some reason, Head Doyle was moving in with them. Head didn't really know either one of them, but he went to St. Mary's, had a sexy blonde girl friend, and as well played Junior B hockey. Head was part of our Flying Club.

The first time I went over to the apartment, Serge and I did some LSD. We were trippin' on the Milky Way when Mike made one of his few visits to this, his apartment... his home away from homes. We rocketed through the afternoon, and came down just long enough for Serge to ask Mike if I could move in. I hadn't known them for long, but there was just something insane enough in Serge's eyes, and my grin, that we knew this might be an interesting Trip for a while.

The next day we ambled out of our nooks and crannies that we ended up in the previous distorted night, and Serge announced he was going to Vancouver. Philip Mainline directed Serge to his brother Manshika's rented house/commune, on Oxford Street in Vancouver. Manshika was our West Coast Guru, who we Youngsters considered we knew quite well, because we had befriended his younger brothers in High School. In reality, almost none of us had even met him.

But that was Serge. He knew he would be accepted wherever he went. He had that captivatingly look and that crazy smile.

He said, "Come on John. We'll hitch hike. It'll be great." Now I was still in grade eleven, and I was now living in my new apartment, a short walk away from St. Mary's. I was getting to know Mike, which was intriguing. And I knew the moment we got to Vancouver, Serge would go off on a tear somewhere and I would be piecing together enough for a cup of coffee, while searching out the location of the next Dead Concert.

The more I thought about it, the more I thought, "I can't miss out on this... This is the Next Thing!" But somehow I reconsidered going, at the last moment, and convinced Serge I would finish my School Year, and then see him out there in mid-June... There was a Grateful Dead concert at the PNE grounds on June 21. I told him I'd be there. I missed all my exams, but Father O'Riley passed me for them all anyway.

So suddenly Mike had this apartment, which he only got for Serge, and neither of them resided there within a week. But Head and I threw some legendary high school parties there, in *Ode to their Abstinences*, along with some *Early Seventies Happenings*, and some weird stuff on the side. But Head took off soon as school ended, and I was soon at Serge's house in *Freaksville,* Vancouver. It was a house stashed full of Freaks and interesting people from Dundas, Ontario.

Dundas was a tight *Bedroom Community* that belonged in a Freak's Brothers Comic Book. It was the coolest town of the Seventies, anywhere. I was there for good hunks of a few decades. A town full of sex, drugs and great bars. It was legendary, as we found out for ourselves one night at the *Last Chance Hotel.* The TV, playing to nobody in the back ground, was airing Johnny Carson's 'The Tonight Show'. Suddenly it was announced, in one of those skits called, *'Interesting things Johnny read in the paper today',* "That the town of Dundas, in the 'state' of Ontario, Canada, apparently has more illegitimate children born, per capita, than anywhere else in North America." Ed McMahon gave it the big Whoooooo as we howled and cheered our dusky accomplishment, in the Last Chance Hotel.

Many students from St. Mary's dropped into Vancouver that summer, on their way down the West Coast with their copies of Tom Wolfe's, "The Electric Kool-aide Acid Test" in their nap sacks and sandals on their feet. And they all stopped off at Manshika's little four bedroom Commune, to their teen-aged heightened grins, and Manshika's chagrin. Serge was first, and I followed in June with Trent Haliday and Craig, who was now off speed, and basically off any side of reality. But that's what we did back then. We just kept on truckin' on! Our first night in Town we all went to the Dead concert. We would have missed it, but they cancelled it for a couple days, so the day we rolled into Town, it was a buzzin'!

Once we arrived at the PNE Grounds for the 'first-come-first-serve', standing-room- only concert, there were Bikers guzzling down bottles of whiskey on one side of the floor by the stage, and Exotic Scenes like this beautiful, long haired Hippie Temptress with quarter ounces of blonde Lebanese hash on a pin, burning for whoever was in need, which Serge and I were over and over again all night!

There were speed freaks watching a show that wasn't even in the building. There were old freaks from down the road. There were teenagers swimming on waves of peyote, mescaline, mush-rooms, bottles of wine, Mexican pot, and the sweet, sweet voice of Jerry, cryptically wailing away, "Shake it, Shake it, Sugaree; Just don't tell you knowooooowo, Me!!!" Everybody was standing belly up to the Stage to groove to Pig Pen on the Hammond, Billy on the drums, Bob makin' sounds on his guitar, Phil interacting on bass, and Jerry makin' the best guitar riffs on the West Coast (along with Jorma Kaukonan).

Jerry had opened up the evening, for an hour and a half with the 'New Riders of the Purple Sage', playing pedal steel while singing along with Dawson and Nelson. The Dead then came on and played for three and a half straight hours. The only time they stopped was when Garcia took a step back, took a King-Kong drag off a cigarette, then would lead on for another forty five minutes, then have another puff. This was the period of time when the lads had just started to haul around Owsley 's own private *Wall of Sound*; massive speakers and amps that took trucks and trailers to transport from city to city, orchestrated by gruff and ready tough Union Roadies. You didn't want to mess with these guys... the rule was the Show Must Go On!!!

After the concert, Serge and I went back to Manshikas, where Serge was living. There was a party going on, and after a while we got our hands on some more acid. We decided to go down to Wreck Beach; UBC's own public nudist beach. We ended up staying there a week, until all our acid ran out, and we were looking for something with a New Buzz.

We got back to Oxford Street, and everybody was heading down to a Gas Town bar to see Buddy Guy and Junior Wells. We drank all night, and the next morning we were looking for something to do. Serge and Trent were heading down to Mexico the next day, and I headed to Portland for the next concert with the Dead, Jefferson Airplane and Quick Silver Messenger Service. I didn't dig the vibes there so I made the Haight Scene, and tripped off following the Dead for a week, hitch hiking from scene to scene. It was a Stone Groove!

Rochdale College;

Rochdale College, located at 341 Bloor Street West in Toronto, was an experiment in student-run alternative education and cooperative living. It was a double joined building, eleven stories tall. It became an alternative to the brutal University of Toronto scene, where students were told to get haircuts, and were often thrown against, or through wooden doors.

Rochdale was originally designed as a Student Dorm, so traffic through the city would become more manageable. Construction started in 1965 but by '66 the investors were tipped off that they could beat the taxes by introducing a Curriculum for College Students. And *BOom*! Rochdale College was innocently introduced to the tax payers of Toronto.

The philosophy of Rochdale was certainly equal to teachings of Plato and preaching of Socrates, in their prime. It was based on a concept that the students would decide what subjects would be taught, and they even had the autonomy for the selection of professors and educators, at their own discretions. By 1967 construction of the building was forging ahead on time. Professors and School Faculties worked day and night in innovative sessions, creating a curriculum for knowledge-craving students.

It was a productive and fertile time across the globe; an age of change. Out with the old and in with whatever. These concepts challenged the Old World. Johnson's Democrats in Washington had passed many encouraging Civil Rights in the U.S., providing voting rights for Negroes, and launching a War on Poverty. He was calling it all a Great Society! So were Grace and Jerry Slick.

Toronto was a city in the front lines of progress, and Rochdale was a huge part of it. In the spring of 1968, I remember a cement strike threatened to stop construction of the building, with only the first two floors of the Towers completed. But they had accomplished so much in the past two years creating the College Curriculum, that they decided to open on time for the September 1968 College Year. They decided to finish the building, one floor at a time, until completed. It was a good decision. Rochdale College opened on time.

It was just at this time that Yorkville's *Needle Crowd* and *Biker Vermin* were bounced from the streets of Yorkville. The purged population went like ants, in a straight line, for the unsuspecting Towers of Rochdale. Once there they set up shop, and caused elbow to elbow Freak Congestion in the Main Lobby, while sleeping in elevators, empty rooms, closets, stair cases, benches, storage rooms, gymnasiums, sleeping standing up, speeding, never sleeping, jolting in washrooms, plunging in back rooms, never eating, drinking J.D., playing guitars, shaved heads, Krishna's, Buddha's, as well as being rather disruptive to the College as a whole. And many of the Dorms became inhabited by big time drug dealers, who set the scene for the biggest public tax supported Drug Dealing Emporium in Canadian, rather America's history at that time. And definitely since!

I was introduced to the concept of Rochdale early in 1968, before the cement strike, by my teacher Mrs. Griffiths. She thought I was a good candidate for Rochdale, and wanted me to consider going there eventually. My Aunty Gert resided and taught in Toronto. She took me down to 341 Bloor to investigate the future... my future! I was excited. I thought, "This is cool; a chance to control my own fate. Evolve. Darwin had a theory..."

I dreamed of conducting my education at Rochdale by 1973, but it was not meant to be. The hippies running the College (Paul Evitts) decided to take the chains off the front doors in 1969; chains that were on the doors to restore some semblance of order. Fools! Without them the Freaks and Needles moved back in.

Unfortunately, that was the end of one of the greatest notions of educational concepts ever assembled anywhere, unsuccessfully. Right Place at the Wrong Time! But at the end of the first fiscal year, they realized they couldn't pay any of the bills, and they closed the Curriculum down after only one year. Rochdale became one of the counter-culture's most bizarre White Elephants in history.

But it was an Elephant in a Zoo that could get you any kind of drug, in any amount. It was the home of Inner Space. It was the *show-down* of the Enlightened and Distorted Intellects... the home of Bikers and Misfits. We tried to score eight days a week. I used to walk in there with three, five, ten thousand dollars in my pockets, as a fifteen, sixteen year-old.

They soon screened the entrance, but by '73 I knew somebody who had lived there for a couple years. They set up a Security Force in the Main Lobby to curtail the drug traffic flow as early as 1971. We had a friend/dealer (friendly dealer?) in room 605, who would vouch for us as his visitor, to grant us access. I continued shopping there after high school. I got ripped off for a wack of cash on one deal in '74, enough to buy a new Camaro. My dealer hi-tailed it to Europe and it seemed I was paying for the trip. I phoned him one night in London.

He said, "Well what do you want to do about this John? I'll be here for six months, and I can't give you any money right now".

I immediately said, "I wanna stay in your suite (605), until you return."

He said "Sure", and I hung in, off and on, as I had a house rented inside the Gates of Dundurn Park, in Hamilton. It was copasetic for me after '74, until they closed it down in 1975, to the tax payer's glee. It was like a line of rats reluctantly leaving a burning building. Eventually we all came out, or were carried out. It was the end of a legend, a legacy, and a legal liability.

So I moved back out west. After High School, it was a time when our tight clique split up for the first time in four years. Some of us went west, some went east, and some went to Europe. High school seemed like twenty years... or at least like a Long Strange Trip. Now and it was time to Travel.

Ted Toakley had bought some virgin forest on an Island off the East Coast, and set up a Commune for anybody to enjoy. I knew some connections, musicians, and some Ladies in B.C. I loved the Ocean Pacific. I loved the whole West Coast scene. It still had that simple magic at that time. I knew I'd follow my heart. Some followed their souls, and chased the Dead around Europe. It was a Legendary Tour the Dead made into a triple album called, 'European Tour', of course. We all had great Adventures. We shared Magical Stories. It was a hell of a phase. It was merely part of growing up I guess.

The Seventies were experimental. They were change. And they were fun. They were even kind of innocent. From Kent State to Studio 54, we were so Young! Everything was a learning experience. The Eagle was flying! Mountains were moving. We were evolving. It was natural.

So it was Natural to Change. With new technologies and progress, we were up to the Next Challenge. And with change, it's always time to leave some things behind; school, beliefs, superstitions, parents, fears, weights, religions, bicycles, heroes, and villains. It was finally time to start the next phase.

Is it the end of the beginning?
Or beginning of the end?
Am I going or coming?
What's the message round the bend?
Cruising down new avenues
Head lights, high lights, shadows sinning
Stroke of midnight but I'm not sure
Is it the end or the beginning?

Wreck Beach

We used to hang out a lot at Wreck Beach, over by UBC. Serge and I lived there for a week once, and saw some fun times. People from Dundas would come to Vancouver, and they would be directed our way before they returned to the *'Land where the Sun rises first'*. Police at Wreck Beach were friendly, so were the smiling sun gazers.

If you've never been, you cruise Maine Drive westward until arriving at the top of the Sandy Cliffs. Well-worn paths then take still-clothed tourists down to the Strait of Georgia. One early afternoon Serge and I were heading down to the water for a game of *Football in the Strait*. For some reason, Serge was mucking about on one of the sandy patches that overlooked the water in steep, terrace-like cliffs. For another reason just as quizzical, I followed him.

I realized we were just chillin' and I sat on my haunches. Suddenly the entire huge piece of sandy real estate started moving towards the edge, as one chunk of sand. We sensed quickly we were doomed! There was no recourse. No way to stop this slide. No second chance! This was not the Last Chance Hotel! We both rode this mass of sand down to the edge of the cliff, and at the very last second I grabbed at some stalks and roots, and precariously managed to hold on. Serge went right over the edge. At the brink of the cliff I lay holding on, watching him fall.

It was an incredible distance, hundreds of feet. And there were levels of sandy cliffs, just like the one I was still clinging to, all the way down to the beach. And I watched Serge bounce off each cliff; again and again and again, until he rolled down the hill all the way to the Strait. People flocked to him. Then looked up at me! I tried and tried, and finally grabbed some more roots further up, and was finally able to climb to safety. I hustled down the paths to find Serge, and everyone, shoeless and clueless, already in the water picking teams for tackle football. In typical form, Serge gleamed at me and said "What took ya?"

Later that day Serge saved me from drowning on a rip tide. More acid please!

Headin' Home

Gas Town, adjacent to China Town and Downtown Vancouver, was a central location for fun when I worked for the Attorney General, on Cordova Street in the Eighties. There were authentic Chinese Restaurants, and it's close to entertainment establishments like the Commodore Ballroom, the Orpheum Theater, and all of The *Water Holes* that were downtown before the Granville Strip pulled all the entertainment establishments and *late night drinking scenes* into one area on Granville. This was done in the early Nineties, in an attempt to better manage drunks leaving Drinking Taprooms at 3 am (Devil's Hour), drunkenly on their way to a Taxi before they got assaulted and robbed.

I saw Buddy Guy and Junior Wells play in Gas Town back in '72. Serge and Craig, along with most of the Dundas wrecking crew were there. A character I met from Penticton was passed out in the alley, and no one noticed him gone until it was time to drive home. He was our ride home, of course. A search found him happily curled up between two garbage cans, eyes shut tight, and crooked smile on his face.

He said he had scored the car that day for sixty dollars. He and I decided to drive to Dundas for a beer the next day. Trent and Zorro were going as far as Penticton. We drove through the Mountains, stopping in every little town to pan-handle gas money, and share some of our wicked joints with the Locals. There we were; four Roman Catholic lads from hard working, church going, bill paying, God-fearing families, that never took a nickel that wasn't there's, and raised kids who should have known better. Blame it on Beatle Ed!

But it was an age when there was still time and space around for Older People to just stare, gawk, and scratch their heads at us Teenagers out on the road. Hippies with long hair, faded jeans, worn running shoes, Grateful Dead t-shirts, and not a cent in our pockets! And not a care in the world! It was a time that was maybe like the *Dirty Thirties*, when people picked up hitch hikers travelling across Oklahoma, Northern Texas and New Mexico; all leaving something behind, and looking for a brighter future. They had to have Faith. And Confidence! And be Resourceful. They too were exploring new boundaries on the *'pay-later-with-your-soul-plan'*. And they were listening to Woodie Guthrie for peace and harmony.

We were trying to believe in ourselves out on-the-road too! We were asking questions others wouldn't. And we were never satisfied with the answers. That was status quo. There was a bond between us youngsters in those golden moments of the Magic Years. I'd walk down the street in Penticton and pass someone with shoulder length hair, a guitar strapped over his back, and a glaze in the ol' eyes that made us both smirk, cause we knew there was something going on; an unsaid thing.

I could glimpse at his face and see the moon he slept under the night before.

I saw the battle scars of a *Soldier of the New Consciousness*. Scars that had been spreading since the first flickers of a New Age back in '66. It was that feeling that was alive that very day in 1972. And it was getting stronger, and we both knew it and grew it in our minds! Screw Nixon and the cops. We were basking in the glare of that Brave New World Huxley had predicted in his genius in '32. It was in the books we read and the trips we took, and it lingered like the breath, way down deep, in the lungs of a lone wolf about to howl.

We *dead-headed* our way through *Rocky Mountain Towns,* on Highway 3, through Princeton and Osoyoos, before heading north on *97* towards Penticton, where the Coolest of Dundas were hanging out there that summer, thank you. We saw Derick Music, the Wetherpains, Betty Boop, and all those on migration from Dundas who were leaving behind their schools, parents, hassles, commitments, promises, break-ups, shake-ups, families, good times, crummy blow, politics, lies, truths, friends, churches, doubts, the Coach House (aka the Last Chance Hotel), noise, green lawns, apartments, connections, relatives, The Collins Hotel, Rochdale, the El Mocambo, Maple Leaf Gardens, roller skating halls, Massey Hall, the Toronto Concert Hall, the Elfin Theater, the Dollar Fifty Delta, girlfriends, over population, Trudeau, Perth County and the Dundas Peak.

We used up our panhandled gas getting there, but were able to sell some pot in Penticton, and we eventually motored on to Kelowna. Kelowna is one of the most beautiful cities on a lake, in B.C. You only have to go there to see how this daring statement can be made. But there are just *too many people* there these days!

We headed north to Vernon and dug the mountains for a day. Vernon is like some forgotten mountain ghost town, where Lost Tribes gather every few years and plant seeds with beautiful maidens who are from Cornwall, Montreal, Toronto, Vancouver; any place other than Vernon. Then they awaken one morning, feel a chill in the air, and scamper down holes from which they came. Scurrying and skedaddling, grappling with graphic roots and rocks, while not seeing sun until the next spring, when they might consider exploring Colorado for a season of Passion and Experimentation.

When we arrived at the Trans-Canada Hi-way, Trent and Zorro turned west to travel through the desert to Kamloops, Cache Creek, and Lytton, to get to Hope. The town of Hope is like the Khyber Pass. All traffic, and life, is funneled through

Hope to get to the Fraser Valley. Travellers then continue through Chilliwack towards the lights of Vancouver; through old Native Lands and Burial Grounds, missing Totem Poles and broken leaves of sage, all blowing you towards the Pacific. It was a different time. Cultures were lost. It became a British Columbia.

Meanwhile, Trent was waiting for Serge to come back from Dundas, where he had mailed himself a bunch of buds, which would finance his way to Mexico. Meanwhile, my new compatriot and I turned east at Salmon Arm. We panhandled a little extra gas money, cause we had been warned that Revelstoke, next on the agenda, was a kick ass, red-neck town. Now I wouldn't have worried as much if I was travelling with Serge; he was crazy. But this lad was too tall and too lean for any real redneck retribution recourse.

So we cruised, well maybe slithered and crept, through Revelstoke. Next we arrived at the Ski Mountains of Golden. God, we rolled a big one, and commenced just groovin' and diggin' the snowy peaks above us. This was just preparing us for Banff, where Easy Breezy, from St. Mary's, worked at the Banff Hotel. We felt like the Who, when they used to straggle into L.A. and stay at the Hyatt House, aka the Riot House. But I didn't swing from any chandeliers, or join Keith Moon breaking through the walls into other suites in search of his stash. I was good for everybody's sake.

Down the road (literally) from Banff is Canmore, and then you're suddenly out of the Rockies. And just as suddenly you're suddenly on some shit kickin' dusty plain, in the shadow of the perky past peaks, and in a dude-ass place called Calgary. The *Calgary Stampede* was on when Trent, Craig, and I passed through weeks earlier, westward bound. So it was kind of peaceful then, considering all the tourist money that was there to coddle. But it wasn't a Stampede Party now, and a couple long hairs in a shit brown Chevy, with dirt under their finger nails and nothing in their stomachs, were not feeling too welcome here, looking way too Liberal in a totally Conservative Town.

Alberta Bound, Alberta Bound
It's good to b*e*, Alberta Bound…

We would just have to keep telling ourselves that all the way to Saskatoon!

It was Easy Rider all over again. Just that feeling out on the road that has you pressing a little harder on the gas pedal, so to put that much more space between us and the Cowboys. A little quicker pulse was now in the cards. It took all our remaining pot-cash to motor across this menacing mad-town of cowboy hats and shit-kickin' cowpuncher boots. We were careful to not reveal any *bad habits* until we got to *Sweeter Pastures*. I felt like we were leaving a lysergic trail behind us, one that dripped in our eyes and sweated out on our foreheads. But we put on some Merle Haggard, and looked convincing. With 'We don't smoke marijuana in Muskogee' blaring away in the back ground, we made it to the Saskatchewan border, and like Bobby D, didn't look back!

A couple years down the road, Oak and I would hitch-hike through these same kinda towns and cities that were lost out on the horizon, and never thought twice about it cause trouble loves company. When I got back to Mike's apartment (yes Mike had kept it going while we were all either on the coast at Ted Toakley's Commune, or out on the West Coast, or in Mexico, Europe, or somewhere in between; Limbo!) I was just in time for a concert at Watkins Glen, New York, where there was another Woodstock sized event going down… never enough time in a day!

Chapter 10
My Plastic Jesus

Serge had this great pair of blue jeans that he had started patching in Vancouver, ala 1972. The patches were made of suede and leather, and there was an array of complementing colours weaving through the pant legs. My jeans were a vintage *'Classically Ripped'*, and I traded the hippie look for articulately sewn, respectable, good ol' attire that would probably get me stomped in the wrong bar. Serge was more into stitchery than I. He kept me in stitches.

I tried to delve into the different coloured threads and leathers, and just kinda make it all work. I gladly let the Girls sew them for me sometimes. Serge wouldn't hear of this. He must have been sewing for years because his *pant's collage* of hides and colours were outstandingly sown. At fifteen, sewing was not on my to-do list. But Serge didn't leave home till he was seventeen, leaving him with three years of experience in everything one does as a teenager that has boundaries and results. But sowing? He was born and bred to 'forever dare the Gods', which he inherited from his father, 'Fast Eddie'.

But I saw Serge was like another Jim Morrison, in as much as he was his own worst enemy. He was running in the Trial Runs for the Olympics, early in '72. He was clearly a favorite to win. So, just as the Lizard King Himself would have done, he got pissed on gut-rot rouge vino the night before, and puked his chances away. Some people just have a bad time with success, so they battle against it, until they feel secure that they have lost it. Gram Parsons died with a syringe in his arm, while some Ditty throated Him until he passed over the Great Divide. Maybe there was some Lenny Bruce mentality involved about Serge, or an unassembled 'Bruce Lee Path to Destruction' kit within him. His mother was Oriental…

So Serge traded in his one-time chance at Olympic success and fame, for a dollar and seventy five cent trip to the *comfort station*. 1972 evolved into 1973, as we were all back at St. Mary's, pretending we were going to graduate in this year.

The usual lads and I were living in a nice big house on Gibson Street, with nice big rose gardens, and a proper-looking wooden floor in the downstairs living room. It was completed with a massive stone fire place. There were five bedrooms and one bathroom. The staircase was imposing in size and length, and I was putting up bets with my buddy, Eno, on how long it would take Craig, or Cecil to drunkenly stumble down them.

Cecil was from Longville Quebec, where he had just turned nineteen. He was into Chicago Blues, Delta Blues, British blues, Boogie-Woogie, African blues, and Cornwall blues. Cecil was a little beer bellied, had hair to his waste, and the Girls liked him. Cecil often drank till he dropped. But it took a keg, and a least a 26er to drop him. Eno had turned us onto Cecil. He was a Classic! A man's man, but only when he wasn't too drunk. He was a legendary drinker. He eventually died after years of smack.

The last I can remember of Eno was one crazy night, when one half of the house (with probably fifteen visitors included) did some Purple Microdot acid, and the other half got Almighty Drunk. Cecil did both. Craig tried to play Eno's violin and destroyed it. Havoc wreaked (nothing new), as next Eno's Peter Max painting was knocked off the wall. But Cecil took the *biscuit*. *D*espite repeated advice from the acid-trippers who kept warning him that he was getting too blotto, and that maybe he should stop pouring bottles of Southern Comfort down his throat, he finished guzzling anyway, and started pissing on Eno's new chair.

He had just purchased it that day, and Cecil distortedly thought it looked like a toilet.

Vaboom! Eno then stormed out of our confines at three in the AM, yea yea the Devil's hour, and only returned to move the rest of his stuff out the next day. Stepping over our motionless bodies scattered all over the floor, Eno declared, to anyone who could listen, that we were insane. Guilty as charged!

Trent

Now Trent was smooth. He was your short but muscular Taurus, with curly blonde hair, and a smile that put everyone to ease. He was eighteen when he came to St. Mary's to finish off his grade thirteen, with Mike. He was immediately appointed, I mean voted, to be the Entertainment Committee Chief, and he had real rock acts like Kim Mitchell and Crowbar playing at our school dances.

Trent was intelligent and mature. And charismatic as all get-out! Trent worked part time/full time at the Beverly Hills Hotel. He was the kind of stoner who would show up Monday morning at St. Mary's with a brand new TR 6. There were many trips to Rochdale and R&R concerts in this Golden Sports Coupe. Trent's dad was admired and respected by all the kids in the neighbourhood, and he was a Classic to us kids at St. Mary's.

Everything Trent did was cool. You put on your *best act* and brought your *best stash* to visit Trent Haliday, and his younger brother Cid, who was another Classic. Trent had a savage sound system, and everybody went over there for some intelligent listening and conversation, and whatever. Like I say, you showed up at Trent's and Cid's in your *best fashion*. If Cecil went over, it was when he was not drinking, hopefully! It was cool to smoke a joint, and then maybe have a good conversation with his parents, or discuss the latest musical happenings with the lads. It was wholesome at Trent's, and a lot of fun.

At the other end of town lived the Mainlines. Ken and Babs Mainline were industrious, respectable Catholics whose two sons attended St. Mary's, while another lived out west. Philip and Rock liked to party in their parent's basement. Their parents were tolerant because they accurately assessed that it was better to have them party at home instead of at the Bar, or all over town (like me). So we did our best to alleviate their *suspicions and fears of the road* by partying in their basement like there was no tomorrow! Thanks Mr. and Mrs. Mainline!

We would smuggle in the odd bottle of wine and liqueur. Craig would show up 'craiged', and a good (and bad) cross-section of St. Mary's stoners would show up, stoned and drunk. At least I know I did. What made everything wholesome were the great games of hoops we played out on their black-topped laneway. The Mainline boys were all ball players. They were a lot of fun.

There were some comical times. As I said we got lunched down there; I mean it was the early Seventies! However, we had all read our Thomas Wolfe Bible with the philosophy that we had to 'pass the acid test'. In other words; function while stoned. The preaching's of Ken Kesey professed to translate being high into being productive.

However, even with our best intentions, it was always just a matter of time before someone could not pass the acid test, and be totally indisposed before having to walk up the steps when it was time to leave. It was then time to have to casually ssslither past their parents. We just considered it part of the evening's entertainment to see some Acts aim themselves towards the exit at the top of the stairs. We eventually tried to schedule our visits diplomatically, when they were at work, and we were skipping classes.

But that was life back when parents thought they still had a chance to try and combat their children's bad habits and sins. The parties we had under their noses, and up ours, kept me attached to a family life, of sorts. There was a domestic feeling in my buddy's family homes that was a tad different from *my* place, where someone might be suddenly naked, or a tribe of bikers might cruise by for a drink after *Last Call*. These were my second homes; homes away from home. I know the lads caught threats and earfuls after we left, but the words just fell on brains too bleached to offer any resistance.

With our rented party houses, we became an alternative to our friend's parent's basements. Trent and friends were visiting our Cannon Street scene. Our frequent visits to his parent's houses became more like cameo appearances. Trent traded in his sports car and bought a red hydro van, done-up perfectly for travelling with an eight track player, and about forty *'eight-track'* tapes by the Dead, the Jefferson Airplane, Hot Tuna, Quick Silver Messenger Service, the Flying Burrito Brothers, Commander Cody, etcetera… He drove to Manishkas in Vancouver with Craig and I on his way to Mexico with Serge.

By summers end, Trent and Serge had returned from Mexico to our new house on Cannon, with tans and a lust for tequila. This was right up Cecil's alley. We drank tequila while Cecil guzzled it. One September night, we were drunk, and Cecil had bought a big TV earlier that day. We all began banding together to watch *'Kung Fu'* on Monday nights, even though we weren't really TV watching kinds of dudes. But on this night, Cecil said that *'Cool Hand Luke'* was playing. Now we all knew the legacy of this Paul Newman and Strother Martin movie, with the humour, and pain, and the Plastic Jesus song;

Plastic Jesus Song

I don't care if it rains or freezes

Long as I got my plastic Jesus
Riding on the dashboard of my car.

Through my trials and tribulations
And my travels through the nations
With my plastic Jesus I'll go far.
Plastic Jesus plastic Jesus,
Riding on the dashboard of my car

I'm afraid He'll have to go.
His magnets ruin my radio
And if I have a wreck He'll leave a scar.
Riding down a thoroughfare
With His nose up in the air,
A wreck may be ahead, but He don't mind.

Trouble coming He don't see,
He just keeps His eye on me
And any other thing that lies behind.
Plastic Jesus plastic Jesus,
Riding on the dashboard of my car...

Though the sunshine on His back
Make Him peel, chip and crack,
A little patching keeps Him up to par.
When I'm in a traffic jam
He don't care if I say "damn"
I can let all my curses roll

Plastic Jesus doesn't hear
'Cause he has a plastic ear
The man who invented plastic saved my soul.
Plastic Jesus plastic Jesus,

Riding on the dashboard of my car...

Once His robe was snowy white,
Now it isn't quite so bright -
Stained by the smoke of my cigar.
If I weave around at night,
And policemen think I'm tight,
They never find my bottle - though they ask.

Plastic Jesus shelters me,
For His head comes off, you see
He's hollow, and I use Him for a flask.
Plastic Jesus plastic Jesus,

Riding on the dashboard of my car...
Ride with me and have a dram
Of the blood of the Lamb -
Plastic Jesus is a holy bar.

[Plastic Jesus has become quite entrenched in the folk tradition,
so there are considerably more folk verses than there were
original ones.]

I don't care if it rains or freezes,
As long as I got my plastic Jesus
Sittin' on the dashboard of my car.

Comes in colors pink and pleasant,
Glows in the dark cause he's iridescent
Take him with you when you travel far.

Get yourself a sweet Madonna
Dressed in rhinestones sittin' on a
Pedestal of abalone shell.

Going ninety I ain't scary
Cause I got the Virgin Mary
Assurin' me that I won't go to Hell.

Get yourself a sweet Madonna
Dressed in rhinestones sittin' on a
Pedestal of abalone shell.

Going ninety I ain't scary
Cause I got the Virgin Mary Assurin' me that I won't go to Hell.

Well Luke eventually ate those fifty eggs, and it was only a matter of time before Trent was buzzing Serge that, if he ate fifty eggs, he would give him a half ounce of his nice black hash. Serge put Paul Newman to shame the way he mowed down those eggs. But the bet came with the clause that if Serge puked once, he forfeited half the hash, and if he puked twice, he got nauda. Of course Serge got to forty-eight eggs before he puked, then scoffed down the last two.

As we were puffing Serge's winnings he looked at me and said, "John, you eat fifty eggs. Trent's still got some hash!" Now I was double tokin' and seriously smoking a lung full, and I didn't figure I needed to be bloated to kingdom-come with fifty eggs in me gulliver! But everyone knew Serge and I were a two-way punch, and soon they started tempting me with some hash, and then Pierre threw in some pot. I knew I couldn't say no. Imagine…I couldn't say no!?!

Suddenly Trent announced we didn't have nearly enough eggs left to do the bet. A reprieve! Before I could savour my luck, Pierre said,

"But we have plenty or potatoes!"

Serge, burping and slurping, exclaimed, "thirty-five baked potatoes for all Trent's hash, and that pot too!"

Serge claimed we would smoke all the hash and pot that night, or at least until he got the munchies. Now that was gonna take some smoking, but I was up to it. Of course I had to win it first, so Pierre and Trent loaded the oven and baked thirty-five potatoes for my *midnight snack*. Our *clause* was I lost half for puking, and all for puking twice. To make the story short, I couldn't eat more than twenty-eight dusty-dry baked potatoes. And to this day Serge still figures I owe him the pot and hash.

The next day I was too tired for school, and Serge was too bloated for work.

I don't know how *Luke* handled the load, but I was just lying on my mattress, which was flopped on my bedroom floor, puffing some of Serge's hash. I was rollin' a *special joint* mixed with black and green when she made her first visit. A pleasant little lady, ok girl, was makin' the rounds I guess, and she suddenly appeared before me. She said she knew somebody, or maybe she said screwed somebody, who knows, but anyway she said she had come to visit someone named Ken. I told her she was probably in the wrong house. I passed her the joint and she sat down and started petting my patched jeans. She commented that "They were groovy." Groovy? I hadn't heard that adjective in a couple mega-years, but hey, I dug it!

A couple hours later Serge walked in, wearing his suede and leather patched trousers. She was captivated. She started pawing his pants next, and once again exclaimed that the stitching must have taken a long time. Serge said it took him a couple of years. She said "Groovy."

Serge grinned and said, "Groovy?"

She said "Yea, you know what groovy means, don't you?" Before Serge could say a word, I picked up my Webster's and blurted out;

"Groovy... First heard amongst jazz musicians in the 1920s, groovy — or groovey — was a word used to describe music that was played with feeling and finesse. It was based on the phrase 'in the groove', which referred to the way a phonograph needle on a record player followed the grooves of a record."

Neither of them said a thing. I said Tina, "Why don't you show Serge that thing you were showing me," so they disappeared to the attic. The next morning the police showed up and demanded the girl. I told Serge that Tina had Company as I stashed dope that was everywhere. She then left with the 'le boys in blue' for whatever reason. Maybe they wanted to show her their OPP patches...

Chapter 11
Hot Tuna

We all met back at St. Mary's by Labour Day. Mike, Serge and I were ready to try a house together, this time with two *characters* from Longville, Quebec, and a couple of girls who were a little older than me, and Craig, who wouldn't go away. I was getting close to sixteen years old by this time. But this latest grouping of peoples at this house was different from the others. We were all a little older, and perhaps also a little wiser? I doubt it. But Serge was a little crazier after a month in Mexico.

I went back to St. Mary's for my final year, while Serge worked at National Steel Car, in the dirty North End. The Girls had jobs, and Mike continued to work with children at the Center. We all had possessions that we carted to this house. That meant we had an extended collection of albums, speakers and turn tables. I stopped attending classes as I simply played albums all day long. Or at least until it was time to go out on an Adventure.

It was a wonderful time to be young. All our Parents wanted as little as possible to do with us, the police hated us, our Teachers plotted against us, Society had no use for us, and straight students at our R.C. Separate School thought we were collectively the anti-Christs. Obviously they were all right. But like when the Nazi's bombed London, the Blitz only brought the people closer together, and we were unified by Society's Cause; Us against Them, Them against Us, Generation verses Generation, War verses Peace, Freaks verses Squares, Old verses Young, Good versed Evil, Enslaved Minds verses Freed Frontal Lobes, Beatles verses Stones...

Anyway, I was in the *upstairs living room* one morning reading Craw Daddy Magazine, and suddenly an advertisement for a *Hot Tuna* concert leapt out of the mag, past my eyes, and into my cerebral gray matter. When Serge came home that afternoon from National Steel Car, I told him that we were going to see Jorma Kaukonan and Jack Cassady with Sammy Piazza, aka Hot Tuna, on Fifth Avenue, in New York City. I told him he needed to thumb to Ottawa and grab a concert ticket for each person in the house. He promptly skipped the next day's work, and made it to Ottawa and back, with tickets in hand. Another house hombre, Pierre, and the Girls at that point, said they wouldn't be going. We gave the tickets to Fraser Fried, his brother Freddy, and Serge's and Mike's younger brother, Pete.

Now Freddy and Fraser's father was a Professor at Humber College. He most practically decided they should drive down in his car. But when he heard there were six of us, he pointed out that there were only five seat belts, and considering we were crossing the Border, someone was going to find another way down.

Well we all looked at Pete. After all, it was my idea; so I was in. Serge grabbed the tickets, and Mike was driving, so they were in. It was Fraser and Freddy's car, basically, so they would be travelling in the Fried-mobile likewise. Pete, looking defeated and dejected, said, "I can't hitch-hike alone down to Fifth Avenue".

He gave Serge his ticket and asked him to sell it down in New York City. Pete was my age, and Serge was two years older. Mike was another two years yet. Suddenly something happened. Serge slapped Pete on the shoulder and said, "Don't worry Pete. You can have my seat. I'll hitch hike". And like that, Serge was suddenly thumbing down to New York City, in late November, in the snow and the cold. Serge didn't care... it was part of the Adventure to him. And I liked Adventures!

I was never so awe struck in my life! I thought, wow, what a Character! What Bravery! How Chivalric! How James Dean! How Neil Cassidy! I casually went over to where Serge was standing, in the upstairs kitchen, and offered that I would hitch hike down with him... if he didn't mind...

Now Serge and I were friends who had gone on a lot of Adventures together in our relatively short time of knowing each other. But this was different! This bonded us together against the elements of cold, snow, border crossings, hitch hiking hundreds of miles into who-knows-what, border guards, police, unexplored territories, smuggling drugs over the border, going into a broken nation, Nixon, Freaks, war vets, a crumbling economy, and New York back then looked like a burnt out military zone. But what an Adventure! It was my immersing myself into the crazy world of Serge... and baby, this sounded kinda crazy!

We left on Tuesday night when Serge made it home from work. It was blizzardy out; the wind swept in tons of snow. It was cold! The perfect setting for such an Adventure! It was dark out when we left the house. Deep in the City, we just started hitching a ride out towards the freeway that took us towards the Peace Bridge. As we were approaching the border, Serge noticed a Bus Station through the blizzard. He told the driver that had picked' us up to let us out there. He had a plan to get on an Albany Bound Bus, and that would take care of crossing the Border.

We boarded the chock full Gray Hound bus. Serge sat in the second to front seat, on the driver's side. I sat on the other side, at the back. As we pulled into the Bridge Crossing, a Border Guard entered the bus. He quickly grabbed Serge from his seat, then me from mine, and took us off the bus and corralled us into a Little White Room. We knew the drill. They would search us, question us, leave us alone to contemplate our unworthy existences, and then send us back to Stompin' Tom's Northland.

Serge took five grams of honey oil out of his pocket and shoved it into his sock, when we were left alone for a minute. The Guards searched us, and then demanded to see our monies and tickets. We had fifty one dollars between us, and our tickets were in order, so we figured we were ok. Regardless of our obvious intent, they classified us both *Risks* of never coming back, insane as that sounded to us. But it was an Insane Time in the early Seventies.

We were taken in a Taxi back to the Canadian side of the Peace Bridge, and dropped off in the snow. While I was thinking how good an effort we had put out, and *'oh well what-cha-gonna-do'* was running cross my mind, I suddenly noticed Serge yell, "Let's go", and he started sprinting across the bridge towards Uncle Sam. I was stunned. What was the Plan? They would be over there just waiting for us. Was this a good idea? Why was I running after him? While I was just fifteen, Serge was seventeen. I wasn't looking forward to hitching back myself through the blizzard. So I followed...

As we approached the American side, I ran along wondering where we were going. What were we going to do? How was this going to turn out? And before I could think of another question for the Dark Evening, Serge suddenly just jumped blindly into the air, over the side of the Peace Bridge, and Disappeared!

I glimpsed over the steel hand railing and stared at least thirty feet below. Serge was reeling in pain on the surface of a stone parking lot, waaaaay below. I have to admit, even I was stunned. But Serge jumped, so I had to jump. Before I prepared for this eventuality, Serge yelled up that he had damaged his ankle, and he had broken the vial of honey oil lodged in his sock. He then yelled, "Jump!"

The night nipped at my extremities. The snow came down in torrents. I was hiding on the Peace Bridge, and probably on my way to Jail. Or Heaven, or Hell! Serge yelled for me to, "Hurry up." He had just jumped blindly. But I was strategically sizing up the situation. I started to methodically climb over the hand rail, and descended the frame until I was hanging from the bottom of the railing, with my feet kicking in open air. I suddenly realized there was three strands of barbed wire, equally spaced, attached to *out reaching posts,* which ran along the bridge for about for a couple hundred feet.

And this was all arranged to keep people from doing *exactly* what we were doing. Really! They actually figured somebody would actually do something this crazy? Really?! But there I was, holding on to the bottom of the steel railing, while trying to untangle my pants which were caught-up in the barbed wire. Nothing I had ever done before could prepare me for this. As I hung there, kicking and picking at the barbed wire, while judging the likelihood of surviving or dying, Serge yelled up his coup de grace… "Hurry up John or I'm leaving!" Serge was easily getting to recognize my boundaries, because that was all I needed to hear. Besides, there was no climbing back up. And I began to realize I couldn't hang there much longer.

I kicked at the barbed wire, tore it away from my pants, and dropped! Over thirty feet straight down! As soon as I reached the frozen stones I rolled and was fine for the fall. Serge's ankle was swelling, and there was honey oil dripping everywhere. The very first thing I did was wipe it all on my map. I got almost all of it. Now all we had to do was smoke the map!

We scampered off, and tried to examine exactly where we were. It was like a demilitarized zone. It was dark everywhere down there. Buildings were all closed up. And luckily there was no one around… until suddenly a Police Car pulled up, with two cops who were surprised to find us, to say the least. When they asked what we could possibly be doing here, we showed him our tickets, and told them we had just crossed the Border. Now at fifteen years old, I just sat back and pondered,

"What's wrong with this picture?" But the one Crow turned to the other, as they huddled together on the snowy branch of this moonless night, and said,

"O well. They let them over the Border, so I guess there's no problem."

No problem? We were in the middle of Absolutely Nowhere, directly under the Peace Bridge, six hours after any Shops (that might actually be in business in this Abyss) were closed, we had only the shirts and coats on our backs, and we were wandering aimlessly in the dark. Did I mention I was fifteen? Serge's ankle is sprained, he in massive pain, and this cop says that he guesses everything is "OK." So they left us there, in this precarious position, and drove off to protect people from the Baffling Night. We smoked a big chunk of the map and carried on, feeling somewhat invincible to the Night!

We thumbed down to Albany, where we smoked more of the map, and tunneled into a snow bank to sleep. I told Serge if we slept in a snow drift, it wouldn't go under thirty-two degrees Fahrenheit, and we wouldn't freeze. We froze! But we kept hitching, and it was afternoon when we entered Poughkeepsie. We didn't 'pick our toes' but Serge decided we would catch a train to Fifth Street. He purchased two tickets with our dwindling cash, while I fought off a Big Black Cat who kept insisting I was too skinny, and he wanted to buy me a hamburger. I felt like I was home!

We made it to the Concert Hall by seven, one hour before the Hot Tuna concert started. To celebrate, we took off to find the Nearest Bar. We found one a half block away, and we entered triumphantly. At the first table we came across, there was Mike, Pete, Fraser and Freddy. They were actually stunned that we made it. They were amazed that we were alive! They bought us each a beer, and we started to recount the last twenty-six hours on the road. After another beer we eagerly went over and watched the Concert. It was more than worth the effort! It was a Stone Groove!

We chummed around Fifth Avenue for a while after the Concert. Freddy wanted to score a strumpet for his efforts, but Mike said if he was going to drive all the way home, we had to leave now! Well, we made it all the way to the New Jersey Turn Pike before Mike fell asleep at the wheel, hitting the guard railing.

A steel pipe came through the side of the car, missing Fraser's head by inches. We decided that telling Fraser's Dad that he was miraculously alive would have to overshadow the damages to the car. It was a close call. But we were all alive. We stayed pulled over on the side of the New Jersey Turn Pike for Mike to collect himself. When he shook it all off, and concluded the car would be ok to continue driving, Mike said, "What shall we do now?"

I looked up and said, "Hey, Poppa John Creech is playing tonight in Boston. Think the car will make it?"

Chapter 12
Moon River

Serge and I sat in the back of the small imported car, watching as Heinz pointed and flailed his finger in the face of B Cautious. He said, again, that he was warning him for the last time. Serge and I looked at each other and smirked. We were expecting a blow-out at any second. And when it came, I wanted to have no part of it. Heinz was a Red Devil Motorcycle Club Member. B Cautious was simply a drug dealer with no charisma, and as this little scene was revealing, even less common sense.

Minutes earlier, we were having a fresh beer on a stale spring afternoon in April, 1976, at the Red Lion Hotel in downtown Hamilton. B had approached us, and asked the question he always started conversations with Serge and I with, "Do you have any money for me?" We usually did, but it was never enough, and always with an excuse... you know how it goes... the bank was closed ... I left it in my other jacket... my dog ate my wallet... I was abducted by aliens... did I not pay you last week? I got my foot caught in a bear trap... I've got leprosy... (now for the leprosy excuse, it helps if you glue rice- crispies to your face with honey, and add make-up that makes you look like Lon Chaney Jr.). B must have been intrigued by some of our excuses, because he always came back for more.

But he was in no mood for excuses that early spring day, as he had to pay this fellow for a front he had taken on a deal a couple days earlier. He was disappointed with us both, again! He used to threaten us with imaginary mercenary madmen that he claimed were his friends, but, Serge and I already knew that you can't be friends with mercenaries.

You just pay them off. Never too much though, so they need
to keep coming back. Something like when Hannibal contracted
the Carthaginian Army, having them cross the Alps on rented
elephants. But they don't work for peanuts! B kept prompting us
for some cash, like he didn't hear our creative, yet valid excuses.
He insisted he was over five hundred dollars short of his obliga-
tion, and we had let him down, again!

B's idea of business was that he could buy a quarter pound of
'honey oil', or a ten pound hunk of hash, then front it to people
all over the City, at his profit margin over cost, and then think
that he actually owned the amount of uncollected money owed
to him. But the only dudes who collect the *full share* of money
owed on fronted drugs are bikers, and mob enforcement agents.

But the *full share* was often a Shakespearian Saga; of some
cash, and usually a pound of flesh. Every time the saga unfolded,
B was Shylock, Serge was Antonio, and I was Bassanio. I suppose
Koran (Serge's girlfriend) would have been Portia.

I guess Shylock had his problems, but did he ever learn? B
didn't, but that was part of his atrophy, and degeneracy.

Speaking of which, the biker had arrived and was making his
way toward B. He looked like a surfer, adrift from Laguna Beach.
He had sweeping blonde hair, a muscular, but not bulging build,
and blue eyes that he must have borrowed from Sinatra himself.
B told him he needed to speak to him, and then introduced him
to Serge and I as, "Heinz." Heinz told him to come out to his
Volkswagen for his speech. B immediately told him that Serge
and I would accompany him to the car. Heinz didn't care, as
he only wanted one thing... money... and as little of his flesh
as possible.

Nobody ever paid B off on time because his deals were always
tinged and tainted with shitty dope. One quarter pound of black
oil he gave us once was actually mixed with lighter fluid! Pot was
always shrouded with seeds, and hash was stale. But this version

of Shylock never learned. That reality explained this slightly comical scene of four large men in a tiny car. And one was pointing and flailing his finger in another's face. There were warnings, threats, intimidations, menaces, perils, risks, forebodings, thunder, lightning, fulminations, impendences, foreshadowing, and definitely some writing on the wall coming to light in his conversation with B.

I diplomatically suggested to B that we should take a quick ride over to the North End, where someone owed me more than the five hundred in question. Fear has a funny way of being passed on from entity to entity, until it stops somewhere. B had his fear of Heinz passed on to us, and I made it clear to the next recipient of this fear, that the comical scene of four large characters in a small car, which was now parked in front of his house, was getting more serious, minute by minute. I asked him if he ever read, *The Merchant of Venice.*

Somehow this suddenly made an impact on him, as he admitted to having the money he owed me, safely stashed in his bank. He quickly took Serge's place in the little car, and we drove to the bank where he withdrew enough to make everyone's day substantially brighter. B almost needed sun glasses.

We reclaimed Serge as the lost Antonio, and went back to the Hotel for a beer, and to celebrate B not going on a one pound diet. After a few beers, Heinz offered Serge and I a ride to wherever we were going. He then told me he liked the way I operated, and invited us over to his dwelling. He told B to hit the road... Shylock never learned...

Over at Heinz's place there were paintings of devils, ghosts, and ghouls all over the walls. I followed the monsters throughout the household until I turned one corner, and discovered the Artist busy painting. Her name was Rhonda, and she looked like she could punch out anybody who pizzed her off. I thought, "Wow, B was lucky to get off with just Heinz!" We drank a few brews, and Heinz dropped Serge and me off at my house, which was located inside the gates of Dundurn Park. I visited him at his house a few more times, with Heinz introducing me to some of his Brother Bikers and Behemoth Buddies.

Heinz showed me his white Norton 850 Commando, which was 'resting' in his bedroom. I found him interesting, and had him over to my house more frequently. Serge declared that I was playing with fire, buddying up with these bikers. But he didn't understand that almost everyone I went to Flamborough Center School with became a biker, for one Group or another.

I partied at their Club Houses, but I was just an old acquaintance, not a Runner, or a Striker, or a Wanna-be. They were buddies, but I didn't trust them because I didn't have to, or need to. So havin' Heinz and his buddies drop over was not a big deal. Usually it was just to try out a quarter pound of weed, or a tank of nitric oxide, or just some beers.

I told Heinz I loved the new Norton 850 Commando that had just come out, which he had one of in his bedroom. He giggled, and said he couldn't take it out of his bedroom until summer, as he was keeping it on ice and it was too hot for the streets yet. He stopped giggling and told me a story of how, when he was *barrowing* a Harley in the North End, the owner and a few friends burst out the front door and chased him away. He ran frantically until he crapped his pants, coincidently, because he was sure to get a good shit-kickin'. While on the run a couple blocks away he ran by this Norton 850, and he made a mental note of it, for the next evening's adventure...

We all howled at the thought, and after another hit off the nitric tank, Heinz and his Droogs grunted goodbyes and sauntered out my front door. It was the end of winter, and Heinz and his buddies were driving cars that day. As I sat on my couch, I suddenly heard a repeated clanging and banging for a minute or two. I went to peek out my front door, and witnessed the Lads running over every garbage can on the street… it was garbage day I guess…

Anyway my landlord came over an hour later, and tried to reason with me that my 'friends' had been reported to the cops by some neighbours, who saw them come out of my house to commit the garbage-can-thuggery. They suggested that these garbage-can-criminals were 'Motorcycle Bandits', and he fumbled to find the word 'evicted'. I told him I was done with the house anyway. It was the year of the Outlaws, Charlie Daniels, and Marshall Tucker. I was moving out to the Country.

I grabbed the newspaper when he graciously departed, and immediately found a forty acre farm up on the Mountain, which loomed above Lake Ontario from a distance. So I travelled up with my Yamaha and surveyed that this Farm consisted of a huge six bedroom house, a large wooden barn with a stone barn-hill, and a pole barn behind it. There were ten acres of apple orchards, and thirty acres of grapes, both in neglected shape, but redeemable. I rented the Farm immediately, and decided to ask Serge, his girlfriend Koran, and my brother Paul to move in. Sometime over the next week Craig materialized and never left.

We cleaned and renovated the house and barns quickly with Paul's help. We were happy with the status quo, and settled back for the spring, Country Style!

Oak was in his prime, and Serge had two new dogs of his own. Whenever Serge went out I would receive a visit in my bedroom. I figured I'd tell him about it later. In the meantime there was music to make, adventures to stumble upon, and new invitations to extend to old friends. It all happened quickly.

One day a dirt bike came screaming in the laneway. A couple Freaks got off and introduced themselves as the neighbours on the one hundred acre Farm, located just down the road. They invited us to *come over and visit,* and learn to party 'Mountain

Style'! We assured them we would be over, but Serge and I had to go to Court that day. We both had interesting arrests involving a strange evening at the American House Hotel a week earlier. We had been arrested for gambling on a chess game that we were playing in the Hotel one evening. Punches were thrown and police were called to escort us away. They were just a bunch of rednecks, but as usual, Serge and I were up to our half of it.

So we went to Court and received a one hundred dollar fine, each, for 'unlawful gambling in a Hotel'. Of course Serge went into the Court's Washroom to smoke a joint, and of course I followed. When we came out, Serge recognized a character from the Mountain named 'Otter', who was with an astonishingly beautiful girl. He said he had a car and would take us home. When we told him were we were going, he marvelled at the coincidence, as he was going to the Farm down the road. This was the farm the two dirt-bikers had come from that morning. I thought bringing this Gorgeous Creature on my first visit was a bonus.

Upon entering the huge abode, she went upstairs and screwed every guy in the house while I chuckled and hunkered in the kitchen with Serge, Otter, and cameo visits from dudes who appeared when they were finished in the bedroom above.

Now these were the carefree, playful days, when the worst sexually transmitted diseases were cured with a shot of penicillin. But I didn't want any sloppy sevenths or more, so I warned Serge to stay with me in the kitchen, and out of harm's way (since I was still being visited occasionally I needed to battle the Jimbo complex for Serge).

Anyways the kitchen had its own entertainment. There was a wooden barrel that the boys had lifted from a Winery Tour, which was originally filled with wine concentrate. As it was guzzled and the volume lowered, bottles of rum, tequila, whiskey, Jack Daniels, and whatever else was there that day was poured in the barrel to keep it topped up. The barrel was kept topped up for a couple months, until we were all rotten within.

After being there for only an hour I realized these guys *Partied Extraordinaire* indeed! After another hour, we grabbed a different girl and took her back to our Farm. No penicillin was needed, but she gave us all scabies. Serge told Craig that nothing was free, and this was the cost of all this *free love*, or *stolen love*, as it were.

We were all part of a Chain, and every Link told a different story. The new 'Mountain Links' played the party game hard. They were at least a couple years older than me, which gave them a couple more years of experience and adventures! There were daily visits from the 'Wild Ones' Motorcycle Club at their Farm. This was the Group some of my Droogs at Flamborough Center School, like Billy Boyd, joined up with, so I was game for most.

But next I discovered that Heinz was living in a quaint little cottage, two minutes from my Farm. He had severed himself from the Club, and he had girls from St. Mary's visiting him frequently. It's a small world, but I always seemed to be in the middle of it. We all lived in harmony on our mountain farms that summer. At least until Heinz moved into my Farmhouse, trying to keep one step ahead of too many people.

One night some Dudes came down from Racken Breakum's Farm when they heard Heinz was living at my Farm. All they knew was that Heinz was blond, about my size, had blue eyes, and that sure seemed to fit my description nicely! Some lads from Racken's Farm came over at about three in the morning (Devil's Hour), and convinced them I was not who they were hunting for. The next week I arranged a deal where Heinz sold some Dundas Dudes I knew twenty-five pounds of pot, unfortunately mixed with hay. It was time for Heinz to hit the road. Little did I know he would be the first person I would run into when I ventured to Vancouver with Oak, the coming autumn. It continued being a small world...

The lads at Racken Breakum's Farm came over one day, and told me I was invited to an all week, annual party they threw up at Moon River. I told Oak he was on his own and I jumped in one of the cars. There were cars and campers, Winnebagos, trailers, motorcycles, and pickup trucks over loaded with drugs, alcohol and women, all looking for a place to plotz.

When we got there I could see this was the perfect place to party. Moon River is a river in the municipalities of Georgian Bay and Muskoka Lakes, District Municipality of Muskoka in Central Ontario. It flows from Lake Muskoka at the community of Bala, to Georgian Bay, Lake Huron, south of Parry Sound. The lads had been coming here for entertainment and excitement since high school, and they had this Party down pat!

When I returned to my Farm the next week, Paul had moved his blonde girlfriend into the house. She thought I was trouble, and while she was right, who was she to say so? Her claim to fame was that she collected door knobs! She was beautiful, but spun. I had places in the City where I could chill out at when the parties got too intense, which was getting more and more often that summer.

I took off in Paul's pick-up one evening to visit a friendly friend in Dundas, when I suddenly noticed there was a cop car that apparently had been trying to pull me over for about ten blocks. It was unmarked, and I was drunk, so good luck having me aware of what was going on. When I finally realized what was up I pulled over; right in front of the Red Lion Hotel, don't ya know. The cop was pissed, and when I got out of Paul's truck he grabbed my hair, and swung me around as he screamed at me that he had been trying to pull me over for ten minutes, and who the @!*)_!? did I think I was?

It was just a reflex action as I sunk my knee in his balls, and well, he let go of my hair. By this time lots of RDs were catching my entertainment out on the street.

I thought about asking them to give me a distraction from the action, but soon there were more cop cars, and I was thrown into one of them. Of course it was the cop's that was looking for me. He kept telling me all the way down to the Prescient that he was gonna rearrange my head, and other such scientific notions. As I was marched inside the door, I loudly claimed I wanted to charge the arresting officer with assault, and that I had about ten witnesses (all RDs of course). So another cop took me down to the next floor, where I was booked and busted.

I spent the night in a cell, but I noticed that the whole jail was filling up with water from a toilet that had been plugged when a fight was ended by stuffing someone's head in the loo. I just kept my feet up on the bed and waited to be bailed out (PTP). Next morning I was charged with dangerous driving, resisting arrest, drunk driving, and possession of about three ounces of Columbian pot, and driving without a valid license, ownership or insurance. I told Oak it was time to head out west to greener pastures. As usual, Oak agreed.

Paul got his pick-up back the next week, and by then he realized Serge and I were too unpredictable and crazy to live with. Of course he was right. Koran's mother had put her on a plane to send her to live with her sister. Of course Serge followed her, and now Paul just had to deal with me. But I think he was doing the Bump with Heinz's girlfriend, and suddenly she was living at our Farm. I had just been fired from my position Paul got me with the Conservation Authority, the cops were looking for me, Oak was on the fritz for killing a neighbour's chickens.

It was time to run!

Oak and I went out to the 403 Ramp and stuck out our thumbs. It was an illustrious time to travel. Hitch hiking was the norm at that time, and Oak got us a few good rides. We were outside North Bay when it started to rain. Oak mentioned that he had noticed a coffee shop that we had passed a small walk back, and

I said, "Lead the way!" We weren't hitch-hiking, just walking, as Oak led me to the waiting hot coffee. Suddenly a 1975 blue Ford Econoline Van stopped, as we were walking against the traffic. A lovely blonde stuck her head out the driver's window and said playfully, "Hop in... the *doggee's* getting wet!" Oak smiled and hopped in. I followed.

She said she was Penny, I said I was John. Oak said nothing. As usual, he was chillin'. We said some stuff, like she was going to Edmonton, I said so was I. She had to stop off in Calgary, but then was heading north. She claimed to have a house there that I could move into, and help rent it. She had just performed in a TV commercial, in Toronto, and was headed home to Edmonton. She had a job in the Oil Business doing something, and she said she could get me a job there too. At some point she was visiting San Francisco for an audition, or an acting part. She thought with my strawberry blonde hair that I should try out for a 'beach part' in some movie.

Penny had the Van stocked with a big bag of buds, and some so-so coke. She drank Southern Comfort. I drank beer, and wondered how long this would last. Life goes fast. I just try to keep up. We were having a good time being westward bound together, and Oak was diggin' it. A couple-three-days-later we pulled into Calgary, where Penny said she has some business for a couple hours. We pulled into a restaurant, and Penny said she would be back in a while. I asked her what kind of business she was attending. She laughed, and said she was actually going to visit her two year old daughter.

Penny said she had been married, and one day she '*walked*' when she got some small part in a movie, in Toronto. She told me she left her daughter with the father. Boom*!? When she left I talked it over with Oak, and we decided to go visit Vancouver instead.

Chapter 13
English Bay

English Bay is located behind English Bay Beach, in Vancouver. It is comprised of a series of quaint, various English-era shops, and personal residences. These include English-influenced, and designed series of two level, studio and converted 'flats', and terraces, bungalows and cottages, that lead to lovely, busy beaches. Tourists and residents can watch volley ball games while enjoying the sun, or perhaps just stare off at the great ships in the Burrard Inlet as they disperse into the Pacific Ocean. This was where my best four legged friend and I found ourselves when we returned to the West Coast, in the mid- Seventies.

We had hitch-hiked out together in September, after years of interesting adventures and serious partying in Ontario. Upon leaving I had nothing but the clothes on my back, with an over-sized stash of pot in my pocket. The only identification I carried was an old, original, faded and ripped *Birth-Certificate.*

It was worn with serious folds in it, leaving it barely legible. Oak just had his Rabies-shot certificate, which was new.

We were leaving the Farm that we had shared with Serge, his blonde girlfriend, brother Paul, his blonde girl-friend, Rhonda, Heinz, some RDs, some characters looking for other characters, Craig, some misplaced ladies, and lots of Lost Souls. It was time to leave. The parties, freaks, bikers and newly spawned Cowboys I met that summer had taken me to a level of amusement and pleasure I didn't know about, until I was there.

There was a *country western* Waylon-Willie-Man in Black theme that summer. Ghost Riders crowded the Skies, and there was always another love song on the way. Oak and I were the last to leave the Farm. Koran and Rhonda were living in Vancouver, as was my craziest mentor of my motherless years, Serge. Serge had actually just left Vancouver, for new adventures on the Island.

Oak and I were *on the road*, lookin' for some *elbow room,* and some new adventures for ourselves. There are always enough unusual, and undocumented, fortuitousness contingencies available on the avenues weaving across Canada. But I rarely seemed to ever have any money in my pocket when I hitched across Canada. Maybe it was the *Dean Moriarti* in me, or in us all, but in my tender teen years, I had criss-crossed the country at least a dozen times; ala driving and hitching. Oak and I were partial to just sticking our thumbs out whenever the *travelling bug* hit us. Which had a lot to do with my empty pockets, I guess.

Oak and I had tripped across the Continent eight or nine times together. But on this trip, we had lots of time and space, and enough Invitations to know that when the rains turned cool, we would be able to move off the beach, and onto or into, someone's couch or bed. It was a sandy stage of our beings, featuring smooth, young faces, and the twinkles that get caught between blue eyes and the stars. Oak and I appeared on the beach one day, with only our grins and sins, and ventured out and found an *almost-finished* attic-apartment in English Bay.

This little penthouse rocked! It was hap-hazzardly adorned with bricks, mingled with some mason stones, old wooden floors, and some big-ass boss French-windows that opened out onto a little porch. Once opened, they conspicuously overlooked English Bay; with the drifting beach, cruising sail boats, larger ships, bluer skies chasing away distant clouds, people walking along the Sea Wall, pine trees dropping needles underfoot, and dogs out walking their people along the shore. This attic had a mid- sized bed-room, with a door, when needed. This nook had a semi-hidden kitchen, tucked away behind a chimney that came up through the floor, then up and out to the roof. A young lady from the floor down below helped me paint the old bricks rustic rouge. There was a laundry matt half a block away, she was down stairs, and Oak approved of it all.

Serge was a former long distance runner, who had a deep rooted Jim Morrison complex. He was really the spitting image of his father, Ed; Fast Eddie. Not the first Fast Eddie I ever knew, but the truest form to fit that name I ever witnessed. Serge was muscular. A true runner, like a Greek from twenty three hundred years ago that sprinted from town to town in a Spartan Rage, stopped not by rain nor wind, darkness nor light, fear nor sickness, nor reason itself. He had the body of a Dionysian God (when sober), and the mind of Ludwig the second. He was charismatic, and he was always telling me that he was crazy. He said he was proud of it. I dug it. He was just ahead of his time.

When he met me the first time, we smoked some hash I had, outside the he Basilica Church. It was his first experience, or experiment, with anything other than cheap alcohol, which he handled poorly and usually puked up. He was an Olympic Runner try-out, who also was a top fifteen runner at the Boston Marathon, the year I met him. He just stopped running one day, and met me the next. After toking his first hash, or any drug, with me, he asked how much it would cost to buy some.

Now I would have been fifteen years old, and five dollars for a nickel of hashish, or ten bucks for a dime, was my budget. Rich kids bought quarter ounces for twenty five skins so they could sell nickels and dimes, and get the last chunk free for their troubles. So when Serge says 'I'll take an ounce' I thought, "Holy crap. Who buys ounces?" So, as I alluded to earlier in my non-fiction, I took Serge to Rochdale College for his first education into *the other side of this life*.

Serge was young and vulnerable, but had a great grin. Girls went ape over him. But they made him nervous. I can't imagine why, but then it comes back to me; he said he was crazy! Serge and I used to try out-doing each other to see who was the craziest. Were both were proud of our insane notions. And now in 1976, he exiled himself to the Isle of Vancouver, with his women, dogmas, and dogs.

Life in places like English Bay, and UBC, were some of the last bastilles where the Hippies still out-numbered the Yippies and Punks. Viet Nam was over at that time for a couple years, and 'Apocalypse Now' wasn't released yet. It was mid-Seventies. Now everybody knew a veteran who was smuggling Thai weed in ships or planes, but with the war over, weed smugglers were getting picked up by the North Vietnamese as Spies, and tortured, then killed. A new strain of *Indicia* was immigrating north from Washington State into Vancouver. Yea Vancouver;

'I'm headin' for the nearest Foreign Border
Vancouver may be just my kind of Town
Cause They don't need the kind of Law and Order
That tends to keep a good man underground' …

You da man, Gram …

Oak and I were hanging out, often taking hikes out on the beach where we would meet some of the last Survivors of *Beatle Ed days*. Good ol' Survivors who hadn't gotten married yet, and didn't have any children who challenged them for moments which were *magic* in a different kind of way. I found such Survivors in Gas Town for a hoot and Downtown on Davie Street for a good time (in the bush). They could also be found late night, in off-beat Kitsilano piano bars that stirred our drinks, and then our minds.

It was a couple of years still before the Masses became slaves to Escobar, and other cartels. Freaks were still hanging out. They were going to Frescoes for a greasy burg, and then travelled over to West Van to visit the Macro- Biotics food stores, to take health supplies home for the girl friend. Survivors built the Sea Wall, they strolled through Stanley Park, dug the Zoo, and sashayed, joint in hand, to the beach. English Bay was far out.

And what a perfect location it was! It was walking distance from the Beach, close to Down Town, next to Stanley Park. This was all just two minutes from my living room! My dealer lived just over in West Van, and there were close-by *night clubs* to browse over on Fraser, Robson, and Burrard Streets.

There was a maple tree on English Beach that I could see from my kitchen window. Oak and I went past it every day to stretch our legs, and throw a stick, or ten. Oak was a '*stick dog*'. You've seen them before; with smiles on their lips, and branches in their mugs. However, Oak really played it to the Psychotic Level. It was always '*Get the Stick Time*', and Oak would go through walls, panes of glass; even barbed wire, unfortunately, to relish and retrieve one.

Oak would bring me the first *morning stick* on the beach as if it was the morning paper at the table. He then would grin at me until I threw it for him to retrieve. It was a living... Putting the world on hold one morning, I stuck the wooden cylindrical shaped *pain-in-the-butt* (stick) up on a branch in this maple tree, for momentary relief from Oak's maniacal gaze. I stepped away for a toke, and when I returned, there was Oak, jumping up to get the stick out of the tree. Over and over Oak jumped until there was suddenly ten people surrounding him, applauding wildly every time he got the stick. I would replace the stick back up on the branch each time he captured it. When he did, he would then do his victory walk before giving it back to me.

Pretty soon there were twenty five, forty, fifty new Oak fans orbiting and orating hysterically each time he got the stick. As if rehearsed ahead of time, they would all let out a spontaneous, "Awwww" each time his efforts were unrewarded. We were soon doing this every day, to a new crowd each time.

Oak was becoming an English Bay Icon. He was a cosmic Canuck hero. Team Oak! In interviews on the beach, he came on like a chiasmic and cultural canine! In the following weeks, Oak and I would appear at the beach, and there would already be a crowd waiting for us when we got there... that is, for when Oak got there.

I was chillin' in my attic one afternoon when I got a phone call from Rhonda. She was a friend of some of my friends, but not mine. She told me she was watching Oak on television. I assumed she was joking, and went back to sanding on a log I had recently collected off Wreck beach. I called it my Zen Log. I sanded it, and then stared into the new grains that I brought out each time I continued sanding. I swung around to grab my Heineken when I noticed the TV that was on. Suddenly there was Oak! He was running at full pace, with a stick in his mouth and ears flapping in the wind. He was grinning, and below him read;

Come Visit Stanley Park
Supernatural B.C.
BCTV

After this exposure, Oak got his nick-name; *'Joker'*, aka, *'No Joke Oak'*. His intensity of performing left him a star at English Bay Beach. Oak was dedicated to his craft; he was sometimes successful, sometimes not, sometimes injured, but always with a sly grin on his face!

Emmy Lou Harris;

In 1977, with no other options on the coast at that time, I took some Columbian Candy to an Emmy Lou Harris concert at the Orpheum Ballroom, located on Smithe Street in Vancouver. I had been drying this Columbian under a heat lamp all day, until departure time for the Ballroom. It was good stuff, but the maintenance was killer. I wasn't going to become one of the *Brief Case Brigade* and free base through the concert. Besides looking like Hunter Thompson on the Lurch, with drugs and paraphernalia leaking out of his suspicious satchel, I would miss the whole concert.

Free basing addicts rarely look up at anything, except to desperately secure the next hit. So I took my seat, along with my girl-fiend at that time, and just whipped out quick snorts on top of the cigarette package that I used to transport the insidious stuff. When in public, this shit needs to be protected from everything, except my frontal lobe! Packaged protection to ensure encapsulated and expensive eloquence, one might say. Just as Bruce Lee described; how to be the Closest, and most Silent, while completely Disguised, "Be water my friend", as the Dragon whips your tail for a hundred bucks a gram!

As the lights began to dim I put another quick line up my nose. I decided to put it away until Intermission, and listen to the eloquent Emmy Lou. Emmy was admired by Gram Parsons, years before, when he was turned on her act *back east* in Baltimore. They became an inspiring duet on Gram's '*GP*' album, with unbelievable songs like, 'We'll sweep out the Ashes in the Morning' and, 'That's All it Took'.

They also sang together on Gram's masterpiece album, '*Grievous Angel*', on monster melodies including, 'Hearts on Fire', 'I Can't Dance, 'Brass Buttons', 'Cash on the Barrelhead', 'Love Hurts', and 'In My Hour of Darkness'. Elvis Presley's Band played on these sessions.

When Gram died at the Joshua-Tree, later that year of '73, Emmy Lou took what Gram had taught her and released her first solo album called 'Luxury Liner'. It was magnificent, and touched all the hearts of those that loved The Flying Burrito Brothers Band, and Gram. It was Gram who had inspired Roger McGuinn to the milestone Country Rock album, 'Sweet Heart of the Rodeo'. It was a masterpiece album. It touches my country soul, deeply and divinely.

Every time I have ever played Emmy's Lou's 'Luxury Liner' album, her rendition of 'Lefty & Poncho' leaves me weeping. Every time!

I had plans of speaking to Emmy Lou when the concert was over. I knew when I spoke to her about her music, and threw in a few Gram references, she would understand how much her music, and time she spent with Gram, meant to me.

I was wading through the crowd until I came to the Backstage Area. I met with some guy who looked like he couldn't care about Gram, Chris Hillman, Sneeky Pete, Kris Ethridge, Sin City, Wheels, or Women who Do Right with an All-Night Man! He just looked like he was in a hurry to get out of B.C., even though Gram had sung, 'Vancouver maybe just my kind of Town'.

I approached him anyway, and before I said a word, that last snort I had done was still too moist, and suddenly this big chunk of snow popped right out of my nose and onto my outstretched hand! I immediately tried to snort it off my hand, and this guy looked unimpressed, dismissing me any further audience.

I guess I had made a choice between that snort, and maybe meeting Emmy Lou. I found my date and we headed back to my condo. I had a plateful of this more *copulas than copasetic* substance drying out under a heat lamp, waiting to be snorted into our delicate lungs and respiratory systems, on its way to numb our minds. It was now a more manageable mound of madness, and we glutted ourselves while raving about Emmy Lou's performance.

Oak came over and told me it was time for a walk. At least I think that's what he said. Anyways, the three of us were strolling down the Avenue, letting Oak get ahead of us as he was on a Mission! We were very high, and still full of wanderlust for

Emmy Lou, when this black *Town Car* pulled up. A Black man and a White dude jumped out of the car, while flashing some ID to show they were cops; just like they do in the movies! They told us to '*spread 'em*', and lean against the car for a search.

We were just too high to do anything, except maybe have another snort. But that did not seem to be an option at that moment. My hapless lady friend and I, now helpless, looked at each other. The jig was up! But how did they know? Maybe my *Dealer* was being watched. Maybe that dude backstage told the '*Police Palace in the Clouds*' of my ba*d-intentions* of having a drugged out conversation with the Luxurious Miss Lou!?

Am I paranoid if they are really after me? Maybe this Columbian cartel was silencing us Canadian customers who bitched about this Snowy Shipment's moisture content! Maybe it was Karma! Luck of the Irish? Maybe Oak had pawed and clawed his way on the phone, trying to call anyone to come let him out for a pee, and called the cops by mistake? I was trying out all the options and scenarios when suddenly they both stopped yelling and padding us down, and looked at each other. They manically broke out into an insane laughter together.

So hapless and helpless, we just stood there, peaking and freaking, when they admitted their actions to being a ruse. They then jumped back into their *Get-Away Cadillac* and screeched off! They just left us standing there. Oak came over and told me he was ready to go back inside. At least I think it was Oak who said it. Anyway, we ambled inside, and ingested everything on the plate, and decided to go visit my bud Mazzahoff, over on Straight Street. We felt somewhat raped, and did not want to stay at the scene of the non-crime.

Chapter 14
Same Ol' Same Ol'

Oak and I were living the Life of Ramses on our newly rented forty acre farm located on Old Clayburn Road, in Abbotsford. Oak's (and my) girlfriend had moved in with Adriana, a mutual friend of ours. We had just moved on, in one of Nature's most Natural Separations ever. I woke up one morning and politely said,

"Let's separate",

To which she just smiled and said "Ok".

Our friends were shocked. But we just felt we had been doing *Trips* together long enough. We split, with not a bang, or a whimper. Well, Oak did some whimpering I guess. He liked female affection, and he would take off to visit the ladies by himself at Adriana's if I did not take him over for a visit often enough.

Life on *this* farm was laid back just enough for the Joker and I. We were enjoying ourselves, while raising a herd of Steers and Heifers (sounds like a Millstone Prairie Pub with live entertainment). I did so with a little help from my one of my newer friends, and Prairie Vanguard, Marlon Dean. Marlon worked on his father-in-law's huge dairy farm. So huge, that Marlon figured no one would miss the odd bale of alfalfa for calves that are always hungry.

In the mid Seventies, the price of milk quota went up in B.C. from ten dollars a pound, to over two hundred dollars a pound! Choice milking cows went up in value to as much as a quarter million dollars each. Suddenly, these hick Dutch Farmers out on the Millstone Prairie were multi- millionaires. Kind of like Jed Clampett striking oil!

I worked for one of these *'too-rich-to-milk-themselves'* farmers for a year.

I milked two hundred and forty cows a day, and three hundred and sixty on weekends. This is where I met Marlon. One day in 1978 he pulled up on a Harley dirt bike in a field I was working in. I looked up and saw him looking me over, suspiciously, but with a grin. He must have liked what he saw, because he scarfed up a joint and lit it up.

Soon Marlon introduced me to his gorgeous wife, Pamela, who had two other incredibly gorgeous younger sisters. Pam also had a tall skinny brother, who their father was strict with for some reason... something like, 'If it didn't kill him, it would make him stronger, kinda thing'? Marlon was the most popular kid in school, and was now the number one Madman on the Millstone Prairie. One Saturday morning after breakfast, at his brand new ranch house, I innocently beat Marlon in an arm wrestle. I suddenly, and unexpectedly, became the newest *Top Dog* on the Prairie to beat.

It was a challenge to contest Marlon at anything, win or lose. I must have had to defend this unwanted position of *'new-guy-to-beat'* every time I surfaced on the Prairie. One day I let Marlon beat me, just to put it behind me... Just for some peace of mind, ya understand? But don't tell him that! He would hunt me down to this day for a rematch; a second chance at dominating this 'Red-Headed, Long-Haired Sasquatch', as he called me.

Marlon and I became best friends in no time. He was the top Welterweight Boxer in B.C. But he was currently being controlled, perhaps for the first time in his life, by Pamela's father. He was a redneck, who thought Marlon wasn't good enough for his Daughter. Eventually they got married, but like Bud, his opinion of his daughter's choice never changed.

Marlon was always looking for extra cash, as his paycheque was largely in the form of a brand new house to live in, free food, free gas, and a brand new car for a wedding present. But cash was another matter. Marlon signed a contract that promised him a substantial bonus after a few years. In the meantime cash was short. But Marlon and Pamela were happy on Millstone Prairie.

When one of Marlon's friends, Troy, found out I had coke connections in Vancouver, he and I would travel in and buy all we could afford, so we could snort as much as we could for free. Marlon kept away from such deals. He was always too busy for such shenanigans. Busy, busy boy!

One day Troy and I bought some ounces of Columbian snow, but I got bogged down with the bong all afternoon with a buddy. Troy came over for his snowstorm after work. I had been free basing all day, and was hanging back when Troy busted in, all excited about this big bag awaiting him. We had half of it on the counter, weighing out his share.

As I was fidgeting with the scales, I kept hearing this tap tap-tap sound behind me. I finally turned around and followed the tap sounds to the back door, which had a window in half of it; for looking out… and looking in! Zonked to my stomp, I looked out the window. There was someone with a ski mask on, with a shot gun pointed at me, gently tapping on the window with the end of the barrel. He yelled, "Open the door."

I thought I recognized him as a friend of Rick's. Rick had driven with us into Vancouver and back that day, then went off to enjoy some Italian wine and French female company at his place. I had been free basing for hours in Vancouver, and I yelled at the dude who was holding the shot gun, whom I thought was just making a bad joke,

"Hey that ain't cool. Knock it off."

He said again, "Open the door!"

When I didn't look shocked, or make a move to let him in, he took the butt of his shot gun and smashed the door off its hinges. I suddenly, well, maybe that is, *finally* clued in that this dude was serious. In an attempt to run, I slipped and fell on the spot three times in a row, and then got some traction and ran into my bedroom. Coincidently, Troy had given me his shot gun a few days earlier, to duck hunt with. He warned me it was big for ducks, but I took it anyway. It was still loaded, and I was about to come back out but Troy frantically yelled at me to drop his gun and get out there, as this dude was about to blow his head off.

I threw down the gun and reluctantly went out, looking at Troy lying on the floor, spread eagle. I was invited to do the same. When I was face down, I glimpsed up at the gun covering us.

He yelled, "Don't look up! Where's the rest of the coke?"

I ululated "Troy, he's got a one shot!"

Recognizing his unpredictable next few seconds, he started kicking Troy mercilessly. I insisted to him that was all the coke there was. At this point, I realized he was kicking Troy, and not me. Everyone knew I was getting over a few broken bones from a motorcycle accident I had a few weeks earlier. I thought maybe it was a hired biker who had been informed I was in potentially *fragile shape.*

You don't ever win fighting bikers if you're not a fairly tough psycho. Count your losses and live!! At that point it didn't matter. He took Troy's keys and sped away in his car. We followed Troy's car into Town in my old pick-up, but we didn't really want to catch up. What were we gonna do? We didn't know who it was, and we didn't really want to know, anyway. But what we did do was drive over to Rodeo Vespucci's place, and I told him to put on some Lynyrd Skynyrd. Rodeo replied 'Skynyrd? I said, "You got that right!" He sure had that right…

A few weeks later, a new friend, Jewels, myself, and a few old buddies, had been abusing ourselves all day. Jewels left at about one ante meridiem. I remained, working overtime with my chunk of granite by myself, when a car slowly pulled up on the shoulder of the road at the end of my laneway. I was wired, going on the third day with no sleep. The car had been parked there for about an hour. I worked at ingesting everything on the table before I finally decided to check this scene out. I was like a bird on a wire; one part wired on blow, two parts wired on adrenaline, and ninety-seven parts Pure Paranoia!

And I was now ready to investigate this car that was at the end of my laneway for over an hour at this point? OK. Wiped, wacked-out, and wasted, I wobbled down the lane way. Ready for anything and ready for nothing, I cautiously edged my way to the end of the lane towards the precariously parked Pontiac. At one point, I wasn't walking that quickly, but my cautiousness and fear were now behind me. Curiosity led the way. I wanted to know who this was. A cop? Ok, my stashes were stashed. A bandit? Bring it on! A psycho? More psycho than I was, taking on this car in the darkness, wired to the teeth, during the Devil's Hour at 3 AM?

I ambled on towards the car. I soon found myself staring in the window yelling, "What do you want?" Hey, what are you doing buddy?"

He gave no response, and kept staring forward like I wasn't even here. I started banging on the window. Nothing. I banged again. Nothing again! As I continued banging the third time, I must have needed another snort, cause I suddenly wondered, "What the hell am I doing out here?" I receded and went back to the house for a snort. I was up the rest of the night, snorting, and staring at this car!

I must have really gotten into it, because I suddenly looked and saw he was gone.

My neighbour told me some time later, when I asked him if he knew anything about the blue Pontiac, at three in the morning, with the moron in it who only stared at the moon? He replied that it was an ex-boyfriend of his daughter's.

Well, I guess I was just paranoid after all eh?

Dean Moriarty

I have owned some fast Motorcycles. I had the fastest stock bike thrice; a '72 Combat 650 Norton, a '73 350 RD Yamaha Road Racer that possessed six gears and (first year of) Torque Induction, and the '82 Eleven hundred Kawasaki Spectre.

The first car I ever bought was a 1957 Chevrolet Bel Air. It had an original 235.5 cubic inch engine in it, which had just been rebuilt. It was geared with a Power Glide Automatic Transmission, had two fins on the Hood, fourteen inch wheels for a lower stance, mesh grille insert, front fender chevrons, wide-look tail fins, a chrome Chevrolet signature on the hood and trunk, distinctive chrome head lights, and a magnificent emblem on the front of the hood, balanced between the two fins, and crowning the top of the hood. The emblem was worth as much as the car. It was a black and white Bell Air. It was Clean Machine.

I actually purchased the car for a *friend with benefits*. I bought this Bell Air on Hornby Island, from a lumber-jack Zeppelin fan who called himself Cashmere. That about summed it up for 'Shmere'. He and his buddies liked Zepplin the way we Dead Heads followed the Dead. Cashmere once told me, "I lived with a Dead Head once. We used to hide albums on each other, and charge hashish tokens for their returns." He smiled and said it was, "All good!"

Cashmere had been a lumber jack for fifteen years. I can't tell you how much that surprised me, but hey, Zepplin freaks cut down trees too! He had been on Hornby for years, and harvested trees on the Coast. Manshika told me 'Shmere was selling his '57 Chev Bel Air for seven hundred bucks. I figured that was just about the right price for this expedition. I loved the Islands off the coast, and this would be a good visit with Cashmere.

I was killing time before catching the Ferry, at Straight Street, when I was suddenly summoned to Manshika's room . I shuffled in and took a puff. Manshika was the guy to see. He was our west coast Guru.

Manshika was the Vancouver version of who Leonardo was in the rest of the Fraser Valley. Manshika wasn't loved like Leon though. Shika was respected for his business prowess that made people trust him. And like all Gurus, he was put on the top pillow, because he had all the prerequisites to be a Sultan. The Musicians all knew him. He knew people that shared our lust for the morning dew. He was charismatic and smart. And like a wise Guru, or Sultan, he calls me over, just before I head out to Horseshoe Bay to jump on the Ferry. He gave me some helpful advice on 235.5 cubic inch engines FMI. Anything Manshika said was worth listening to.

I had to hustle now, because I was meeting someone on Main Street who was giving me a ten pound lot of good pot to trade for the car; for my transporting fees. A fee which came to... exactly! The price of a '57 Chevy Bel Air! Hornby Island would be happy.

My *friend* and I arrived on Hornby that afternoon. I made the drop off and picked up the Chevy. I asked him if Serge was around. Cashmere said he was in Victoria. I was reminded that we had no time for such a visit, so I took a rain cheque. I would literally save it for a rainy day, and on the West Coast, there were lots of those.

Serge was just like Dean Moriarty, or Neil Cassidy, with his wild eyes, his protrusive sweating, his fearless attitude, his athletic body, the Women that always got left behind, his lust for drugs and excitement, his magnetism, his guaranteed notion that things never worked out as planned, his lack of a plan, everything he conjured but never conceived, his need for attention, his natural leadership he possessed, his passion, his confusion, the books that needed to be written about him, and that Smile! And he said he was crazier than I was!

I was always finding the time to write down my thoughts, notions, and concepts; concepts of notions. When I was with Katrina (later), I was Shaman Paradise. But when I was on the move with Serge, I was Sal Paradise. Serge would try to write things at times, but his rhythm was all about being on the move. He couldn't slow down. So I tried to keep up.

But in the end, people were circumspect of Serge; too many calamities with too many smiles left on his face. Too many spectators left wondering. Too many people left behind. There was no start or finish lines. He just ran on adrenaline, full out, full time, until there was nowhere left to run. He eventually ended up in Mission City, with kids, and dogs, and mechanical parts besides piles of things that just got higher. Eventually Time coaxed him to join it wallowing in the mire. Serge was crazy. But sly crazy... Like in a Dean Moriarty, real-life, fictional kind of way.

A Biting Grip on Reality;

Luther Medici (older brother of Leonardo), and I, were sitting in my 1950 GMC candy-apple-red pick-up truck on a cool spring day, after being on a coke binge for three days at my kitchen table. That was what we did in the Seventies as we tumbled blindly, and helplessly, into the Eighties. Jewels tried to keep up, but had to leave during the night, a few times. I had given her a gram before she left, again, but she had gone home, twice, and both times came back up within half an hour for more. She was partying with Matta Ravenscliff, and you never wanted to keep

Mizz Matta wanting too long. Matta was a slight figured politician, who most people naturally respected, and some unnaturally feared. She was extremely intellectual, with a Biting Grip on Reality.

You had to be on the ball, and have a pair, to drink and snort with her. I was ok because she admired my poetry. This made some people jealous. Matta's father had been born in a German prison camp during WW2, and the whole Family, though French predominantly, always reflected Eastern Influences in everyday life. Her father was a proud, intellectual man, who was one of those *silent cogs* in the Ministry of Defence.

Anyway, yes, Luther was in the red Chev's Custom Cab, spaced out and patiently waiting for me to drive him home. A friend from Victoria B.C. was staying with Oak and I for the last week, but she had not made it to three days of insanity like the rest of us. But we were loud partyers, and she let me know that she was sick of being woken up constantly. She was sick of Jewels constantly calling, and sick of hearing Luther's astronomically loud laugh every thirty seconds, she was sick of my not sleeping for seventy-five hours, sick of the parties, and sick of us all around the kitchen table. She reflected that every time she came out, we were sitting upright like icicles' that were afraid to melt. She said it was time for Luther to skedaddle, and everybody else too. She wanted to go back to sleep before Jewels phoned again, in her hopeless efforts to console Matta. It was time to take her to the Ferry so she could return to her quiet life in Victoria… tomorrow.

With congeniality in mind and anyways looking to please my Island Girl, I told Luther it was time to head down Old Clayburn Hill and visit his father/my friend Tucano Medici. He would be having his first beer of the day soon (never before five) and I thought the change of scenery, and a cold one, would help me knock off the White Line Fever within my soul. I went outside where Luther was all perched and waiting. As I crawled into the cab, Luther's eyes were suddenly the Size of Saucers. Flying Saucers! He said, "Did you see that?" I said I wasn't sure, and what the hell was he talking about?! He said a white baggie had just come exploding out of the kitchen window, in full view of the pick-up. Then his eyes got wider.

"What?" I think I asked? Luther had the eyes of a hawk. He told me the eighteen by twelve by four inch thick piece of granite that we had been worshipping for three days was now out the window and on the lawn, by the plastic bag. I told Luther the party was moving to his house.

It was just better for everyone if I just disappeared for a day or so. I bailed out of the GMC and gathered the implements and the plastic baggie, ready to start the Next Party down the hill at Tucano's. I was thinking what a favour I would do the red-headed raven inside the house by disappearing for an extended amount of time. I fed the calves, shut the barn door, and once again crawled into the newly chromed and painted elegant Cab to make my get-away. And once again, Luther's eyes were the size of football fields this time. I reluctantly groaned, "What now?" Luther didn't answer. He looked confused. Maybe totally messed up would be the better adjective. I saw I would need to drag it out of him. I told him I had half an Eight Ball, the hunk of granite, and that I was ready to go so,

"What the hell?!"

Luther grappled with words and finally came up with, "Holy shit John! Look!"

I turned my head, though I had serious reservations about doing so, and glanced in the direction Luther was gaping at. There was an eight month Holstein steer, with a rope around its neck, hanging, suspended in the air. It had been grazing on its rope '*leash*', and had jumped, or fallen, off a cliff that separated the top fields from the lush lower dell.

I raced over to cut it down. Its feet were hanging just inches from the ground.

It was slowly hanging itself. Its tongue was blue and its eyes red. And they were bulging out of its head! By the time I ran to the barn and grabbed a knife and returned, the steer was quietly in another world. So, with a ring of white powder around my nostrils, I left the yellow nylon rope around its neck, strung the free end over a thick brown tree branch ten feet up, and then tied the rope to the truck frame under the bumper. I hit the gas and dragged the calf up the hill, then dragged the rope over the branch until the steer's body started rising upwards. It quickly hung securely in place; totally off the ground. I grabbed the knife, and slit its throat to bleed it out. I then slit it the length of its body, and degutted the carcass. I washed my hands, phoned Marlon, and told him to send over his friend Roy over. Roy owed me a favour for ripping off fifty pot plants out of my garden the previous autumn.

He could skin the carcass, and prepare it to hang for a couple days. The weather was still cool enough to let it hang for a few days, outside. I jumped one more time into the pick-up, with the coke and chunk of granite waiting patiently in place. I then roared down to Tucano's place, still in time for the first beer of the day. It was like a movie with no ending, and too many commercials!

Time for a change, Again

Vancouver is where the band Chilliwack comes from. Founding member Bill Henderson could have remained closer to home and called them, say, 'Coquitlam'. Or how about 'Whistler'? 'Kitsilano'? 'Wreck Beach' would have been a classic! But he chose the handle Chilliwack. The word Chilliwack is the name of a local Indian tribe, as well as a geographic description of the area. Originally spelled Chilliwhack, this "Halkomelem" word means "quieter water at the head" or travel by way of a backwater.

Vancouver loved them, and they loved Vancouver. Such a musical relationship brings many to Vancouver's mountains and rivers, to a Culture on the Pacific. I had lived Downtown Vancouver, at English Bay, in the East End, near the 'West End Boys', Burnaby, Port Coquitlam, hell even under the Portman Bridge with the Colony Farmers. I had taken over a Musician's house in West Vancouver with a couple close friends. Oak said he was bored. I told him I knew how he felt.

There was something in the air. It was time for a change once again. It was nothing specific really, but there was something stifling in the breeze. In West Van I was living with Ghosts of incredible scenes of the past; indelible people, times, faces, blow, blow people, musicians, dealers, dopers, telescopers, astrologists, bikers, hikers, cosmic happenings, beautiful women, passers through, hippies, yippies, dudes that skied, amplifiers, guitars, waterbeds stashed with contrabands, cars, motorcycles, pets, and Alice. But this was 1977. Oak and I had just returned from a summer on the road, driving to Dundas and back.

I stayed the summer at Stanley Pack's place, after meeting his wife at a party.

Upon meeting Sweet Sue, I told her I was just off the road from Vancouver, and she said I could stay at her place. She forgot to mention that she lived with Stanley... or that she was his wife. I knew Stanley for years. Such was the Dundas bedroom community, where everybody knows everybody, whether you want it that way or not. We grew up together. When Stanley came in, he said to just sleep on the couch. Well that worked itself out ok.

A very entertaining month later, Oak and I found ourselves out on the road, hitching back to Vancouver. We had a big bag of pot, a knapsack with a change of clothes, a bag of Kibble, and about one hundred dollars. Oak was anxious to get back to the land of the setting sun.

Oak and I had a great week on the road, stopping for another week in Thunder Bay with, sure enough, some original St. Mary's Survivors. We went to Pow Wows on Native Mountains and to parties with people I hadn't seen in a few years. Oak and I were in Good Spirits for hitting the road to Vancouver. We had made this trip across the *Straight Divide* hitch hiking many times, and probably as many times in planes, trains and automobiles. When we returned to the coast, it was the same ol' same ol'. Oak and I were ready for a Change.

Mission City

A faceless prophet came over to my house in West Van, one forgotten day, and happened to mention that *someone* he knew was moving out of a house in Mission City. I checked out M. C. like I was on a mission. It was on the south bank of the Fraser River. I drove over with my roommate Alex, and we looked over the Town. The quaint dwelling was a three bedroom house with a garage, on a peaceful backstreet, not far from the downtown. It was September, and there was a big fireplace, and lots of stacked wood. I told Oak that this place had promise for the coming winter. He concurred. Alex and our mutual friend Maria moved in. Winter quickly did too!

Mission City was close to the Sylvester Mountain Chain, on the way to Harrison Springs in the sierra. Winters there were cold. Do a bunch of mushrooms, and throw another log on the fire! Christmas time meant a lot of snow, which meant we got fewer and fewer visitors as winter progressed. Christmas day saw Alex high-tail it into Maple Ridge, while Oak, Maria, and I stayed behind, with no alcohol, some sandwiches, and next to no Christmas Spirit. In Abbotsford Leonardo was having a party, and we figured we'd make it over there after supper of cold sandwiches. But this was part of *stretchin' about* and movin' on out to the Country. For peace of mind, for the good and the bad, for and what it's worth.

It got on to about noon, and we were stoking the fire, preparing to eat some Christmas Mushrooms. Suddenly we heard someone on the porch.

I opened the door to a knock, and Cashmere strutted in with his new girlfriend Joy. They arrived with an old friend of mine, Jackie Ray. They brought beer and whiskey, with a huge turkey, and potatoes with all the fixings. They figured we were alone on Christmas Day, and thought we should celebrate the day together. What could we say?

We got out the mushrooms, and Cashmere, Jackie, Oak and I hiked up into the Mountains, while the Girls stoked the fire and cooked a meal to melt our mushroom mouths. It makes me hungry right now just to think about it. We drank the beer and whiskey, and fizzled out on the mushrooms at about the Devil's Hour. It was one of the more special Xmases any of us had ever experienced. Well, at least since the one when I got the Abbey Road LP in '69!

We all got up the next day and did more mushrooms. Once again we headed up the Sylvester Mountains to trip about, this time with the ladies. By late afternoon we were scattered from each other, the way you get with mushrooms sometimes. I met up with everyone but Joy. It was getting dark, cold and snowy. The rushing river was all we could hear as it got darker. Our heads were starting to focus enough to realize that we had better find her, or she could freeze up there overnight. 'Here's Johnny'! Sorry Stephen King.

But the roaring river was much louder than we could yell, and it was getting too dark up there to effectively search. With things looking bleak, I pulled Oak towards me and said, "Oak. You have to find Joy." I repeated it to him. He knew exactly what I was saying. He ran back and forth and got all excited. I repeated to him that he had to find her. Oak suddenly got intensely *focused*, and started sniffing and running along the river. It was rough terrain, and tough to keep up. He ran for fifteen minutes, and just as darkness set down, he ran right up to her. Joy looked up and said, "I was wondering when you guys would get here." We went home and gave Oak any kind of food he wished, except live chickens. We praised Him, and made Him know what a Hero He was. Then we ate some more mushrooms.

The Chief;

Leonardo knew every single person in the Fraser Valley, east of Vancouver. Or else they knew of him. When he heard I was living in Mission City, he was intrigued. He knew a lot of Native Indian Peoples in the hills and on the lake out that way. When I was over at his dwelling one day, he introduced me to a couple teen-age Natives. They were friendly, and Leonardo told them I was living in Mission. They asked if when I left, that they could catch a ride with me over the River to the Mission City Tavern. I said sure, and that I'd probably be having a beer there myself. They asked if we could get there around seven, as they were meeting their uncle there. I said sure and we soon took off.

We pulled into the Mission City Tavern around six thirty, and enjoyed a cold one on such a cold night. David suddenly looked up and said, "Here he is." With that I looked up and saw it was Chief Dan George. He walked slowly over to join our table. The Chief was in some such movies I had seen like; 'Little Big Man' and 'The Outlaw Josey Wales', 'Harry and Tonto', 'Shadow of the Hawk', 'Alien Thunder', 'Smith', 'Americathon','The Bears and I', 'Spirit of the Wind', 'Cancel my Reservation', 'Nothing Personal', and 'Cold Journey'. It was an honour to meet him, on so many levels. He was quiet, letting others forge the words that would carve the evening. He asked me where I was from originally.

I told him, "Back east."

He replied, "That's what they all say."

Winter plunged on, and I decided to attend Fraser Valley College. After Christmas, I was sent to farms in the Fraser Valley by the College, where I was hands-on instructed to care for, and properly milk dairy cows. This Course enrolled me, and some other pretty suspect looking characters to be in valuable Milking Establishments, milking cattle that were worth hundreds of thousands of dollars each. Of course I was born on Bud's farm, and I had even worked full time on my neighbour's potato farm, but Dairy Farming is a breed of its own, pardon dos 'pun mon'.

When Alex saw me cash a paycheque from the College, he quickly joined up. Now I don't think Alex was ever on a farm in his life, and here he was about to handle quarter million dollar animals, at three o'clock every Devilish morning. Now you tell me what's wrong with this picture. As a farmer's son, I looked sideways at the whole Program, but I kept cashing those cheques.

I actually did finish the Course, and got a job milking bovines on a huge farm, a stone's throw from Leonardo's. I was milking hundreds of bovine mammals every day. You soon, or eventually if you're frosty, experience special relationships with the cows you are milking. You are responsible for having her bred on time, her healthy calving, and milking her out twice a day for the rest of her milking career, which basically is the rest of her life. Then she becomes part of the McDonald's chain of care. This is sad, because cows are really wonderful beings. One point two billion people can't all be wrong, right? Not properly milking out a heavily lactating animal will kill her. It is a different kind of farming, indeed... farms with scads of money behind every closed barn door. And scads of millionaire cows with blissful smiles. And no egos!

Strange Shit;

Harrison Lake was calling us one day, so Kori, the baby and I headed off for a visit. It was a spectacular Lake which we went to for energy, whenever we had the time or notion. I was soon walking round the lake, with the wife in Adidas, and baby in a stroller. It was a warm and sunny day as we progressed around the water, all care-free like. There was an asphalt strip around the lake, nestled in between the water and the steep base of mountains that replenished the lake each spring. It was a twisty shoreline to follow, though greatly aided by the asphalt path. It was quickly coming up High Noon, as the sun was straight above. A day made for a hike.

A feeling of peace took over the lake as we continued twisting our way around the tranquil surrounding. Oak had taken the day off. He figured he would just stay at home, and maybe attack the neighbor's Chicken Coop later that day. A regular-dog-dangling-afternoon if ever there was one!

We had been strolling round the water and soaking in the sun for about an hour. We were still a long way from circling the lake, and I commented that it was warm, but maybe we would make it all the way round, seeing as the baby was asleep. The rest of the world seemed to be too. I was thinking about lighting up, when the sun suddenly went behind a cloud. I wondered where the cloud came from as the sky was clear a moment before. More clouds suddenly appeared, and the sky around us was rapidly turning dark. Ominously dark! Suddenly there was lightning through the Dark Sky, and a wind hurled itself at everything around us. This had all happened, in just one minute.

We were coming to a blind spot on the pathway, and as we reached the '*Arc of the Bend*' the wind became insane and lightning bolted, like in a Lon Chaney monster movie. We were about to walk around the blind curve on the path ahead when a *Dark Figure* suddenly appeared. It was a Priest, garbed in black, with a black hat, black beard, and Black Eyes! He immediately locked his Eyes into mine, and glared like Beelzebub. He was scowling! His eyes buried deeper and deeper into mine. It became Totally Dark, and the lightning silhouetted his image, as everybody kept in a distorted motion. He never took his eyes off me. His glare became menacing! As we each walked around the bend, leaving each other behind on the rocky curve, the wind died down, and the sky quickly began to clear. The lightning subsided. The sun then came out, and it became warm again, like none of this had even happened. I said, "Did that really just happen?" No one answered, as if no one was really sure.

As we continued our trek we came across two younger girls on the path. I asked them if the weather normally changed so drastically. They commented that they noticed on the rocky outlet that it had gotten dark and stormy, and then disappeared as quickly as it came up. They said they were relieved that it went away, as it looked like a bad one was on its way. I said, "Wait a minute. You mean it didn't get dark and stormy where you were on the lake?" They said that it was all contained in that one outcrop, and that it didn't affect the rest of the lake at all. I went over and stroked my Irreproachable Child's forehead and said to her, "Welcome to the Twilight Zone baby!"

Chapter 15
In-A-Gadda-Da-Vida

The monkey was riding his bicycle down the high-wire, once again. He was vehemently and earnestly watching the thin wire he was straddling. The vigilant anthropoid cautiously rode toward the cessation of his voyage between the steel girders that supported the steel circus-line he mounted with his velocipede. And I swear, the whole time he was smiling!

There were other 'circus-like' acts going on around us as our meal was served. A huge organ was being played much of the time. 'In-A-Gadda-Da-Vida' played every time the monkey balanced his bicycle across the high-wire. Doug Ingle, who wrote the lyrics, and his band Iron Butterfly, guzzled a gallon of Mountain Red Wine before practicing it together the first time, and that's what he slurred out. But that made no difference to me, or the monkey. It fit the mood perfectly.

There were bursts of bubbles exploding from mouths of Roman Statues. Balloons floated down from the ceiling every few minutes. Confetti ruled the air waves. A Cosmic Volcano erupted compellingly, as red and orange fluids oozed down the mountain side and into a lake, then disappeared. The music roared on. There were midgets dressed in uniforms of elves, fairies, Snow White and the Seven Dwarfs, Munchkins from the Wizard of Oz, and of course the Wicked Witch of the West attacked them on her broom with her Flying Monkeys, every thirty minutes. There were Monsters, Vampires, Werewolves, Mummies, Feathered Serpents, and Ghosts were flying, running, and staggering around everywhere. If the World is a Stage, this Restaurant was a Point-in-Time! You didn't need any magic mushrooms in here, though who knows, maybe there were some cooked in your meal for good measure!

It was like something out of a Hunter S. Thompson nightmare, of too much LSD, mixed with some mescaline, for clarity, and MADA, for sensual rhythms and rifts. But this was just lunch. I heard it got Weird at Suppertime! I'd be there to check it out.

This was our first bite to eat since we got to Portland; home of The Keseys, Gus Van Sant, Elliot Smith, James Beard, Beverly Cleary, Carrie Brownstein, Matt Groening, Gage Skidmore, Kaitlin Olson, Sally Struthers, Jane Powell, Ann Curry, (born in Guam, raised in Japan and Ashland), Courtney Love (born in San Francisco, raised in Eugene and Portland), Tommy Thayer, Mel Blanc, Terrell Brandon, Sally Struthers, Silver Skye, Jinkx Monsoon, Ashton Eaton, Jane Powell, Laura Allen, Kaitlan Olson, Katee Sackhoff, and other Famous and Strange Portlanders.

We were taking the scenic Highway SR 4, along the Columbia River when it started to snow. Within an hour I was headed to I-5 Freeway to get into Portland, as I had steel belted radials on my '54 Chev, and I was skidding and sliding uncontrollably south. It turned out to be the biggest snow fall in the last hundred years at that time. I figured soon as we hit Portland I would buy snow tires. But the snow had stopped, so here we were in this Cosmic Restaurant, cheering on the Monkey!

I was talking to some Dude about getting us a bag of pot, of course, and he invited me over to his place. He said he had a friend with some Maui-Wowee buds who dropped by frequently. So we waited. I talked to Pete, my canteen comrade, about the strange weather, while my friend washed the remnants of the day on the road off her face. He introduced me to a couple of his Droogs, and we puffed one while making plans to visit the Restaurant as a group, for supper. It wasn't the food we went there for, particularly. A group was playing there, aptly named,

'Seafood Momma' (formerly called Quarterflash), from eight till nine-thirty, for digestion purposes I suppose. My new comrades promised me I would be impressed. I could hardly wait, but in truth, I wanted to see the Monkey again too!

Well the Lads were talking my language, and we sat back to hear about the Portland Sound... They told me Portland spawned groups like Foghorn String Band, the Kingsmen, Paul Revere and the Raiders, Robert Cray's Band, Curtis Salgado, as well as early Hardcore Punk led by the Wipers. I was surprised, I mean aghast! As Johnny Carson said just enough times; "I did not know that!"

Pete and the fellows educated me that Portland was chock-full of Frat Rock, and Garage Rock, which gave many Groups direction. Fifteen years after I left Portland, it became home of Grunge Bands like Riot Grrrl (my absolute fave!!), alternative sounds, and beginnings of Indie Rock. The millennium has witnessed local Indie Artists like the Decemberists, Floater, Gossip, the Dandy Warhols, M. Ward, Storm Large, and the Pink Martinis, contrive and contribute to make Portland the *Hipster Mecca* of yesterday and today.

Seafood Momma blew my mind, and we were soon back at Pete's house (I'm not sure exactly who actually lived there, but we were now part of their scene). We slept on the couches, ate, drank, toked and joked with them for five days. Every time a bag showed up for me, we smoked it and ordered another. It was a sweet scene. Except that they watched 'Mork and Mindy' as often as possible, which I detested. Robbin Williams put too much energy into his shtick for my slow ambling brain to appreciate. One night when it came on, I went out for a walk with a joint. I had (another) ounce of Maui buds, and we were going to leave for California in the morning. I made it about one block before I stumbled into this lonely, blue, three quarter ton

International Pick-up truck. It was in perfect shape, aside from needing a revitalising new paint job.

But there was more to this vintage Pick-up than I picked up on at first glimpse.

I started banging on the front doors of houses near the truck, enquiring at each one if they owned a 1954 International 4X4 Pick-up truck. It took about five houses until a man, about thirty years old, admitted to owning the conveyance in question. He said flat out it was not for sale. I asked him if he minded if I looked at it. I told him I was from Canada, in a '54 Chev Bel Air. He said he had seen it parked on the street over the last week, and was enticed by it. He asked me if I would sell it to him. I said no, as I was driving to La Honda in the morning. He started out towards his Pick-up, telling me things about it as he walked.

Apparently he had a Vision, and a ton of work into the truck… He had taken the Deluxe body off a 1954 International P.U., and put it on the frame and drive train of a 1956 International 4X4. He claimed he worked at the garage on the corner, and had done all the work himself. He rhymed off a list of problems that arose, and how he conquered the complications simultaneously. Now I was more intrigued than ever. I offered him sums of six, seven, and eight hundred dollars. He said it was very tempting, as he would make a 'good' profit at eight; but still no. I could see his pride in the vehicle, and his work, as well as the patience and skill he displayed.

I had about eleven hundred Canadian dollars left in my pocket. I told him he could have a thousand of it. He said if I gave him a thousand American, he would do it. 1978 was a tough year for the value of the Canuck buck, but I was back the next morning with a thousand George Washingtons. I explained to my travelling companion that the conversation about the California vacation was on hold, and she could drive the Chev, while I maneuvered the 4X4 to the Canadian Border. We had a serious session of Maui *mind-messers*, I changed the ownership over to Moi, grabbed my bag, exchanged mailing addresses with the Lads, and we were northerly Border bound.

As we neared the Sumas U.S.A. Border Crossing that evening, I started getting a little paranoid about the exotic bag of buds. We stopped into a Sumas U.S.A. bar, had a beer, and stashed the bag outside. I figured I'd pick it up the next day, when all the business of crossing with a new vehicle was history. We idled momentarily at the Crossing, and the Border Guard tipped his hat and said, "'Go ahead." No questions, no answers, too easy!!

I drove the short distance to Leonardo's, and showed Luther my new/old 4X4. When I told my story of how dreamy-easy the border crossing was, Leonardo said that he wanted to smoke some of, "That Maui shit." He concluded that Now was the sleepy time for wild west wanderers to slip across lonely latitude lines, so I went back across the Sumas Crossing, had a beer, stuck my stashed stash down my pants, and once again I got the *Good-Night* nod. I went back and smoked with Leonardo till the cows came home... Leon's place was totally surrounded by cow pastures, which was filled with cows who had never smoked Maui before, or at least that's what they claimed. I blew a toke out the window and told them, "Not to hurt themselves." They just stared funny-like at us. Maybe they ate some local Psilocybe Mushrooms that their very own stools had helped germinate and make flourish. Who knows... all they did was smile!

Vintage;

After a stoned night's sleep, I travelled into Town for a few munchies, and to show off my new vintage vestige. I pulled into the Supermarket parking lot, and nonchalantly pulled up to an incredible looking cherry-red, 1950 GMC half ton pick-up truck. A large teenaged lad soon appeared, and I told him I had just bought this 4X4 in Portland, and that I loved his P.U. He said it was totally original, with the 216 engine, and all the chromed parts, inside and out, which had just been re-chromed. The body had just been painted, inside and out, and it ran perfectly.

It had original rims, original 'three-on-the-tree' gear shifter, and the interior was painted original cherry red, and the seats had just been originally restored. I told him he was a lucky man. He agreed indeed that we were both lucky to own these Jewels of the Road. He said he had done all the work, for next to no cost, since it was all accomplished in his Auto Shop in High School. I must have been drooling, because the next thing he said was, "You really like it eh?" Before I could answer, he said he was *'heart-broken'* because it had been in an accident, with his younger brother driving.

I was confused. There were no bangs or dents in the truck, so I asked him if the accident was before he had restored it? He told me to look closer at the driver door. I did, but again saw nothing. He pointed to the center of the door and asked, "Don't you see this crease?" I looked and looked, but saw no deformity in the door. He coaxed me to change my vantage point, and look at it with the sun in the position he was in. I did, and after a minute of looking I finally saw this almost imperceptible *'crease'* he alluded to. I told him I saw it, and he grunted how, "Pissed off he was that his brother had ruined his project."

I told him not to worry so much about it, but he said that now he wanted to sell it, because of the door deformity. He said he worked, "Too long and hard on it to, look at that door every time I get in it." He asked if I wanted to buy the 'Jewel'.

I asked how much it was worth to him. When he said three hundred dollars, I told him it was worth much more. I assured him that as a fellow Vintage Vehicle lover, I didn't want to take advantage of him on his down moment. He said three hundred was what he wanted. I asked him if he wanted to sleep on it, and he retorted that if he didn't sell it to me for three hundred, he would to the next interested person.

I told him to follow me to my bank, and I purchased the beautiful, almost flawless vehicle. The next month, I bought another '57 Bel Air, in better shape than the first one from Hornby Island. I suddenly was assembling a small fleet of crisp vintage autos.

Tucano: The Working Man;

It's a funny thing to be a Working Man, all day long. I felt like such a fraud!

I mean, how do people do it? All day long, all week, years on end; basically a life time! I guess it could be worse. My best friend, of this lifetime, was a six foot, three inch young man name Leonardo. He was one of the most charismatic souls I ever met. He had more people relying on him than most Senators or Politicians. They just made promises but Leonardo always came through. He put things together for people. He was a Drummer in his spare time, when I first met him. He was a businessman. He was a gambler. He was loved. He was exciting. Women were maternal to Him. He was a Guru. He was Cosmic. He was Determined. He was a Dreamer. He was Keen.

Leonardo had muscular dystrophy. Being so tall, he was like a piece of uncooked spaghetti... tall and straight, yet unbending and impenetrable, and easily broken. When he was young he would often fall to the floor, uncontrollably, with no muscles to break the impact! It would have been better if Arnold was cooked and then he would be soft. Then in times when impact came, he could just stick to the wall, or just float gently in the warm water. But Leonardo wasn't cooked, and when he fell, I felt like I fell with him.

Leon's father, Tucano, was a strict man who would tell Leon to go out and cut the lawn, or give him other chores that needed to be done. And Leon somehow would; maybe never on time, because Leonardo never did anything on time. He ran on his own Time, in his own Space.

Tucano raised a tough family out on the cold frozen furrows of his Saskatchewan farm. That is until five of his nine children were all born with M.D. He finally sold the farm, and moved his family to B.C. All the boys were interesting and brave, and all the girls were beautifully Dutch blonde. Leon's older brother, Luther, also had M.D. He quickly became my best friend while Leon was doing business with hundreds of clients who bought exotic champagnes, concert tickets, vehicles, music, and anything that came through Town. Luther played bass guitar. He had the gift of gab. We were made for each other!

However, my most interesting friend of the family Medici, who basically adopted me, was Tucano. He was a Father Figure to most of Arnold's friends, but we were equal frontiersmen. We saw something in each other. I had a forty acre farm on Old Clayburn Road, in Abbotsford, and Tucano would drop by occasionally, to give me support and advice. Tucano was an alcoholic, and me? Well every time I had a nickel I'd spent a dime on blow. But Tucano never drank his first drink of the day until 5 pm. And I had been through enough acid tests over the years that I found it easy to function while stoned. So it was a good relationship. I loved his family and some of them loved me.

Chapter 16
The Eagles Claw

My bedroom in the rented farmhouse on Old Clayburn Road was made of two spacious bedrooms made into one, with a great archway in the middle from wall to wall. It sported four large windows and two doors, obviously. I had an elevated king size waterbed in one end, with a picture of the Quick Silver Messenger Service band on one wall, and a picture of me, at the age of five, on the other. The other end contained my 'therapy log' that I had picked up on Wreck Beach years earlier in my English Bay days. Now it served as a table with a stash, as I used to stuff grams for late night visitors in one of its cracks. There were colourful batiks' stretched out on the walls and East Indian Tapestries on the windows.

The house itself was a Bungalow, with an unfinished basement. It had a front lawn that was really a pasture for horses and cattle, who liked coming up to the house windows and looking in at me. There was a dell of about twenty acres, with forests and deep pastures. There was a barn for calves, and another for the horses. My farm was surrounded by other farms, with fields of cows, bulls and horses. Across the road was a field with a hill that climbed so high that hang-gliders shed their inhibitions to the sky by jumping off the top, and floating on a 'wing and a prayer'. It was picturesque.

The landscape surrounding my farm had sparse patches of trees and blackberry bushes; just perfect for concealing pot plants in the fertile soil. I had hundreds started in a milky-white plastic greenhouse, in April. You could actually see it from Old Clayburn Road. I think everybody knew that there were pot plants in there, but nobody cared. Jimmy Carter was in the White House, and we were all basically waiting, impatiently, for marijuana to be legalized by 1979.

You remember Jimmy Carter… at the time he was known for being the brother of beer-drinkin' Billy Carter. He was a Good-ol' Plains Georgia boy, endorsed by the Allman Brothers, and who made a fortune growing peanuts. But Jimmy got caught up with the Shaw of Iran, who eventually got the Pride, and Disgrace, of Georgia out of Office, when he was beaten for his Second Term by some actor who had done movies with monkeys.

Anyway our hopes, that turned into torrent expectations of legalization, went down with a helicopter that smashed into a transport aircraft containing fuel and servicemen, during the Operation 'Eagles Claw'. Jimmy aborted everybody's hopes and dreams of ending the Seventies on a spectacular note of legalization with this catastrophe.

But I had hundreds of six to ten foot plants all around my property, and I was hoping that everybody continued to not care. Up until September twenty-fifth nobody had, so I harvested over two hundred and fifty plants. I had dozens more in my corn field, which were shorter. Somehow they knew not to out-grow the corn, for their own protection, and mine of course. I eventually brought them inside the house, where I cut off the roots and hung them on nylon ropes which I had erected around my waterbed. I hung the rest up along the walls of the double bedroom. I even got shorter plants to hang along the archway, in the middle of the room. It looked like a room virtually made of leaves and buds.

And what buds! They were huge, and there were virtually thousands of them. When I was finished, I took a step back and admired the horticultural hide-away that was my bed. At that point, I told Oak I was going down to Adriana's to find a volunteer to spend a green evening with. I told him I would be back in a flash.

I then begged him to be good; just like Regina used to beg the same of me... the Cycle! I straddled my Low Rider and rumbled off to Adriana's residence. Oak would head over to a neighbour's farm for *'chicken snacks and adventures'*, just to kill time until my return.

I winded it out on Old Clayburn Road. It was a great stretch for a motorcycle ride; easy curves and then some straight-aways. I continued my way on Clayburn, and then cruised in second gear as I came upon the small residential section. I was enjoying a pleasant and uneventful evening drive when suddenly BAnG#*!.

Some sixteen year-old-kid with a driver's license all of five days old suddenly turned across my lane, in front of me, to make a left hand turn. He totally cut me off for time and space. So I did the only thing I could. I followed the script and smashed right into his daddy's Impala. I hit my knee on his ride, and flew through the air until I came down, unceremoniously, on the pavement, where cars dodged me in the setting sun. I knew Oak would be pissed. He was always left holding the bag, or at least that was always his story.

Anyway I was eventually ambulanced off to the Hospital, where I started a glorious, yet cryptic romance with three shots of Demerol a day. I wasn't in love. It was just a cheap thrill. We've all had 'em. But in the end they always leave ya *'high and dry'*, wanting more when getting less. After a week, I had dozens of visitors from Vancouver, Abbotsford, Mission City, Langley, Surrey, Saskatchewan and anybody new off the plane from Dundas, or beyond.

Now I was still infatuated with Darling Demerol, but everybody was bringing me vials of cocaine, mushrooms (fall batch), Hashish, Mescaline, Stimulants, Depressants, Hallucinogens, Dissociatives, Opioids, Inhalants, and loads of My newly pulled pot. A couple ladies I knew moved into my farmhouse and started stripping leaves off the dangling plants. Everybody was finding their way up there on their way to the Hospital, where I kept receiving more and more dope and drugs every day. It was quite the get-together. I saw faces I hadn't seen in months, and years, and they each had their pockets full of medicaments for me.

As human traffic increased, I began taking visitors and dealers and jokers and smokers up to the Proctology Ward, on the Third Floor, where we could find empty rooms to blow joints in, and I could rap with my guests. These third floor back-room visits increased when they tried to take my only True Love away; my Darling, Darlingest Demerol. I would go through the blow so fast that I started taking mescaline to take the edge off. Puffing was just mechanical; I needed pain blocking anodynes. I bitched about the nurse's clumsy attempts to cut me back. They denied it all the time, but I could see in their eyes it was just another game between nurses and patients. But hey, when you're in love with my Darling, there are no substitutes for the Heart, or subsidies for Lost Souls.

I guess I was obviously having too good a time, because when I returned from the Third Floor one day, there was a cop waiting there for me. At first I thought, "Ah, another Visitor. Man I wonder what drugs he brought me". But as soon as he barked I snapped out of my daze. He growled, "This party is over!"

I guess the Hospital smelled of pot from stem to stern, and I suppose the ones who complained only smoked cigarettes. Anyway 'El-Groucho' said he was going to search my 'Headquarters' for drugs. Now I had just smoked (obviously) too many joints, and I was coming down off some MADA. All I really wanted was just a few minutes alone with a needle, and some Darling Demerol.

But Justice is a brutal beast at best, and he advanced on me like I was caught climbing out of a window with expensive silverware and golden candelabras jangling in my pockets. I suddenly slipped my brain into Overdrive and steered towards my only open lane. I shouted back, "This is my Property, and you aren't touching a thing without a Warrant'! He, "*harrrrrumphed*" at me, and said this was Hospital Property, not mine, and he was indeed going to start searching.

I counter-punched that the *name plate* on the end of the bed frame, which I was now pointing at, said my name on it, **John Organ.** So, it was My Property! I was probably full of shit, but I thought it was worth a try. I guess the Officer saw himself in a Court of Law for too long, fighting about some insignificant bust, without a proper warrant, and all the paperwork, the Judges, Lawyers, Witnesses, more paperwork, and on and on until it looked more like Liability Licking than Law Enforcing. So he stopped, and decreed that he wasn't going to search, but I sure as Haiti's Revenge was going to leave the Hospital Premises! He told me to secure a ride, and hit the road. What? And leave my true Love behind?

But it seemed like a deal I couldn't turn down, so I stashed all my drugs into my casts, and phoned Rick for a ride. He motored me up to my Farmhouse and assisted me, and my hugely swollen left knee, and my broken right wrist, my broken pelvic bone, and my bruised Ego into the front door. Debbie was making spaghetti sauce, and I was escorted to a comfortable chair. I ate a plate of delicious spaghetti, but then made the mistake of downing a second. Turns out everyone had done mushrooms that day, and spiked my spaghetti with some; for my stamina and fortitude. But then Samantha added some, not knowing of the first dose, and then Rick threw some in, because he knew no one else would think of such a dandy idea.

Within twenty-five minutes I started to feel strange. I didn't say anything, as I figured this was now life without my Darling. But thirty minutes later I was seeing colourful flashes, and there seemed to be a musty clump of trees on the couch, next to my chair. I figured it was a spiked meal. I easily identified the mushroom melt down, and I started trying to figure out how much they spiked it with.

But next thing I knew, three dudes in leather jackets and boots appeared at the door. Rick greeted them, so I figured they were cool. I told Debbie to grab a quarter pound of buds and start rolling. Just before dawn we finished off the quarter pound, and the three Lads went drifting out the front door. Debbie looked relieved as she exclaimed, "O well, that was ok I guess."

I asked her what she meant. She explained that the three Visitors were actually Nasty Creatures of the Night, and she was indeed relieved nothing bad had happened. I enquired, "What the hell are you talking about... they were Rick's friends, so what's the problem?" Rick said he didn't know them at all, but he was also aware that they were *no-good-nicks* that were always up to no good. I shrugged and told Debbie to grab another quarter pound and start rolling...

Addictive Personalities

Rick was Matta Ravenscliff's brother. We attended Fraser Valley College together because I was getting my first year of English behind me, and Rick was told by Matta to go to school and get a life. He was on the rebound from his girlfriend leaving him. He was drinking too much, and doing all the wrong drugs.

I was writing poetry and prose, and had ideas about some songs I was writing. Rick had a natural addictive personality.

Rick was a '*colic baby*', and they fed him Phenobarbital to stifle his crying. He was an addict of any drug he could conjure, and he blamed it on Society for dosing him as a baby. Rick was strong and at the same time effete. He was always the one in the washroom with a needle while we were having a fun time snorting at the kitchen table. I free based, but would never give him any because you cannot feed, then fan, the fire.

Now my *buddies* and I were respectable free-basers. We had our own shit, or else we sold all our shit to get shit. Some addicts I met were going through an ounce an evening, and they sold empty empires and *everything they owned*, or eventually stole, to keep it up. Alvin (no past, present, or future references necessary) came by my Farm one night. He was one of the *Briefcase of Blues* boys. By the end of the night, despite my strong objections, I owned his Low Rider Harley, all his cash, and anything else if, I had the blow.

I invented a name for his type; *'stupid-smart'*. Many people are so smart that they end up doing stupid things, because they can. Because they're bored! They know how to work out all the angles, and fix all the holes in an everyday life to make it a *faster trip*. And that only slows down when they run low of eccentric evolutions. A motorcycle, or an exotic car, can only be interesting until it can be traded for something more provocative, or stimulating. In no time you're in Rehab, or dead.

So Rick and I travelled weekly to our English Class at F.V.C. One week we were all assigned poems and prose that we were supposed to recite the following week. I was assigned the poem, 'Machu Picchu' by Irving Layton. But my Guru, Roma Dash, visited me that week. He had sent a 'Flower' for me to help germinate earlier in the year, and I wrote her some words that I decided to recite in Class, instead of Layton's. I asked Roma to escort me to Class that week. I excused myself when it came to my turn to recite. I confessed I admired Irving, but that I had to read my own poetry. Our Professor, Justin, looked perturbed, but I read it anyway. It started;

All along the distant shore
Your body casts a spell
Long legged and Your body tight
Your mind begins to swell,

To guarded days of realty
Casting glances at the beach
You sweep along the Winds of Time
The mantra keeps Your Beat.
It all unfolds before Your Eyes
Sounds keeping to Your Beat
Just follow long the Path of Time
So many Friends to meet.
But are You sitting Consciously
Or have You cast Your Spell?
We play the game and live for Now
Then wait for Time to Tell

I recited a couple more that I wrote to Roma. The Class was strangely enthralled. Many students asked me for copies, and I obliged. Justin was impressed. I rose at the end of class and invited Justin, and the Class Body, to join me at the Mission City Hotel for a beer. Those who didn't borrow their parent's vehicles to drive to class joined us; about half the Class. After a beer or two, Justin came up to me and gushed, "I really liked your writing. Wow John, I'm a Poet too! I'll bring you some of my stuff next week." I grinned. He was like an excited kid who grinned and gawfed. Roma and I travelled across the Mission Bridge home, and then over to Leonardo's. Leon's days started at 11 pm.

Rick never broke the Chain of pharmaceuticals. I watched him get a little more rough and ragged as time went on. Matta kept on keepin' on. I loved everything about Matta's Spirit. Rick drifted away like the receding waves that get lost in the cruel sea. He was killed in an auto accident in 2012. Serge died a couple years later. Most of my Friends from that period have died over the savage years. They are all in my songs. I wish them all Godspeed on their Journeys. Life is cruel, and then we die. Just as long as we understand this, Life goes on.

Chapter 17
Back to the
Drawing Board

The light flickered on and off. And on again. I looked straight up. There was a Negro Man and three younger Negro men. They were looking down upon me. Clarity chased me, but unfortunately I was winning the race; backwards, perhaps. Nobody was saying anything. So I said, "Hello." The elderly Black Man started grinning, and coaxed me to tell him how I liked his smile. I said, "Its ok, I guess."

I asked him who they were. They started looking at each other, uncomfortably. Finally the biggest of the three Lads said to me, "Don't you know who we are? We're your family!"

There was something wrong in this statement, but I couldn't figure what it was. I noticed they kind of looked overly concerned about something, so I innocently asked, "Is everything alright?" And all of them, at the same time, gave me their own reassurances that everything was fine...

"Of course everything's ok."

"It's gonna be alright!" They all seemed to be smiling and in good sorts, so I just let it go at that.

The distant lights were a little gray around the edges, but they were staying on now. They had stopped flickering. The larger Lad once again asked me if I was ok, and I got a little suspicious. That wasn't a normal conversation, I deduced, because I had been asked three times now, not that I was counting, and

I couldn't remember having a conversation before that was all about my being 'ok'.

I tried to divert the dialogue so I enquired, "Where's my car?" All four of them got sort of *antsy*, and were exchanging escaping glances at one another, until I had to say, "Is my car ok?" And they all suddenly got all smiley again, and comforting. They reassured me, each, individually, and collectively, that my car was "Alright'; it was 'ok.'"

The largest Lad said, "Everything's just fine." The youngest Lad said nothing. He never seemed to say anything while the others chattered like cheer-leaders. The four Black Men seemed ok to me, and had spot-on answers. They were still re-assuring me that my car was sweet, or did they say it was a sweet ride, when the lights started flickering again. Then I guess they went out.

The lights had flickered before. But this was the first time I remembered them staying on for any length of time. The next time I remembered them staying on long enough to remember, I was with my older brother, Paul, on the front lawn at my farm on Old Clayburn Road, tending to my '55 Chevy Nomad Station Wagon.

The Chevy Nomad was a station wagon model produced by Chevrolet. It was marketed from 1955 to 1961, from 1967 to 1972, and then used as a trim package on the 1976 Vega, as well as for Chevrolet vans during the late 1970s and early 1980s. In South Africa, the Nomad name was actually used on a small utility vehicle. The Nomad is now best remembered in its two-door Tri-Five form that was considered a halo model. It was named for nomads.

1955 Chevrolets received all-new styling. It was advertised as, "The Hot One." The longitudinal new Chevy was crisp, clean, and thoroughly modern-looking. Its popularity was shared with the Tri-Five Chevrolets of this generation. Nomads came loaded with interior carpet, chrome spears on front fenders, chrome window moldings, and full wheel covers. For 1955, Chevrolets offered a V8 engine option. The new 265 cu in (4.3 L) V8 featured a modern, overhead valve, high compression, short stroke design that was so excellent it remained in production in various forms for many decades. The base V8 had a two-barrel carburetor and was rated at 162 hp (121 kW). The "Power Pack" option featured a four-barrel carburetor and other upgrades yielding 180 bhp (134 kW). Later in 1955, a "Super Power Pack" option added high-compression and a further 15 bhp (11 kW). It had ample room for six passengers.

It was all going as planned for me and Paul; smoking a quick one before we hit the road, piling any supplies we might need on the trip, and generally preparing my newly rebuilt 327 cu in V8, by Saskatchewan Auto Rebuilders, for the drive. It had a brand newly rebuilt 350 Turbo-Hydromantic Transmission, dual-exhaust, brand new Pirelli Anniversary Special Tires, imported rosewood for the decks, deep blue leather for the seats that were imprinted with batik design, spirited with an 850 Double Pumper carburetor, etcetera, etcetera... I had been working on the 'shell' all spring. It was re-chromed, and ready for paint!

But suddenly I could not move my legs. I did not understand what was happening to me. I was uncompassionated. I yelled at Paul! I told him I could not move! He didn't seem to be listening... He started driving the Chevy himself, and seemed to be leaving me behind... I yelled again. No one was listening. Then the lights went out again.

When they came back on, Paul and I, and Bim, who was a friend from Ontario, were together for a curry meal at 'The Himalia Restaurant', in Vancouver. Everyone was sitting cross-legged at the table for some reason, but I once again could not control my legs. They would not fold beneath me, so I could not sit with Paul and Bim. When I voiced that I could not bend my legs, everyone in the Restaurant seemed to ignore me again, and spent their time talking with their backs turned to me. Then the lights went out again.

When they came on again this time, I found that I had been taken to the upstairs of the Himalia Restaurant, and deposited in a bed. This seemed very strange to me... I came here with friends for a meal, and here I was being kept, seemingly tied down against my free will. I shouted out for help! I needed to be freed of this bed; of this restaurant, of this nightmare! I rationalized being kept up here in this bed was my punishment for not bending my legs. But it was not my fault! I would bend them if I could!

Suddenly, the smallest Negro who never spoke was there. I begged him to help me escape this Madness! It appeared I was indeed tied down to the bed, and I told him that if he untied me, I would not run away. I just wanted to find out why all this was happening. A simple explanation for my being held like this! I almost had The Quiet One release me, but just as he was untying me, others came in the room and made him stop. I was retied. I struggled. Then the lights went out again.

The next time the lights came on I was astounded that my mother, Regina, my oldest sister Mary, and my younger brother Mike, were all in the room with me.

I asked them what they were doing there. They said they had been there for weeks. They had been alerted that the steering column had broken in the '55 Chev Nomad, as Paul and I were driving across the desert near Kamloops. We swerved at fifty miles an hour into a piece of the Rocky Mountains. Paul had gone through the front wind shield and died. I was in this bed, apparently, because I had been in a coma for a month, and had broken some bones, and I damaged certain organs, within/ without, it seemed.

The morphine rocked my brain while subsiding my pain. Regina, Mary and Mike had been portrayed to me as four Negro

Men (four?). I can't even touch my reasoning for that. Perhaps the Spirits sent Prophets to break me the news of Paul's death… Messengers who have understood the pain, torment, agony and misery on a scale that left me devastated. But the message seemed to be that Pain is the same for everyone, and no one is immune. These hallucinations disguised the truth for my heart, and the despair from my soul. Six months later I could run for miles at a time. Paul is still running with the Spirits that called Him.

Like Sam Kinison and Henry the Eighth before me, receiving a *'nock on the noggin'* had an after-effect on me. Many of my friends remembered me as a quiet lad, who had now returned much more outspoken, post palpitated and pounded.

Blows to the head seem to suggest some symmetry between many Artists. To save time and ink, we'll just assume that most Survivors of the first and second British Rock Invasions, were at one time or another attacked by a 'Teddy Boy', or a Teacher, or their Father, or vivacious bandmates. Early Sixties Europe was a brutal existence… not for the weak. I can remember many stories how many Artists got their noggins noodled… Stuart Sutcliffe, Keith Moon, Marty Balin …

Cass Elliot could only finally reach a note Poppa John Philips wanted her to sing after being struck on the head with a blunt object. In the end, whether it changed his voice or not, Ozzy Osbourne used to get thumped on the noggin' regularly. What's a band mate for, anyways…

WLIR

WLIR was a radio station based out of western Long Island, New York. They broadcasted on the air waves from 1959, to that fateful day in 1987, when they lost a fifteen year legal battle and shut shop. This Station didn't have the Wave Power to compete with rivaling stations on the Island, but it brought in a change of music and culture, never seen since the Beatles broke the ice themselves.

WLIR researchers would do their homework to see who was *new and noticed* in the British New Wave World. They also investigated the next phase in the U.S. that was busy distancing itself from Punk since Sid sang his own Epitaph.

WLIR Buyers would travel to England and cop the latest *'Punk'* and *'New-Wave'* singles and albums. As soon as they appeared in the NY harbour, DJs would simply throw them on their *'New Sound'* Radio Station turn tables the very next day. This was a gutsy, mind blowing concept that speeded the air play of new Artists by up by six months. This helped put food in the bellies, and coke up the noses of over seven hundred Artists like; Sting, Blondie, Thompson Twins, Prince, U-2, Talking Heads, Good Rats, Ramones, New Order, Depeche Mode, Ultravox, Yazoo, Joan Jett, Suzi Quatro, Human Sexual Response, Yellow Magic Orchestra, Waitresses, Stray Cats, Pearl Harbour, Dead Kennedys, Producers, Missing Persons, Split Enz, Sad Café, Teardrops, Joe Jackson, Clash, Nick Lowe, Human League, Dregs, Asia, Hair Cut One Hundred, the Falcons, Duran Duran, Flock of Sea Gulls, Go Gos, Lords of New Church, Missing Persons, Modern English, Dexy's Midnight Riders, Flirts, Q-Feel, Pretenders, Squeeze, Thomas Dolby, Culture Club, Devo, Madness, Falco, Elvis Costello, Naked Eyes, Tears for Fears, Men without Hats, Polecats, Eddie Grant, The Eurythmics, B-52s, Electric Guitars, Alarm, Nena, Hilary, Made for TV, Billy Idol, Ebn-Ozn, the Bunnymen, Fiction Factory, General Public, Psychedelic Furs, Nik Kershaw, the Fixx, REM, Bronski Beat, Orchestral Manoeuvres in the Dark, Frankie Goes to Hollywood, A Bigger Splash, Wham, Pet Shop Boys, Flying Lizards, Stranglers, Simple Minds, Paul Young, Adam Ant, Kate Bush, Screaming Tribesmen, Boys Don't Cry, Dyvinals, Blow

Monkeys, Quick, Bananarama, Smiths, Burns Sister Band, UB40, INYS, Medics, Patti Smith, China Crisis, Nina Hagen, Flesh for Lula, Beastie Boys, Cure, Replacements, Thrashing Doves, Public Image, Bangles, Camouflage and more. They called it 'New Wave' and they 'Dared us to be Different'!

While WLIR was chchchchanging the strain for Artists and the Recording World, this coincided with some changes that were taking place under my own skin at the time. The Seventies were a whirl wind, with the Beatles breaking up, as did Jefferson Airplane, Simon & Garfunkle, and even the Grateful Dead for a couple of years. We'd been to the moon, maybe too many times for the effort involved. Nixon finally ended that horrid war, and then his despicable Presidency. Norton Motorcycle Company went on strike right after I bought my Commando 750, and never returned. We were led to believe that gasoline was unobtainable in America as before, and then the Economy went for a loop. New York City resembled a toilet bowl... Life became full of Bad Choices and Slim Promises.

Canada beat the crap out of the Russian Hockey Team in the Summit Series in '72, and T.V., which was my baby sitter of the Sixties, became a drag, and furthermore extinct to me for the decade. Rock and roll had died, and a thing called Disco was tearing up the charts for the Ladies at the Discotheques. Men of Rock crowded baseball fields, and anywhere they could to protest this new genre, before sneaking off to the closest night club to listen to Donna Summer Wannabes, and score women dressed tightly to kill, as opposed to the girls we grew up with in jeans and loose t-shirts.

In New York, Studio 54 is where Mick and a Bubbly Generation went, while Keith was getting busted after the gig at the El Mocambo, in Toronto, which is where I happened to be on that night while on my way in from the Coast. Paul McCartney became a billionaire, and almost ended up on Saturday Night Live playing with John Lennon for $3000! Sex was everywhere, and there were no diseases yet that a simple shot of penicillin couldn't fix. Hi-jacking airplanes and International Terrorists became a new kind of war, for those who couldn't live, or die, without one. What a Long Strange Trip it was!

Afflictions and Addictions

By the end of the decade, ten years of stomping and romping saw half of us still supporting our nasty afflictions and addictions. The other half were supporting their new Families; planned, or many simply due to decisions of not wearing an antiquated piece of plastic on our *Flags of Freedom*. I was no different. I had settled in Vancouver since '72, off and on, and after years of dabbling and dealing and gall darn dogmas, I was actually looking for a job to support my own unexpected, but exciting new Family.

When I was a young teen, and beyond, the good life of dealing drugs and grooving at Rochdale justified, in my mind, that working for a living was for those who couldn't be bothered doing anything more creative. I myself, even though I came out of the womb writing, still hadn't progressed past poetry, Abby Hoffman propaganda, and hippie proprieties. When I was young and *King of the Road*, I always had the means, and momentum, to be everywhere the Cause needed me; be it at anti-war rallies, collecting classic cars and motorcycles, closing the Bar every night, and never missing a Dead concert, whenever plausible.

But somehow, when there is a New Family to support, drug money becomes dirty money to the Young Things that were attracted to us for having it in the first place! And it came with a price. You remember, back when life was about telling the System, and our Parents, that Ours was the better way; a nobler way. A wayward way, equipped with a modern day conscience.

So much for dat Hippie shat by the Eighties! It was back to the drawing board!

So I was twenty three, and off to find a job. Really, for the first time since I picked beans or berries in Grade School. When I was five years old, I remember listening to an interview with Elvis Presley, yea the King Himself! The media pestered Him, stupidly, trying him to make him pay for all his successes, and their lack of any. The question that stuck out to me was when they asked Elvis what he had done before making it big. The King said that he had been a truck driver, but that he didn't like it. He said he had been fired from most jobs he tried, mainly because he wasn't into them. He was in a Band, and doing the Ssshiverrr on stage! One day, on his lunch hour, Elvis said he went into Sun Records, and with the help of Sam Philips, made a record.

But he was different from the Talent back then. He was Young. He was White. And he was good! I was enthralled by his answer. I saw my father work like a dog every long day, and I thought, "I don't want to do that. I wanna be like Elvis." At that time, I thought it meant the easy way out… Chicks and Music!

But there is no easy way out. I saw him being polite on Ed Sullivan, and tell the cameras that he loved his Mother. Ed even said that he was truly a, "Nice boy." What could be better? But it wasn't easy. Just like for Dylan, and the Fabs afterwards, there were monsters that were jealous of them. They had fought in the Second World War. Some also saw the Depression, and most of all, they weren't talented. They weren't Artists.

They were factory workers, plumbers, carpenters, drivers, drillers, doctors, drafters and dentists. They all punched time-cards. And even worse, there were reporters; horribly mentally mutated morons that formed opinions in print of those with Grins worth Millions. The questions they asked were imbecilic, and their attitudes were ignorant. But Elvis was different; he was polite, and courteous, and I thought he was simply better than these dogs fighting over his bone.

So with Elvis in mind, along with the latest Little Feat album and a good joint, I decided to apply for Government Jobs only. The NDP had come into power in B.C., with Premier Billy Bennett Jr at the helm. The year before, on their first day of being elected into power, they doubled the salaries of all the Unionized Government Workers. I thought, "Ok then." And I was suddenly working on a Government Farm in Port Coquitlam, located under the Port Mann Bridge.

Though I had a house in Abbotsford for my Girlfriend and our new Papoose, this job came with a free bunk house, which was inhabited by a bunch of crazy freaks, drug addicts and bikers. It was the perfect work atmosphere to indulge myself into on my glorious return to the Work Scene, after a decade off. We were captured by the night life of Granville Street, and the Pubs and Rock Shows of Downtown Vancouver. This job also came with free food, so we were cashed up, well rested, and fed for hard core partying.

I knew a guy who sailed on a ship that was smuggling tons of Cambodian pot into Seattle. It was great stuff, except sometimes it got mouldy. Exotic bootlegged marijuana from overseas was the precursor to the good Indica home-grown taste from Washington State. By the mid-Seventies, Purple Kush took the hassle out of smuggling in a good high from dangerous places. The night before I started working for the Ministry of Agriculture, I had scored a pound of fantastic Thai bud. That was my ticket to living in this bunk house with these diehard alcoholic partiers.

We all bought nice new motorcycles to go on the hunt with. It was unimaginable that someone, in some capacity, had hired such a Crew of Crazies, to work and live on this government dairy farm. As a matter of a fact, this unimaginable person that did this dastardly deed of assembling 'Us', was a timid little man named Alvin, who mumbled, stuttered and could never look you in the eye. Which was convenient, I suppose... Maybe he would have actually seen who/what he was hiring if he had of even glimpsed up once!

I mean, there was one guy from Florida who had escaped from prison after being convicted for stealing dozens of cars. Then there was a country *bunker*, I mean *bumpkin*, who never came out of his room, but always had sweet young things visiting him all week long. There was another biker from Surrey, B.C., who was on the road and Alvin gave him a home too. There was a dirt track rider who had broken his ankles so many times he couldn't even recollect how many. There was a friendly secretary that kept Alvin in line. There was one fella who had been a Banker all his life. Well he was now a Cosmic Farmer! There were young rebels and older misfits, ex needles, and serious alcoholics. And now here was me, with this big bag of good pot. Thanks Bill Bennett!

There were just too many crazy nights, too many rock concerts, too many run in's out on the road, too many hang overs and just enough infidelities. I made it home most weekends. Word got out to Alvin that the Bunkhouse Bourgeoisie was lost out on the road. We hadn't work for days. This was usually accepted as the price of getting the job done in the past, but word was out that I had this bag of buds that was putting former non-puffing workers prematurely out to pasture.. It was pretty apparent, even to Alvin, that workers would just disappear for days at a time, coming back to the farm just to recoup enough for another ride with the razor. I knew my time was marked. Even here I was gonna get fired! I thought at the time, 'How Elvis of me'!

I then thought it might be time to relocate my act, and I took an application across the road for a position with the Ministry of Health. I was strongly advised by the secretary in no time, that my time was marked with Alvin, and to get the application in that day.

"Ironic," she ventured."

"What's that?" I reciprocated.

"That you're getting the boot here for drugs, and this job at Central Medical and Pharmacy is filled with ..."

"Drugs" I said.

"Yeah", she said, "Good luck!"

My interview for the position was typically one for the books, or for this book at least. A bud from the Farm and I had been up all night with my granite rock, at my house in Abbotsford. I remember kind of sitting on the floor in my underwear, when another Colony Farmer pulled in the lane-way, in his 1974 Phantom V1. He had been busted DWD, and was about to lose his driver's license. He wanted me to be his Chauffeur.

He asked if I had my job interview that day. I said, "What day is it?" Upon hearing Wednesday, I said, "Shit yea, I'm supposed to be there in a couple hours." He tied my tie for me, guided me into the Phantom V1, and drove me sixty kilometers to the interview. He parked in the lot to wait for it to be over, and then drove me back to the bunker, across the road.

Somehow, the elderly Chap who interviewed me thought I was the best thing since sliced bread. He hired me on the spot. In the basement of the warehouse, where I would toil, there were three pharmacists brewing up every kind of drug dispensed to B.C. hospitals. ... Johnny's in the basement mixing up the medicine...Ironic indeed, thought I.

After a year of working downstairs dealing in Dialysis, I was requested to work on the Main Floor for a day, to handle

Receivables on the loading dock. Now downstairs, I worked hand in hand with clients who needed information, drugs, and supplies to properly dialyze their kidneys at home. I wasn't a Receiver, but I was glad to help, as most of the crew was on vacation. I didn't care anyways, as I had my daily gram of blow in my pocket to make it through the day.

The first items I received were sixty unmarked boxes tied together on a wooden skid, with no paperwork or no indication at all about the who's, where's or whatever's about this mysterious load. I remember someone telling me earlier that morning, that if such a situation came about, to open a box and see what was in it, of course. There was nobody there as it was lunch time, so I diligently opened one of the boxes. I looked within. Each box had four quarter pound bottles, with a label on each stating it contained ninety two percent, pharmaceutically refined cocaine. Jack pot!

With a gram already in my pocket, and more at home, I thought "Ok. Take it easy John. There's probably a camera watching my suspicious, I mean paranoid ass right now! Just be cool." I grabbed a fork lift and took the sixty pounds of blow down to the Pharmacists. When they worked with it the next day, I noticed they put packages in boxes, loaded them on skids, and put stickers on them that addressed them to every Hospital in British Columbia. I decided to volunteer to go with the Driver that would be transporting these boxes to the Hospitals the next day. I thought it would be helpful to go observe some Clients, in their homes, with their supplies. My notion was considered commendable, and it was OK by the boss.

I was having a beer in Abbotsford with my Dealer that Friday night. He asked me, between gulps, what it was like to work in a Pharmaceutical Warehouse.

I explained to him that our warehouse received different drugs, to make different drugs, for clients throughout British

Columbia. Now Marvin was an imaginative guy, and the first thing he blurted out was, "Look John, I've got a Beretta. Let me hold you up in a public place, and we'll split one of those one pound boxes of that 92 percent blizzard material." Strangely someone else had made me the same offer a couple weeks earlier in Vancouver. It sounded absurd to me at the time…

Marvin's next stint was a trifle unexpected for me. He checked to see no one was looking, and prompted, "Watch me" as he grabbed the piece out of his coat pocket, and proceeded to show me there were no bullets in it… "I'll see you Wednesday. It'll be no problem! See! No bullets!" It all sounded so normal. Obviously, this was the only logical thing to do! Then we hustled out to his car and had another hit off the bong.

Wednesday came, and I went out in the Ministry truck containing many boxes of bottles of ninety-two percent, pharmaceutically refined cocaine products. We travelled off to White Rock to visit one of my clients; a four year old girl named September. We had already dropped off some supplies at Vancouver General Hospital, and at a few dialyzing Client's homes. I was absently thinking that this was going be like a Moving Picture Scene, with us ready to be held up by some dangerous drug addict who had hit the Big Time! We got to the designated corner of the scam, but I couldn't see anyone. The client's house was on the next block ahead. We were stopped at a stop sign. There was nothing or nobody happening at all. What the hell? I told the unionized driver to pull over, and that I was going into a ma/pa shop on the corner. I got out. Nothing! No Beretta! No Marvin! No Columbo! So I got back in the truck and we drove to the next client's residence.

I soon entered September's house. My head started swirling when I thought about narrowly avoiding such a bad-news-scam! But suddenly I looked at this young and brave, lovely child, with only one functioning kidney, and I suddenly reassessed Marvin, and this screwy plan.

I wondered to myself, "Why was I was listening to a nut-bar like Marvin?!" I just thought I hoped September would be ok. The Spirits might give her a break. Maybe someone could give her a kidney. The world became sober. I finished the day and went out and got plastered. Marvin had scored an ounce for some scary guys the night before in Chilliwack, and they free based most of it during our cancelled prime time potential disaster. Mission accomplished. Just as well!!

Chapter 18
Another Decade
that had to End

I think if Jerry Garcia hadn't met Robert Hunter, he would have been a great Punk Musician. I think of him like Johnny Rotten (J.J. Lydon). Both were natural Leaders and resourceful Gurus of their day. Punk was always there. Like a nasal drip it just wouldn't go away. Mick Jagger....John Lennon...Eric Burden... Punks! The Clash kept it a British thing, but Wayne Kramer and Iggy Pop, in America, were on it first. Back then, 'CBGB's were about crafty and cheeky smiles, while British Punk was totally political. Back in the Seventies, I called Punk "alternative music with a Bloody Edge, thank you." Bloody edges like Black Flag, Teen Idols, Bad Brains, the Ramones, Fear, Germs, We're Desperate, X, the Circle Jerks with Group Sex, the Gears, the Controllers, the Bags with a female point of view, Joan Jett, the Decline of Western Civilization, DOA, the Negatives, Sub Humans, Richard Hell, Regan Youth, The Mob, Heart Attack, 3 Teens Kill 4, Stimulators, Konk, Crazy Hearts, the Beastie Boys, and the High Sheriffs, the Uncalled, the Undead, Search and Destiny, Duff, Dead Kennedys screaming Nazi Punks Fuck Off, a Minor Threat, and scattered in Dave Grohl, Keith Morris, Flea, Henry Rollins, Harley Flanagan, Vinnie Stigma, Darryl Jennifer, the lovely Alice Bag with or without Bag, John Doe, Duff McKagen, Don Bolles, Joey Shithead Renthly, Jello Biafro, Winston Smith and Kathleen Hana.

Personal and social violence had created the 'Hard Core' phase of punk that oozed with Mosh Pit Attacks, and Nazi Punks poised to keep the world from ever generally accepting Punk again. Then there is the argument, that if Punk was accepted by the Norm, it wouldn't be Punk anymore.

Arrests and void numbness turned it back into Punk again, with dudes leading the charge like Fat Mikey, Ian MacKaye, Mike Ness, Donnita Sparks, Jim Limberg, the first we heard from Billie Joe Armstrong, No Effects, Suffer with Bad Religion, Penny Wise, NOPX, the Off Spring, Rancid, Noodles, my personal favorite Josh Homme, Noodles, and eventually/quickly, the grand sell out of Green Day (chuckle).

With nothing better to do in dirty Seattle than stay inside and practice, the Grunge movement suddenly provided incomes and time-monitored careers for Punk/Grunge Artists, when Kurt Cobain shared Nirvana with the world. Suddenly the Chili Peppers were stretching out and Green Day were selling out... Of every great record they had pressed that is! And dig L7, and the immortal Riot Grrrl ! Quicksand, Bratmobile, Offspring, Operation Ivy, Isocrateaze, and Sublime, all tested this new Punk spin-off in the Great Northwest also. No Effects, the Moron Brothers, No Man Army and Flogging Molly all suddenly had jobs. But alas, this was just in time for a new generation to mug Artists with the aid of the internet, for 'free songs... in theory... to share'. But in reality, it was theft on a ten billion dollar level, and Punk suddenly/finally came Crashing Down. Along with the Punk Artists and fans, who were getting too old to dig the basic rule of Punk; it was only for Punks! It's amazing, when you play the garbage posing as music today, how absolutely much we miss what was once there for ridicule, recourse, and divine retribution.

Chapter 19
The Real Thing;

It was 1982. I was being applauded by Chairman Philip McNamara for my work with Home Dialysing Clients in B.C. He was discussing the personal relationships that we all forged, daily, with our Clients. My *Partner-on-the-Job* was on annual leave. So I had to run the daily operations myself, after only one week on the job. Our Teams at the Medical and Pharmacy Warehouses in Vancouver offered our services and equipment, for the convenience of Patients-turned-Clients, who could now dialyse in their own private homes.

This was serious stuff... Patients were being hooked up to dialyzers, in certain equipped Hospitals, for days at a time with needles and tubes and peritoneal solutions and various apparatus sticking in them, while Nurses and Doctors come by to remind them to be prepared to do it again the next day. This Government Institution I worked at offered them their dignity back again. With help from our Support Team, they could now dialyse in their own spaces and times, as an alternative to being accommodated in sterilized white hospital rooms, for fifty one hours a week!

But a year later, Mr. McNamara was aware of my *cheeky smile* and *distant glare*. Maybe he was suspicious of my being around such large shipments of drugs inside our building. Maybe he had heard stories of how we spent our *spare time* at Colony Farm, which was just across the road. Maybe it was my Fu Manchu and sudden shoulder lengthened hair...Perhaps it was the eight ball a week I was going through at the time. Silly Rabbit!

Whatever the reason, Mr. McNamara had a personal meeting with me to let me know, in his most esteemed way that, *"The jig was up."* He told me about job opportunities with the Ministry of the Attorney General Downtown Vancouver, where 'Reputations and Careers' were to be made. He told me to be downtown Friday afternoon with an application, for my sake, and his. He said, "D*on't blow it*." Such a man of worldly clichés; 'the jig is up'; 'don't blow it'… I guess it's merely a matter of semantics. But I had a whiff, and headed downtown.

I got a little bogged down at first with downtown traffic, then with a place to park, and then with the Spiffy Bar on the corner of Burrard and Smithe. I shuffled out of the Bar an hour later, with what I figured was plenty of time to spare to drop off my application to the Office of 'Damaged Reputations and Careers'.

I would then head to Davie Street for more 'opportunities and damaged reputations' that evening!

My world, however, took one of those 'Lost in the Ozone' turns, as I soon realized that I was now searching for some little office that seemed to be hidden within a bureaucracy of streets, doors, steps and numbers, that somehow didn't make sense after a few vodkas. Before too long I was wandering past blocks and buildings, trying to decide if there was a good ending to all this confusion.

Government Offices close at 4:30 sharp, and here it was, minutes before making public offices private again. It was 4:25. A lady with whom I sought directions from, in yet another wrong office, directed me that I actually needed to go back a block and a half, go up a cement flight of stairs, walk across a roof top, then find a glass door that said 'Attorney General: Human Resources'. She elaborated that there would be a *kindly lady* at her desk to take my application, and inevitably save me from a shortage of pay cheques to pay for my addictions and lack of resources.

I hustled and made it there, but it was 4:31. The glass door was locked! Some Conformists believe that *'everything happens for a reason'*, but this happened because I had too many drinks over in the Bar on Burrard! But I was not hiding from the Truth. I was beginning to think of the conversation Monday morning with Mr. McNamara. I was thinking of going back to that Bar. And while I was thinking about these little tidbits of reality, a Janitor suddenly walked up to the glass door, then opened it and said,

"Can I help you with anything?"

I said, "Yes, would you put this on that desk please?"

He took the application, dropped it on the desk, and went off like I never really existed. Maybe I didn't. But I was going back to that Bar on Burrard, and then to rewards on Davie Street, just to make sure!

Reality is always better than the script. You simply can't create Fantasy that is as crazy, or ill-conceived as The Real Thing. It's too complicated, and too much to remember. Reality was, however, that in a week, I received a notification of an interview with the 'Repentant Reputations and Careers People', which would save my ass. McNamara was anxious to dump this problem off, which he affectionately called 'John Organ', on the first Ministry with such a *twisted need*.

A couple days later I successfully won the interview, unanimously, and they told McNamara that the Ministry of the Attorney General was the newest home for this outstanding *British Columbia Government Employee Union* member. I made my way downtown, carefully...

I was hired as an 'Administration Requisition Stockman', to outfit a brand new fifty two million dollar amalgamated building, that contained an Administration Section, a Pre-Trial Tower, a Kitchen, a Stores Complex, a Control Room for administrating the entire computer-operated complex , a Command Center, a Lounge, Washrooms, cars, vans, Visiting Rooms, a Prisoner Admittance Section, and Classrooms etcetera, etcetera, etcetera ...

The Tower, as it was referred to, was connected to a Bail Section, a Probation section, an O.I.C. Office, prisoner cells, and everything needed to keep them happy, or sad. Under-ground tunnels took you over to the Court Rooms, as well as the Police Station. This layout was a huge conglomeration which accommodated 155 Prisoners, as well as Correctional Officers, Police, Straights, Admin workers, Bail Officers, Probation Officers, Social Workers, Priests, Chefs, Judges, Lawyers and Bailiffs and every other member of the *World of Twisted Truths and Justice.* And I was the guy who would buy what was required to run it, and stock it accordingly. Far Out, I thought!

One of the first things I bought was a kick-ass stereo for my Office. My main 'boss' that I would be working with was a Business Manager named Clifford Corey. And his right-hand-Clerk was an attractive, dark haired, North American born Asian named Shelly. She was on the Board that had interviewed and hired me. They had both been working on how this Complex would run for a long time now. I was introduced to my Partner-in-Crime, excuse the pun, whose name was Malcom.

Malcom was from Colony Farm. He was nervous and high strung. He did not meet our admittedly laid back criteria for working on the Farm. His reallocation to a new ministry was proof Colony Farm was closing down. Man the stoner stories from days of yore...

Prisons are militaristic and brutal. But Pre Trials have money poured into them, by comparison, for the sakes and comforts of the Prisoners who have not yet gone to Court, so they have been convicted of nothing wrong, so far. But time ticks on and pressures mount. However it was different at Vancouver Pre-Trial Service Center. There was a gigantic wave of Liberalism being introduced here, in an attempt to take notice away from classic, dirty, old and violent Institutions like *Ocala Prison* that had armed guards enforcing order, at every turn. Vancouver Pre Trial only hired young Graduate Students, who all had at least a four-year Degree in Criminology. They also were hiring male and female guards!

As a matter of a fact, there were some absolute gorgeous young women there that were hired as Correctional Officers. Their job was to basically baby sit potentially criminal male 'tenants', who were there for a good time, not a long one. Prisoners only bunked at V.P.S.C. until their trial dates sorted out their immediate, and distant futures. Some of the competent Lady Officers wore gold ankle bracelets. They felt secure with our computer-ran system, but even in jails sometimes you just had to stand in profile at some points. Be careful!

The comfortable 'digs' these 'tenants' stayed in were all brand new. This liberal environment was designed to accommodate this non-convicted population in functional comforts and philosophies. They had comfortable chairs and couches to watch, what we considered back then large televisions, encased in Eighties designed wooden oak cases. They ate off creamy coloured maple tables, and sat on strong wooden chairs that were built to last in this sometimes rugged environment.

I had crappy chairs by comparison in my home. But I did not share forced accommodations on a Unit with fifteen other Strangers that were soon to be tried, and possibly convicted for various criminal offences. I went home and sat on second hand chairs and couches at my ten acre Horse Farm in Langley, with my girlfriend, who split one day. I continued driving into Gas Town each day, for a paycheque and a New Adventure, which happened too often for legal reasons, on Davie Street.

So I was working in an enlightened environment for the Attorney General Ministry, where we as Officers were creating our *Own Space* with liberal attitudes. This environment supported our *notions of concepts* that these 'Indentured Tenants' deserved Human Rights as they fought the allegations against them, in Court Systems that they would not understand, and that they could not afford. We felt obliged to *over-do-it* occasionally, as we were funded fruitfully to make sure they did not go without anything that technically 'innocent' people craved. As I transcribed the quarterly and fiscal budgets with Business Manager Clifford Corey, I observed that the *'bottom-crust'* of Society was being treated fairly. Society was still changing, and we were the equitable and legal dimension of it.

It was a real education working for the A.G. I learned to answer questions with as few words as possible. I learned never to admit anything. I learned that I was always innocent until proven guilty, just like in the movies. And I quickly learned which Ladies in this Maze I could date. Meanwhile, one of my Gurus sent a young Adventurer to my house that I could help with *her* version of being 'On-the-Road' for a summer!

Chapter 20
The Template

I was doing ok *Romancing my Stone* until I lost my license one evening after drinking with Rachel, a red-haired friend of mine at V.P.S.C., at the Officer's Lounge, which was located on the sixth floor of some swanky hotel that overlooked the bay. Rachel was the lone phone officer at V.P.S.C. that every call coming into, or out of, went through. This was a crucial and sometimes adventurous position to maintain, as she constantly directed calls from the Police, Judges, Attorney Generals, Regional Directors, confused callers, etcetera... And sometimes the calls were just as confusing for her.

I was *'baching it'in '85* , sharing the rent at my horse farm in Langley with a former Colony Farmer, Collin. I had a few pot plants in my garden, but they were more like projects than just plants. I fed them on three different kinds of well-rotted manures, as well as rich organic liquid fertilizers. They were like trees. Big trees! Now a traffic-helicopter went over my property twice a day. Though it was reason for raising-my-eyebrows, it was only a few plants, and back then it was an unwritten law that seven plants, or less, was considered 'personal' crop, usually ending in fines but not jail time.

I was having a marvelous time in Windsor, when I received a phone call from my Colonial *'rentee'* at my farm. Apparently the Police had inevitably busted the plants, and he told them that I was out of town, but that he would give me their message. I gave Collin instructions to phone the Police back, give them the V.P.S.C. phone number, and to ask them to phone me at noon the next day. In the meantime I told Rachel to expect the call, and to make me sound like a big-wig when it came... I told her to advise them that I was meeting with the Regional Director, or somebody important.

When the call came in, Rachel passed the call onto, "Mr. Organ". They sounded a little surprised, and hesitant when I answered. They told me to come down to their Precinct after work that day. When I arrived, there were three Officers standing in a small room. On the desk were the plants, dried and in a huge lump. Apparently it weighed out to over twenty-six pounds. I was impressed. They were nearing the end of their shift. The O.I.C. came over, greeted me, and got straight to the point that I would not be charged with anything, but that I should take this as a warning. I said "Thanks".

The O.I.C. then clasped my shoulder, and proclaimed, "Officers look out for Officers".

I looked at them, then I looked at the open door, then back at them, so I said,

"Can I take the plants with me and get them out of your way"

The Officer had reached the end of being polite and yelled, "No... now get out of here!" Well it's always worth a try...

Rachel and I were soon joined by Sheila, who was a talented Artist that also worked at V.P.S.C. She was special. I should have tried harder to get to know her better, but she was pizzed at me for some artwork she had done that I didn't get published as promised. I was honestly too busy, but from that point on, so was she...

Next we were joined by Officer Willie Kramer, from V.P.S.C., who took Rachel, Sheila and I over to a large ship that was lumbering in the harbour. We had all been drinking since leaving work at V.P.S.C., and Willie was bellowing that he used to be in the Navy, on this ship, when it was stationed in the Maritimes. As we boarded, he warned me not to, "mess up" on the Ship, "Cause the Sailors were in town for a good time." And anybody who needed a good ass kicking was in luck with these dudes. So we finished ambling aboard the Ship and entered a room that was filled with tables, lined up in rows, one beside another, all the way across the length of the room. And each table was loaded with jars of drinks. They didn't use glasses. They filled mason jars full of Rum, or Whiskey, at a nickel apiece.

So after all Willie's warnings about not waking the bears, I walked into their cave, and the first thing I did was bump my knee on the initial table I approached. This sent a shock wave to all the adjacent tables, spilling every jar on every table down one entire row, as they connected abruptly with each other. It was Anarchy! It was a Tragedy! It was a Mess!

There was a dead silence for about ten seconds... Then a massive, drunken cheer went up. Thirty Sailors each tried to buy me a drink for my brazen effort. Now Willie had also warned me never to turn down a drink, or they would consider this an insult. With my head already filled with too many rules, I was just happy to be alive, and drank as many mason jars of rum as I could! The Girls eventually wanted to drive all the way to Coquitlam, to a Keg Restaurant there that accommodated respectable families, and characters looking to get lucky. Always a good gathering...

As we were entering the Keg I started lagging behind, as it had been a hard day's night, and I was slogged! I could see the Port Mann Bridge's lights in the distance. Once on the other side I was home free to my farm in Langley. So I slipped away as our party entered the building. I figured I would make it up to Rachel and Sheila the next day (I didn't care what Willie thought).

I was cruising-on-fire towards the Bridge when I noticed there were flashing red lights behind me. I was escorted into the Cop Shop which was located immediately after the Bridge. I entered the quiet Precinct and started shouting; drunkenly, according to some Officers, or just, comically, to others, "Do you know who I am? I'm Moe Fucking Green!" I pulled out my wallet and

showed them my Attorney General card, which conveniently
stated I had all the rights of an Officer of the Law. But nowhere
on it did it say I was Moe.

The Chief rolled his eyes and said, "Is there anybody you can
call to come pick you up?" I phoned my buddy Collin in Surrey,
and he came roarin' up on his beautiful, new 1300 Yamaha, with
an extra helmet in tow. The Precinct gladly sent me out, but
instructed me to go straight home, and not touch my pick-up,
still parked on the side of the road.

Collin knew me well from Colony Farm, so he was not surprised when I instructed him to pull up to my truck, which he
did. I jumped off the 1300, plotted myself behind the steering
wheel and screeched off, in what looked like the direction of my
Farm. They probably wrote in their report that night that there
was a visit from a UFO that evening, and left it at that. Ah, to be
young, and then to do everything in our power to turn it against
ourselves... kind of like the theory that if there was no god, it
would be necessary to create one...

Maybe it's time to state the obvious, in as much as I did not
represent the average V.P.S.C. Officer. They were not like me.
They acted responsibly. It was just miscasting for the wrong
movie all over again for me. But as they say, "It's hard to get
good help these days..."

Chronologically and mentally, I was still young enough that it
wasn't like I needed to *return* to the Dating Scene. Being Young
kind of keeps you in the flow of everything. Young people in bars
do not arouse suspicions, in anyone's mind, that you might be
married, or that you carry too much baggage for just one simple
evening of fun. Being Young means you're game for about anything. A forty year old who walks in a bar had better have money
to ascertain what a Young Man merely expects. I think I'll always

be Young, because I'm still doing the same things to entertain myself, and others, that I did as a Youngster; namely talking to Young People in bars, writing and recording music, supporting the Arts, and enjoying the company of interesting people.

But chasing young Tigresses through the Jungle can be exhausting, once you catch up with them. This is true, especially after a long day's work. The hunt then has really just begun; wining, dining, and dancing in bars, then making it through Vancouver Landmarks until it's time to go home. And then returning back to Gas Town, *too early* the next morning, and starting all over again. It's just easier to do the Dance on Davie Street. But that's only real for half an hour or so. And it can get expensive! I thought I had to devise a plan to simplify a simple night out, without burning the candle at every end. I designed myself a *Template* for my 'organ overtures and maneuvers.'

I thought about entertaining events around Town that I'd indiscriminately attended with dates over the years that offered the best-Bang-for-the-Buck. Whatever worked best, I'd rinse and repeat two, sometimes three times a week. The Offices, since the days of Fred McMurray have always been equipped with Young Ladies with plenty to prove to Quid Pro Quos such as *moi*. So I would alternate with infinitives throughout the week, and use the *candy of the decade* to make it to the weekends. It's a rat race scrambling for that piece of cheese!

It's dangerous to be too devoted to love and its intangibles, too early in life. There's too much to do! But for too many, life is over in a flash; in the time it takes to say,

"I do!" Oscar Wilde commented that,

"Men marry because they are tired, Women marry because they are curious; both are disappointed!"

So marry when you are tired, or if you are still curious (or naïve), but not when you're Young. Unless you are desperate for company, in which case I would recommend to start with a dog. If it doesn't leave you after five years, or vise-versa, maybe you can endure commitment.

My *Template* for *duplicable affairs,* designed to not burn my bridges, too badly, would start out in my old back yard of English Bay. Here we could enjoy the beach, while exploring familiar nooks (and crannies!). The early afternoon would lead us to the Rhimbrant Hotel on English Bay Beach. Here we would toast our Dubonnet Rouges at 3 o'clock (Angel's Hour), and discuss who we were that day, or whom we wanted to be tomorrow. When we were rouged and ready, we would hike from 'First Beach' up to 'Seventh Beach' along ocean landmarks like Gull Rock, Eagle Isle, and the Sea Wall. These beaches led us to Stanley Park, and the Vancouver Zoo. The Zoo starts with Sea World, and ends over an hour later at the Polar Bears Den (or it could take you all day if you weren't loosely following a Template). By then, our appetites would be stirred by the hike, and the Dubonnet Rouges.

We would then be off, escorting each other's appetites, perhaps to a curry supper either at 'The Hymalia' Restaurant on Main Street, or 'The Sitar' in Gas Town, or the 'Indian Restaurant', where I had been close friends for years with the owners. They were invigorating Sikhs, who played Sitar while we ate. I often stopped in at one of these nooks for my *mental energy*, on my way to classes at SFU. After we consumed our curries, I would steer my ol' Volvo down to Main & 1rst Street, to the newest Lazar-Shows (Laser Floyd, Laser Beatles etcetera...). And always best on a full stomach! We would then drive into the setting sun, and watch it bath in the Pacific to refresh itself until tomorrow.

By that point of the early evening, we were properly primed to search out the latest *sounds* in Town. Our search would take us travelling over to West Vancouver to perhaps dig Doc Fingers (he's in three of my songs) boggee and rock the night away on piano. From there we would follow the moonlight to my Farm. Once there we would feed my horses, then start our own party. We would revamp ourselves from the drive with a joint and a snort; and get comfy by the fireplace.

I would always start our late night, or early morning, by reading the first three pages of Hunter Thompson's, 'Fear & Loathing in Los Vegas'. This would set the mood, silhouetted by the flames, and we would work things out on the couch. Before going to work later that morning, we would feed & water my horses, as the sun came up. We would have a toot & drive back to work in Gas Town, where it all started. Ahhhhh to be Young!

Three AM; aka The Devil's Hour;

It was about three a.m. and the car was still out on the side of the road at the end of my stone laneway of my farm at 3865 Old Clayburn Road. I'd been up for three days with an ounce of Peruvian blow. An old friend from my St. Mary's 'World Religions' class had driven in from Mission City with an ounce of Columbian *'snow tires'*. I was always skeptical of Columbian blow going around because we'd had a couple batches in the past that were moist, and ya had to get into putting it under heat lamps to dry, like I was babbling out during my Emmy-Lou story. But when it wasn't worth the effort we'd just start as soon start free basing. Too easy!

I first free based in '77 in White Rock BC. (yea, that's really the town's name) and from that moment on, I lost friends and dealers; basically anybody who went down that path. I mean, by '78, some guys I dealt with were walking around Town with brief cases containing a bong, some pre made 'based product', a propane tank with igniter, some water, and a test tube. This was the only way some could leave home when they free base an ounce in an evening; an ounce that is, if they lock their door! And don't answer it. No matter who claims to be on the other side!

These numbnoids with the Brief Case Syndrome were at one point resourceful and successful professionals, with the beautiful women, the house, cottage and boat, with the hangers-on, etcetera… The types that could get most anything they wanted in life. That is until they had the syndrome of *Brief Cases Full of Blues*! They were now challenged just to leave home without some *serious back up,* for when it got rough out there. About every fifteen minutes that is! Damn!

At least with smack you just do a hit and you're ok for a matter of hours. But with blow, the better it becomes is why you gotta have it!! And the more ways you refine how you can get it into your system makes it that much more Impossible to be without it. Until there are Zombies walking down the street with brief cases fueling the Time and Space it takes them to get the hell back off the street. Or out of the Board Rooms they are trapped in, or just away from their friends, if they still have any, as to give some *distance* from the Society that is pressing too closely and not allowing them, without resorting to ridiculous measures, to just have a god damn hit!

Chapter 21
Kori with a K

Patty and I were on our hands and knees rummaging on the grass. Sash and Gary, Clint and Karen, Todd and Angie, Phil and Alison, and Fred and Jim were on all fours around us, on the lush green grass. No one was saying anything, but our eyes were open! We had been crawling around for over half an hour now. Some had already left but we were the 'Hard Cores'. I talked occasionally to Patty, to try to relieve her anxiety and tension.

Tension defined as a noun means 'mental or emotional strain'. A mind affected by anxiety or stress cannot think as clearly. I could see the strain, stress and tensity in her eyes. She spoke, only to say this was giving her a headache, and that she could feel the pressure building. I could hear the quiver in her voice, and the hopelessness that had begun to own a crease in her forehead when suddenly I yelled,

"OK. I found it!"

Patty squealed, "Let me see!"

I picked it up, and she held out her hand for me to plop her wedding ring into her palm. She had lost it an hour before, and it was bumming her out so I had a pile of drunk and stoned 'Low Riders' open their eyes and search for it. Most were out-stretched on the turf anyway.

The 'Low Riders' were a *community group* that organized Trips and Parties and Weekend Bashes, like this one. Many of us had been awake for the last fifty hours at 50 Point Park, on the lake.

It was getting on suppertime, and most everybody had headed back to town after fifty hours of drinking, music, and self-medicating with inhalants, euphoriants, stimulants, depressants, psychoactive drugs, hallucinogens, opiates, pot, hash, benzodiazepines, MDMA, club drugs, psychotropic substances, gymnopilus subpurpuratus, pluteus villosus, and my choice of the weekend after the blow was gone; psilocybe villarrealiae! While we barely made a dent in the world of available drugs that weekend, it's fair to assume we had one of every brand of whiskeys, gins, rums vodkas, tequilas, absinthes, everclear, brandies, ciders, beers, and a wine selection of most colours and nationalities.

Harley, his buddy Kato, and I were the last ones still there. For an hour or so, we had been performing 'Batman-like' or 'Kill Bill-billed' fight scenes. One of us would make a *super-punch* while the other would make the sound of the swing and impact. The stricken one would take ten, twenty punches, while flailing, thrashing and knocking about as he was super pummeled by the Super Being. We might still be there now if I hadn't of declared how badly I needed a beer. It was pleasantly warm on this July 23rd afternoon, in 1986, and we weren't done yet! None of us had any money, but Harley had a plan!

After fifty hours of intense intake and no sleep, I was just glad somebody had a plan. We herded inside Kato's beige Diplomat car, and drove down to the New Bar in town, where anything went; usually in the Wash Rooms. Harley explained he had a contest in mind… We would pick out women at the bar, for each other, and we would then approach these selected Gals and tell them how we were "Cosmic Partiers, left over from the *Low Riders Weekend Bash*"… and after astute consideration, they were chosen to anoint our thirsty throats with cold beers!

We would party with them until we needed another frosty, and then go to the next Patron, who would already be picked out, unknowingly to them. It was like to be their pleasure to bask in our broke and breathless charms. After my second successful cold barley pop, Harley told me I should go up and try the Lady at the bar named Kori. I was still thirsty, so I ambled over.

Kori bought my pint, and told me she had seen me around town, mostly in the Bars. She remembered me once at the Last Chance Hotel, sitting at the bar, reading a copy of 'Robert Kennedy; Life and Times', while drinking water. She noticed my drinking water, and not beer. I told her I had ran to the Last Chance that day, and that I ran home afterwards, so I partook of water that day. She said,

"You ran all the way into Town to read at the bar?"

I said 'Yes'.

There was nothing else to explain. I read there at the bar often. We all had lived vicariously through the Last Chance for years and yarns.

After another cold one, I asked Kori if she had a joint. She slyly took me into the alley behind the Hotel, and we puffed 'er back. We went back in for another cold one, and then she took me to her apartment. It was cool! It was the apartment that some friends of mine had lived in in the late Sixties and early Seventies. 'Snake-Bit' had lived in the closet there for six months, strung out on speed. In a *bedroom community* like Dundas, strangely Kori made it clear we wouldn't have sex on the first *date*, so to speak. I gave her my address and she made plans to visit me the next day.

Sure enough she came over, and we made plans to hitch-hike into Toronto together to see Tom Petty with Bob Dylan. After a few cars went by, we went back to my place again. We recognized there was something going on between us. Something that was *obvious and unmistakable.* Had we really just met the afternoon before? Was that even possible?

Kori went from a bosomy curly headed girl, into an incredible, slinky lady. She truly had the best legs in town. Now I'm not being naïve or arrogant when I say she did it for me. It just hit us both like that! We did everything for each other, from that moment on. Kori, transforming herself into a Sensual Goddess, was just a Natural Progression. I moved into her apartment after she suggested it about three dozen times. I had many broken relationships out west. I was wary about getting intimate too quickly, but by that time I realized there was no use in fighting it; it was meant to be. So we did it! She became my young daughter's best friend and influence in no time. Try and fight it as I indeed did, but it was meant to be. I guess we were the Towns Items for the rest of the summer.

I was attending McMaster U at the time. It was a care-free time of much fun and no regrets. Our apartment was on the Main Drag, between the two most popular Hotels in town. A location everybody dropped in on 24/7.

I was kickin' back one evening when the door knocked, but not by itself. I answered it to one of the *original characters* from St. Mary's bolting in. Behind him was a large figure named Bronco, in a *'Charlie I Horse'* cowboy hat, yelling 'Buongiorno' at the top of his lungs!! They were both *high on adrenaline* after coming from the Peace Bridge, where they had smuggled a package across the line for the Black Hand.

Rod Pipe, ol' Basilica Hobnobber, figured he had things in hand as they approached the Border Guard. He was an Insurance Salesman, and the story was, he had just met somebody in Buffalo, on business. His trunk was full of official looking files, and he had a new business-like haircut to complete his professional image.

Rod casually told his boring business-man anecdote to a just as bored Guard, and was about to pull away when they looked at the Large Lad sitting next to him, and casually said,

"Good evening."

To Everybody's surprise, he gave them the same boisterous, "Buongiorno" that he had just given me.

They then casually instructed Rod with the dreaded words "Would you please pull your car over there and turn the engine off please."

Rod was miffed! They were just about to leave! They were about to pull away! And now this! Bronco was holding a Fast-Food plastic drinking vessel; the solid plastic kind with the straw and the lid on top. Rod instructed him to dump out his pop, stuff the package in the empty vessel, put the lid back on, and sip at his discretion. And it obviously worked, because here they were at sixty decibels; front and center! Rod was one of our *original crew*, who was in the right place right time for that Bolivian taste, way back when the Earth was green. Bronco was a Buckaroo that was too loud for words, and not ready for prime time.

Just like at the Emmy Lou concert, this Columbian blow was moist. I hated that Escobar just collected their Bolivian leaves, as the Seventies went on (they eventually processed it for flight) and, according to George Jung's book, threw it all in the same mechanisms and processes, so the taste was lost to time and billion dollar bank accounts. I used to keep ounces of the stuff inside sealed jars of dried rice. It worked to keep it dry somewhat, as rice absorbs moisture. But you couldn't doodle on those hot humid Southern Ontario nights. You had to get it in ya, and forget any formalities or ceremonies. Leave your mechanical jaw in neutral until you have filled your blood cravings, while draining your soul. But we were born to die. So have as good a time as possible in the mean-time...

"Sometimes the lights all shinin; on me
Other times I can barely see
Lately it occurs to me,
What a Long, Strange Trip it's been!"

Out in the barn at Bronco's farm, they owned some nice horses. We'd sneak out for a nose and I'd feel as powerful as the Stallions.

'Conquistador Your Stallion Stands.
In need of Company'!

After a couple years of living and partying together in Dundas, Kori wanted to get married. Neither of us were ever married before, and we travelled to Vegas to do it right. We stayed on the Strip for five days, enjoying Vegas as newlyweds. When Jerry Lee 'The Killer' Lewis found this out, he sent us over a bottle of *Aspe Spumante* Champagne, then gave us a front table. Jerry Lee shared the bill that night with Chuck Berry: 'Family and Friends'.

We finished off the first week by renting a single engine *Cessna* plane to fly over the Grand Canyon, and pick out a place to explore. It actually rained at the Canyon while we were there, so we didn't mule-train-it-down the Canyon as planned. At that time, the Canyon was set up for Family Tourists. There was even a bowling alley there, with lots of kids. Cool.

After a couple days we flew back into Vegas. In 1988, this was still considered 'Old Vegas'. Las Vegas was founded as a City in 1905 when 100 acres were auctioned off by the Union Pacific Railway. *El Rancho Vegas* was a Hotel and Casino, on the dusty Las Vegas Strip. It was located at 2500 Las Vegas Boulevard, at the southwest corner of Las Vegas Boulevard and Sahara

Avenue, what is now known as Winchester, Nevada. The El Rancho Vegas opened on April 3, 1941. The Flamingo was built in 1946 on the concept (and death) of Benjamin 'Bugsy' Siegel. The Golden Nugget was founded later that year. The Desert Inn Casino opened in 1950, followed by Binions Horseshoe Casino I 1951. The Sahara Hotel and Casino followed suit, opening in 1952, along with the Sands Hotel and Casino the same year. Next the Riviera Hotel and Casino opened in 1955, which closed recently in 2015. Coincidently the Dunes Hotel and Casino opened in 1955 and closed in 1993. The Freemont Hotel opened in my birth year of 1956. It took ten years for the next Casino to open in 1966; the Aladdin. Circus-Circus was part of the Sixties expansion, opening in 1969. Vegas was built and ready for more action, and skimming, and even Howard Hughes. Ten years later in 1979, the Liberace Museum opened to a public that loved to be entertained; by the Rat Pack, Jimmy Durante, Sophie Tucker, Milton Berle, Joe E. Lewis, Marlene Dietrich, Harry Belafonte, Dorothy Dandridge, Lena Horne, Elvis Presley, Wayne Newton, and Wladziu Valentino Liberace himself.

After we left the Old Vegas in 1988, it soon became the 'New Vegas', which promised an environment designed to make Vegas more *'Family-Friendly'*. With the opening in 1989 of the Mirage, a Casino aptly named, because the *Family* orientated idea was merely seen for what it was, a mirage! I mean, how do you baby sit babies at a casino?! 'New Vegas' stories of bored children searching for their parents in expensive Hotel lobbies, twenty-four-seven, did not deter the opening of the Excalibur in 1990. 1993 saw the opening of new cash cows called MGM Grand Casino, Treasure Island Casino, and the Luxur Casino. 1994 followed up with the Zen Centre. 1996 saw the openings of the Stratosphere and Monte Carlo Casinos, while 1997 saw the New York New York Hotel and Casino sprout. The Bellagio Hotel and Casino opened in 1998, while 1999 saw the triple bill openings of the

Mandalay, Venetian, and Paris Casinos. The Aladdin was rebuilt in 2000, Palms Casino opened in 2001, the Wynn in 2005, the Palazzo in 2007, The Encore in 2008, and the Cosmopolitan in 2010. The Sahara Casino closed in 2011 and was replaced by the SLS Las Vegas Hotel and Casino in 2013, then changed the name back to Sahara in 2019 before closing months later.

Kori and I paid $21 dollars a night for a hotel on the Strip, and ate more free meals and enjoyed more free drinks than we actually paid for. This was the 'Old Vegas'; the Vegas with all the Characters and Stories too great to make up! It was Frank's and the Rat Pack's Vegas, with Skimmers and Trimmers, and people buried in the Desert. When people travel to Las Vegas today, these are only stories. But these are the Characters that the greatest gambling, scrambling and rambling stories of America came from!

As always when in foreign countries, I was searching Vegas for a big bag of grass. I never thought twice about being on the *hunt*, but then, I didn't ask dudes with short hair and shiny black shoes for a bag, either. But I did ask this slightly built long haired fellow, who worked there as a janitor, if he knew where to grab one. At first he kinda just backed off and said, "No". But twenty minutes later he tracked me down, and said that Kori and I looked cool, so he would help us out with a bag. He instructed us to meet him at the front door at the end of his shift, which was in just a few minutes.

He took us over to his house (on the poor side of Town, which I enjoyed) and indeed got us an ounce. We started rolling and smoking and he started telling stories; about himself, how he came to Vegas, his job, and Nevada. His said he was from Texas, and his name was Jody. Kori told him that since everything in Texas was big, we would call him our 'Little Big Texan'. He grinned and rolled another joint. He told us many stories about his times in Texas, and Vegas, as we rocked and rolled more joints.

I always talk to the Locals wherever I've travelled. They are the ones that make you one of them. Kori often worried about my out-front style when I needed to get high, but it always was all good. We told him some wild stories from Dundas. After a few more joints we exchanged addresses so we could keep in touch.

We had one of those *'like we knew each other forever'* type afternoons that neither of us will forget. I was rolling another joint when his girl-friend suddenly came home from work. Well, she thought this was a strange situation indeed to return home to. These characters from above the forty-ninth parallel had invaded her kitchen, and after buying dope off her Beau (which was a felony there), then rolled joints all afternoon like we owned the place.

She, like so many women in my past, clearly thought I was a bad influence on Jody, and indicated it was time for us to leave. But we had been smoking and joking for a few hours, and our bond was set. We exchanged letters in the mail for a year or so. I won't forget our fun afternoon together. So here's to you, my little friend. Thank You Little Big Texan!

We rented a new Ford Taurus and drove through the desert to Beverly Hills. We got all caught up in a filming session of 'Beverly Hills Cops', so we just hung with the fellow tourists, and did what newly-wed Canadian Tourists do down in Beverly Hills... We got high with our last joint!

I headed towards Downtown Beverly Hills around ten p.m. and started looking around. Kori asked me what I was looking for. I told her I would know soon as I saw it. And after a minute, I saw it... or Him. It was just dark out and I spotted this fellow out on the street. Kori got kinda bug-eyed when I jumped out of the car and chased the guy down. I said, "I'm in from Canada and I need an ounce of good pot." He looked more scared of me than I did of him, so I figured that was a good thing. I told him

I wasn't a cop, so it would be entrapment... etcetera... He saw something in it for himself, and he bargained with me that if he took me to his buddy's place for a bag, I had to take him for his methadone shot first.

I gladly took him for his shot. We then went over for the ounce. He introduced me to a couple guys who lived in this *Apartment Happening*. One was reading some chronicle, and introduced himself as an underground writer who attacked and exposed the Republicans, for sleazy shit they were doing in every district around that part of California. He showed me stuff that revealed corruption, and child molestation in every Child Care Unit in the area. He showed me some pictures and documents from where he travelled to Viet Nam, while looking for ancient MIAs. He was a driven journalist, and he seemed to have his fingers in a dozen different pies of government corruptions and cover-ups.

It suddenly hit me, once again, how absolutely politically involved and entwined Americans are. They are much more comparable to countries like Ireland, Jorden, Israel, Egypt, Iran, Iraq, and well, anywhere that nationality provokes and involves freedom from injustice and human suffering. After Pierre Elliot Trudeau made Canada a multi-cultural country in the early Eighties, today's new legal Canadians just want to leave all their political and social turmoil's behind them the best they can. They are here for freedom and preservation. They deserve this time off in our country-club-like environment called Canada. It's too good here in Canada to get excited about much. We're Sweden with a very dull edge. And we like it that way.

So we scored, and hung around with my new journalist buddy, Steve Spears, for a couple days. We had some great conversations together about his interests, fears, and his visions of the future of California, and beyond. We kept in contact for a couple years by mail. He once mailed me a correspondence called 'Nazi Gate' in which he revealed more bad shit in California that I can't get into for his sake.

It was Friday morning, and I wanted to hang out on Sunset Strip for the evening. We headed down in the Taurus to the spaces west of La La Land. We took in the Whisky a Go-Go for a few acts, and looked for any traces of the Doors. But to no avail of course. The doors were closed. It was like they were only a rumour there twenty years before. We dug it though, and shuffled off to spend an evening on Sunset Strip.

I was wearing my deer-skin, with fringes. Many Freaks had to come up and touch its velvety light brown softness. Everybody on the Strip wore black leather jackets and outfits, and drove rented Corvettes. I stood out the whole evening by the fact maybe that I was the only one not wearing leathers, or ensconced in black.

The whole thing about the Sunset Strip, in 1988, was that everybody there had something to say. They voiced their opinions and advertised their different acts on photo-copied pieces of papers. Each 'act' gave out their papers and there were literally thousand left on the Strip sidewalks at the end of the night. We were virtually knee-deep in papers by ten p.m. The Dudes and Freaks we talked to all night left me with the belief that I've voiced many times since that, "Every street you venture north of Sunset Strip, you lose an ounce of cool!" I collected hundreds of these paper ads at the end of the night, and took them back to the car. I still have them.

One *act* that appeared, and re-appeared throughout the night, were six naked guys, all with waist long hair, that wore only towels tied at their waists. I was naturally inquisitive towards them, to an extent. They handed Kori and I their photo-copied *Written Words*. Hanging out were beautiful blondes, demons dressed in black leathers, Old Acts tellin' it as it was, Freaks spreading the word, New Acts tellin' it as it is, Musicians groovin' on the Scene, always Jim Morrison imitations doing their poses, dudes smokin' and puffin', Beautiful People, and Us.

Kori and I fit in well as we were somehow different; in our dress, our stories, our beliefs, and our Northern Cool. The whole evening seemed to jell together as people frolicked and smiles flowed. At one point the *'Six Naked Conquistadors',* as I referred to them as, were talking to me, and suddenly in unison they all walked across the Strip, upside down on their hands, letting their Freak Towels Fly! What a night!

We travelled back to our Friends in Beverly Hills, where we chilled and crashed. The next day we bid adieu to Steve, his roommate who scored me the buds, and the *heroin-addict* turned *methadone-addict* that turned me on to this interesting scene. But we were now ready to cruise up the Coastal Highway. We were anticipating taking in every site I read about in my youth on our way to San Francisco; home of The Dead, the West Coast Sound, Columbia Street, the Golden Gate Bridge, the Haight, 710 Ashbury Street, The Avalon Ballroom, the corner of Haight-Ashbury, the Fillmore West, the Cow Palace, etcetera, etcetera, etcetera...

Before Kori and I started to drive up the Coastal Highway we stopped in Venice Beach where, unlike Jim, I did not dig the beach scene. Too violent in 1988! Instead I went to a Leather Shop and bought Kori a couple keen leather out-fits, and myself a nice leather jacket. Just perfect for Screaming Eagle rides!

We left Malibu and went off to Santa Barbara. We drove north in our new leathers, around Morro Bay and Pismo Beach to Cambria. The next stop that afternoon was the Hearse Castle. I wanted to see the pool that snaked through the house from room to room but we were late. We hung at Big Sur until we got hungry, and headed towards Monterey. The Pacific Highway just magnifies the Pacific when travelling on its magnificent bridges and roads. We went down to the *docks on the bay,* and I thought about living there at the turn of the nineteenth century, as the west coast slipped conspicuously into twentieth century, when it was still everything Steinbeck was inspired to write about. Salinas was the dream he was raised in.

We spent the night in Carmel, where I purchased a '*Clint for Mayor*' button.

I ambled along the venues of Bukowski, Joan Didion, Robert Frost and Jack London. I could not pass up the Garlic Festival in Gilroy. It was happening too fast, but I had to cruise through Santa Cruise to get to Half Moon Bay. This has to be the most Perfect Bay ever! It's a circular, pool-like bay that has a beach outlining the entire shore. The cliffs at the Ritz-Carlton grandly concede to the mighty Pacific, and prepare you for the San Francisco Bay.

We were keen on getting to San Francisco. I wanted to drive straight to the City Lights Book Store. I had never been there, and it was one of Frisco's cultural icons I craved to explore and enjoy, from Kerouac, to Ginsberg, William S. Burroughs, Neal Cassidy, Gregory Corso, Lawrence Ferlinghetti, Gary Snider, Michael McClure, Caroline Cassidy, Peter Orlovski, John Clellon Holmes, Herbert Huncke, Anne Waldman, Lew Welch, Philip Whalen, Ken Kesey, Hettie Jones, Joanne Kyger, Edie Parker, Elise Cowen, Brion Gysin, Richard Brautigan, Lenore Kandel, Robert Frank, Janine Pommy Vega, Harold Norse, Jan Kerouac, Ruth Weiss, Ed Sanders, Charles Plymell, Barry Gifford, Ronna C. Johnson, Wally Hendrick, Wally Berman, David Meltzer, Regina Weinreich, Jacqueline Herschel Silverman, who have I left out? I drove and drove until I came to the unavoidable reality, that is, in San Francisco you will get lost driving on the streets, and a map doesn't always help.

I finally pulled over to ask for directions, and when the vehicle was stopped, I looked out the car window and there it was! I had pulled over right in front of City Lights. It was meant to be!

Talking to people and reading maps brought out a demographic fact about Frisco up to the late Eighties; Columbia Street divided the rich from the poor; the Freaks and the Yuppies, the Successful Groups from the Starving Artists.

Today, all the old landmarks and spirits of the Sixties, Seventies and Eighties are gone. Disappeared! San Francisco is today home of the 'Rich *Techees*' who are creating the fast paced world we live in today. Even if you own a house in Frisco, it is highly unlikely you could afford to live in the city. San Francisco continues to evolve and change into different economies and cultures. But these are not cultures anybody can belong to. You must be part of the Chain... the Technical Chain that leaves human beings behind while creating the next form of existence for our children, who will fight to survive in it when we are mere memories to the masses.

We spent three days in Frisco before our plane tickets forced us to leave. But we knew where we were going in this great city, and what we wanted to see. And we saw and did it all... with the exception of one thing perhaps. Kori was a hippie down deep, and she wanted me to buy some flowers for her hair, ala Scott McKenzie and John Philips. Instead, as time was running out, I had a street artist sketch our mugs and it was off to the airport for the trip home. It was two weeks later, we were married, and Kori never forgave me for not finding the time, or space, to buy the flowers for her hair... C'est la vie!!

We approached the counter at Frisco Airport to show our plane tickets. There was a quaint young Oriental fellow there to help us. He asked me if I was wary about flying. I said I was, but how did he know? He answered that he had worked there a couple years, and my foreboding feelings stretched perceptibly across my face, to him at least. He said he had something for me, and offered a card with some words and numbers on it. Before I could ask what it was, he offered that this card would supply me, cost free, with as many drinks on the plane as I needed to have a calm flight. Wow! Life sure used to be different, and that's not that long ago!

Kori and I boarded the plane. She was used to flying and was not leery of the jet at all. As we were rising above the clouds, we suddenly started getting sucked into different wind patterns that had the plane suddenly dropping, haphazardly, hundreds of feet at a time. This continued, excitingly, and the Pilot announced he needed to avoid these winds so he was heading south over the Rockies, on the way to Colorado.

But we kept on falling dramatically, and this continued in time as we continued our plummeting descends. People looked alarmed, with some now standing on their seats. The Stewardess started screaming. I looked over at Kori and asked,

"Is this normal? Has this ever happened on a flight you've been on before?"

"No," she screamed! "We're gonna die!"

Suddenly the bar cart on wheels, with no Stewardess attached, started rolling down the aisle until it came to where I was sitting. It forcefully hit my seat's armrest. Every drink on the plane spilled on me! Kori looked at me, and suddenly with no fear left said,

"That guy had it backwards... the drinks aren't on the card, all the drinks are on you!!"

I offered her my soaked sleeve and said, "Here, the vodkas on me!!"

Chapter 22
Sandy Lehmann-Haupt

Borg Gravis was born in Copenhagen, as were his Parents and his adopted brother. Both his parents were Politicians with distinguished careers. Mr. Gravis was an interesting man who did not see any Mountain too high or... etcetera... His philosophy was not challenged, it seemed, when Borg failed the 'Technical Aptitudes Exams' which was still in effect in Denmark in 1964. This exam screened Young Learners for Basic and Advanced skilled Careers. It basically decided, from that day on, whether you might grow up in a Distinguished Career, like his Parents, or if you failed it, a career of unskilled labour.

It was basically equivalent to the Hinduistic Caste System in India, in my humble Goidelic Opinion. But not a life you were born into as much as how you were perceived, and how you could achieve a chance to make it in a Society where there was a shortage of jobs and materials after WW2. Failing this 'test' was the Webster's definition of 'Failure' in Denmark.

His father was distraught that his son, a Prodigy of good education and breeding, should be labelled and shackled for the rest of his working and academic careers. He and his wife resigned their posts, sold their house and possessions, and moved to Canada in 1964. To make such efforts and sacrifices for what he saw as a socially beguiled son sounds noble. Would you do it for your son? Mr. Gravis must have thought the world of Borg. Or perhaps it was vanity. Or even insanity. But anyway, that's what he did.

The family moved to Guelph in their effort to start over again. They bought a house and moved on. A couple blocks over, on Harvest Lane, lived a family who had a lad named Jean Panhead. He took Borg under his wing, and got him on the local hockey team, and introduced him to Canadian girls who loved his accent.

He next introduced Borg to LSD in the eighth grade, and they both entered St. Mary's High School the next year. Here they met me, a big country hick with a likewise appetite for self-destruction. At St. Mary's we all had that hunger for changing the oil in Society's crank case. We were New Riders on the Storm, with coffin tanks eyes and joints between our lips! We were young and smug. The horizon where we strived from was curved and distorted. There was much to learn, goals to be achieved, and things to be discovered. And none of them had to do with St. Mary's academic curriculum.

Within a year Borg had the longest hair, the wildest howl, and surely did the most drugs in the hood. He was Oxford dictionary's portrayal of a 'Hippie'. Life is often cruel to those it doesn't understand, and nobody claimed to understand young Borg. After High School Borg moved back to Denmark and I didn't see him for thirteen years.

In 1986, due to weak National and Global economies, most of the usual Dundas Crew made it back to the Mother Land, unemployed, with defaulted mortgages and families that were struggling. They ventured home hungry for a *new beginning* in the Old Town; the place of their Birth, where it all started. Where old family ties were still there to help, and Old Friends were there to Party!

I had put my Position with the Attorney General on hold to chase a Friend across the country, and to visit my daughter. Dundas had not lost its charm, or hotels that we all grew up in; the Last Chance Roadhouse, the Collins and the Owls Roust Hotels were still there, right beside each other on King Street. But they were as different as possible from each other;

Hippies, and Kickers and Cowboys Angles all in a row, all from the same Town. Rebel Kids drank next door to their Redneck Parents for years. And then they went home and thought they were both cooler than each other, you know... Pink Floyd verses Benny Goodman...

While drinking at the Collins one afternoon, with old and new patrons, I noticed Borg's face, and called him over for a pint. He was no longer a hippie or fragile looking. He was kind of like Sandy Lehmann-Haupt, who was one of Kesey's original 'Merry Pranksters' on the Bus. He was riding a motorcycle, and living with a nasty, small, but scary Lady who could drop you with a single punch. He told me he had been back in Denmark for a dozen years, and was back visiting his parents in Guelph. Ironically, he had been working as the Skilled Tradesman in Copenhagen, where it had been decreed twenty couple years before that he had no talent to do such. I guess it must have been the good cosmic purple microdot LSD in America that straightened Borg out!

Chapter 23
Saloonatics on the Wharf

Jack Straw's Father worked at the *National Steel Car* plant in Hamilton's north east end on the Hamilton Bay, which had been a dead fluidity for decades. But it provided jobs for the Community, and workers like Jack's dad, who came from as far away as Fort Nelson. The Straws lived out in the country, just like their name might suggest. I remember his dad playing guitar and other instruments in my youth, but I can't remember where.

WW2 left the world diverse and somewhat culturally divided. Many nationalities were discriminated against; France for surrendering so early, the Jews (actually for two thousand years), Indians (until, and then after Ghandi), Viet Nam (who did not gain freedom from colonialization from France, even though de-colonialization became globally striven for as a result of the war), and Polish jokes were out in full force when I attended Flamborough Center School.

Being Irish kind of left me immune from the teasing and bullying. We were Natural Born Rebels, just waiting for Bloody Sunday, and it wasn't here yet. Anyways, everybody knew those English Bastards had assaulted and starved us Irish out of our home lands, so who wanted to deal with that? Hell, officially we weren't even in either World War, so it was hard to get an angle on us, exactly. And Kennedy was the first Irish President, whom everybody liked (except for some dudes from the Marseilles Underworld who would one day visit Dallas), so I could stand on my own out on the playground.

There are persecutors all through life. Some souls got persecuted just because they were small. Others were because they

231

were too smart. Some's curse was their tongues; that is their inability to control the papillae textured muscle. Pimples, unexplained rashes, frowned upon clothing styles, being poor, those too fat, those too skinny, being google eyed, those always picked last, those not too bright, those not friendly, those too friendly, those wearing glasses, those sucking up to the *Wrong Side*, those who weren't cool, those who Rushed in as Fools, and those with the wrong haircut. These, and many other reasons undocumented, but were securely cemented in the heads of those who lived out their own insecurities through someone else's hardship and pain, sucked.

Jack didn't have many of these faults at all, but he had to deal with bored and jealous country kids, who were all bigger than him. Dudes are sometimes dudes at best. However Jack was talented. He was skilled at most everything he attempted doing. Some would dare say he was gifted. He was an inspired Artist. Teachers saw he was adroit, and classmates watched the teacher's acknowledgement of his talents. Now that would be a reason to harass him at recess, unless they could find someone smaller or smarter to take out their short-comings upon!

Jack could skate like the wind, and he actually played hockey on artificial ice, in actual arenas! He had proper equipment, and often left us in his dust when he played on Tommy Swamp, or at the Carlisle arena. Players would try to body check him, but few could catch up to him.

Jack played drums and guitar. He brought his 'Ax' to St. Mary's sometimes, once he assessed the Musicians there to groove with. The last time I saw Jack for a while was in the mid- Seventies. He had an apartment in the City, and a beautiful sweet-heart. She was a Musician also. Jack was doing ok where he was. I soon went out west looking for new adventures.

I left Victoria B.C., and my friend of a couple months, Barbara, (whom I think they fashioned Barbie Dolls after), and returned to Dundas in 1986. Many of the Dundas Crew was back in town *licking their wounds* and sniffing out the old stomping grounds. I was cruising freely *on my own,* having rectifiable reunions with many old friends, and meeting new ones. At my new Friend's apartment one day, I received a phone call from Jack Straw, whom I hadn't seen in over ten years. He invited me, and my Friend to watch him, and some other ol' St. Mary's boys who were playing at McMaster U, for Frosh Day festivities.

My new friend, Kori, and I hunted down Jack, who was playing some decent bass guitar on stage, with Ralphy Retro on guitar and vocals, (another ol' St. Mary's rebel). Dag Hayfever was beating the drums, and I met Robbie Bandana playing sick electric guitar. We got together after the gig, and they told us they were playing Friday nights at Doc's Tavern, on the Hamilton Mountain. We caught them there for their next designated Friday night gig. They blew us away with some Grateful Dead tunes, some Blues, Rock, some Band and Dylan. They also mastered some New Riders of the Purple Sage, Lowell George, *Hot Tuna*, some Roger McGuinn, and also electrified us with a couple or their originals. They called themselves the '*Saloonatics*', Retro's hook.

Jack was known as *Wharf Rat* to the Band and his Fans. The handle was an ode to an early Hunter-Garcia composition on the '*Skulls and Roses*' double album', released in '69. We were all classic Dead Heads. I'd met Dead Heads and Warlock Fans from Mexico to Seattle, Vancouver to Montreal, Labrador to Baffin Bay, and Toronto to Dallas. We were around every corner, just pickin' and grinnin'!

I had followed the Dead across America throughout the Seventies, Eighties and Nineties. I actually never saw them until 1972. We Freaks at St. Mary's had been freakin' out over the band since their 1970 releases of *American Beauty* and *Working Man's Dead*. The self-entitled *'Grateful Dead Live'* in 1969 gave a Fan Club address, and all us freaks at St. Mary's joined. They gave us all cosmic alias identities.

I saw them my first time at the Buffalo Auditorium, with so many freaks from St. Mary's that eventually Mr. Mainline rented us a school bus to go down and come back on. We were able to smuggle our drugs to the concert in safety. Thank you Mr. Mainline!

Luxury Dead accommodations! But being out on the road while chasing the Dead was rarely done in luxury, but with Plenty of Style! I've been at concerts where people would arrive in Helicopters, Rolls Royce's, Pink Cadillac's, once a Purple 1958 Vincent Black Shadow! I have seen sweet hearts escorted first class in every way. I've personally driven without sleep for three days to a concert in Seattle, and also hitch hiked in the cold rain and snow, to borrow a phrase from Jerry. I've done much of that hitchin' with my four wheel buddy Oak, who never complained once!

And I've been from
Tucson to Tucumcari
Tehachapi to Tonapah
Driven every kind of rig that's ever been made
Driven the back roads so I wouldn't get weighed
And if you give me; weed, whites and wine
And you show me a sign
I'll be willin', to be movin

Couldn't have said it better myself Lowell.

Kori and I would often catch the Saloonatics, waiting all night for Retro to crack open a dusty Jerry Classic, or for Wharf to pound-out-some solid Phil Lesh riffs on his Bass. Dag would be pleasing his Dag Heads by breaking guitar strings, and Mr. Bandana always had a Righteous Riff for each and every one of us. I chummed round with Robby B for years, but his wife thought I was a bad influence. She was probably right.

Wharf turned me on to the forty acre farm that was the Band's rehearsal house for a decade. Thanks Wharf! The newly married Kori and John moved in in 1988. So did Oak. He was still kickin'. When he passed on the next spring, I buried him out back and planted a Shrine in his Spot. It was the biggest pot plant I ever grew! The best bud with the best taste and high. It was my Best Friend giving to me his all, one last time! Thank you Oak!

We had some memorable parties at the Farm. If a hundred and fifty guests showed up, three quarters would be Musicians, all battling to get on the stage.

I quickly got to meet most Hamilton musicians that year. Many did their apprenticeships while at St. Mary's. Hamilton musicians were Bluesy Waterfront Worriers who played a harder, grittier rhythm sound, the way Artists do in cities on the water, like Liverpool, London, New York and Manhattan, San Francisco, Hamburg, Vancouver, Dublin, L. A., Rio de Janeiro; where music flows artistically in with the waves, and goes out to the wanton world with the tide. Music never dies, no matter how many Artists are left crippled on the beach by the internet.

Chapter 24
I see All in Black
and White

It was a set-up! Kori's parents thought I was the Anti-Christ. They were both proud bankers, and I was everything out of a sixties Tom Wolfe novel.

Like many families in the late sixties, Kori's blood parents divorced early, and her Mother re-married. She worked in a bank, and her new beau was the Bank Manager. I guess it was meant to be. Kori, like many mates, shared stories with me about her life, and many involved her parents. I could see she was an unhappy child. Her family moved around a lot when she was young. That's tough on a lot of kids. I used to pray for my parents to go their own ways. Go figure!

Kori's mother was an Artist in everything she did. She was an accomplished piano player. She was also a professional flower arranger, and sang with the choir, literally.

Kori was raised by her grandparents in her youth, as was her younger brother, Ed. She told me that she used to walk home and cook lunch for her younger brother on her lunch hour. This action might be frowned upon today, but it was a different time back then. We lived in an era of innocence, it seemed, when the State was not so suffocating in our everyday lives. There was no internet yet, and no such insanity ruling our minds and souls like Political Correctness.

Parents were freer to raise their children as they saw fit. It's true that we young kids were unfortunately left alone in cars, and my parents nonchalantly smoked cigarettes at the supper table, but moral standards were not so imposing upon Society back then. Kori's *'Generation X'* must have caught the last days of what I consider (cigarette butts in my mashed potatoes aside), the Golden Days.

We children of the Sixties were bestowed with such freedoms growing up! And obviously, so were our parents and adults generally. Society was more of a Laissez Faire affair. We traded certain safeties that we take for granted today, for simple freedoms that would be soon missed. We were probably the first generation that saw both parents working full time, as TV continued to baby sit us. We would be expected to keep the house clean, keep petty fighting to a minimal, and girls would have supper ready for hungry working parents when they returned home. Kori was expected to know which forks went on which side of the plate, and the difference between Pinot Noir and Chardonnay wine glasses. Boy, do opposites ever attract, eh?

I by no means had many wholesome family stories from my side of the ledger, but I had left my family behind by the time I was fourteen. But it was best for both of us. I had friends to trip with, and adventures to unearth. We were a freak's clique. Kori responded to my life style by becoming a familiar fixture of the mid-Eighties; a Hippie Wannabe. She grew her hair waste-long, stopped smoking cigarettes, lost some weight, and became healthy. I had nick-named Kori; the *"Fifteen-minute-Beauty-Queen."* She had proper curves, and could do more in fifteen minutes than some Ladies I lived with could do in three hours, even though some of them were natural beauties anyway.

Kori's mother and grandmother were alarmed by her 'change'. They thought Kori had lost too much weight, and no women in their family had long hair. They were still waiting to meet me for the first time. When the auspicious occasion finally arrived, they were plainly aghast by my long hair, and the fact that I did not own a suit. They could see Kori more confident and empowered by my presence. They reacted like they had lost some power with my influence on her.

Kori's parents, grandmother and uncle took turns at the supper table being sarcastic. No one took me serious enough to even have an opinion about me.

I ventured into the Lion's Den, but soon I just didn't bother to accompany Kori for her family visits. They never visited us at our Farm once that I can remember. Kori visited them alone without me, until she would go over with our children. But this was psychologically a phase many families sustained in life; one of rebellion against one's parents, until the Child becomes a Parent themselves. And then the feuds are ended, and differences are put aside.

But suddenly one day it all came to an end. Both of Kori's parents died, sadly.

Her step-father had passed on a few years before her mother, and her property was in vast needs of repair. I took it upon myself to reconstruct the property and premises. After one particularly long and winding day, I was tired and in need of a cold beer. I stopped at the Waterdown Beer Store on my way home. It was thirty minutes before closing. I sat in my Pick-up, thirsty and tired, as I mused to myself "Well I'm tired and weak, but not down trodden." Without really noticing it I picked up a pen and scribbled down;

Sky so Dark;

I see all in black and white,
No gray in morning nor orange at night
My inner peace kills the outer fight
So blind at times but with insight.

The sky so dark it shades the sun
Days either over or just begun

I dream to wake now reality's near
With Friends all gone and Enemies so dear.

Never been born I've always been old
Ready for the Beast or the Angel so cold
Face so meek yet eyes so bold
Ears just can't hear what their told.

Foe of dirt lover of order
Never safe; always on the border
Opinions formed from stones and mortar
Leaves my wings of feathers and black tar.

I continue to crash but never burn
Never know just what I yearn
Seems not to be my own concern
Spinning in circles with nowhere to turn.

In the end that's where I start
Too far to go no room for heart
But I'll keep on with eyes a sodden
Tired and weak but not down trodden.

Upon finishing it I went in the store and grabbed some beer.
I went home and for some reason I was able to put the words
to a melody effortlessly. It was the first time I had composed a
song, from start to finish, with a tune that I knew exactly how
the timing would go, what instruments I would use, and words
that were profound, to me at least. I took the paper and threw it
somewhere, unceremoniously. I was engrossed in writing a book
at the time ('Important Exportin' Men'). After a few more beers
I started my overnight writing expedition, once again. I was a
couple months into writing my text, after six weeks of serious
reading and research. I had a couple chapters finished and an

outline of my next twenty chapters already being processed on a couple hundred pieces of paper.

I wrote another song the next day… and got into a groove. I started writing songs every day. But there's never enough time in a day…

There was no Famine;

On October third, in 1992, Sinead O'Connor ripped up the picture of Pope John Paul the second, on SNL, to try to expose who the 'real evil' was. The crowd did not react, or they over reacted by not reacting. It was underwhelming! You could have heard a mouse sobbing in the distant corner of darkness. Many declared her career was over. Indeed she never recovered from it academically.

She was boycotted, so she just went on her way singing songs that mattered to her, and to a hurting world. She revealed, or shall I say confessed, later, that her inspiration came from Bob Geldof ripping up the photo of *'Grease'* stars on 'Top of the Pops', to make a point. So she decided to copy him.

She had been doing a cappella version of War (by Bob Marley), in which she had changed the lyrics, to draw attention to child abuse within the Catholic Church. At her conclusion, she ripped the photo of J.P. in half. SNL producers had not a clue that Sinead was going to do this, as she had held up a photo of a refugee child in every rehearsal. Like many Artists and Prophets, she was merely ahead of her time. She would be applauded today, but like Lennon saying Beatles were bigger than Christianity, the masses still needed to be instructed.

Was Sinead misinterpreted by an ignorant audience, or was the audience really the Constant that the Universe beat to? Ignorance is bliss until someone brings it to our attention and asks, 'Why'? A simple act of naivety became the Devil's Craft of crudeness and callowness. It was a young audience expressing their obtuseness and incomprehension. But was this was not the generation that detested everything that we thought was sciolism and ill-informed for the last twenty years? The *next generation* that was counted on to bring out change and courage? Well it seemed the hip-hoppers were left behind at the Station that Saturday evening. Few had compassion or reaction… Merely gestation of mutation… and fear of truth!

Sinead carried on in a new world of hate and disrespect, even though she fought the Good Fight; for the Young, the Misinterpreted, and the Abused. She wrote a song that someone put on a tape and slid into my pocket once. I carried it around for a couple weeks, still unaware of the content.

One day Kori and I picked up my daughter after school, with her friend who was the same age. I suddenly slipped my hand into my pocket, grabbed the tape and unknowingly began to play it. Roy Orbison's song, '*You Got It*' had just played on the radio. I was singing along with Roy. So was Kori. Half way through I looked behind me and the young girls were gleefully singing along. The car was holy with Roy Orbison! We all sang our hearts out! It was so touching that Kori and I smiled, and held hands. It was wonderful!

It was at this moment I slipped this 'mystery tape' in the tape player. We were still smiling, and we knew we had found the love and tranquility Roy wrote the song about. Suddenly the tape started and a song began. The words began to chisel, slice, and sculpt. We could not get away. It told a strange story! It told the truth! Sinead told us;

Ok, I want to talk about Ireland
Specifically I want to talk about the "famine"
About the fact that there never really was one
There was no "famine"
See Irish people were only allowed to eat potatoes

All of the other food
Meat fish vegetables
Were shipped out of the country under armed guard
To England while the Irish people starved
And then on the middle of all this
They gave us money not to teach our children Irish
And so we lost our history
And this is what I think is still hurting me.

See we're like a child that's been battered
Has to drive itself out of it's head because it's frightened
Still feels all the painful feelings
But they lose contact with the memory
And this leads to massive self-destruction
Alcoholism, drug addiction
All desperate attempts at running
And in its worst form
Becomes actual killing
And if there ever is gonna be healing
There has to be remembering
And then grieving
So that there then can be forgiving
There has to be knowledge and understanding

All the lonely people
where do they all come from?

An American army regulation
Says you mustn't kill more than 10% of a nation
'Cos to do so causes permanent "psychological damage"
It's not permanent but they didn't know that.

Anyway during the supposed "famine"
We lost a lot more than 10% of our nation
Through deaths on land or on ships of emigration

But what finally broke us was not starvation
but it's use in the controlling of our education
School go on about "Black 47"
On and on about "The terrible famine"
But what they don't say is in truth
There really never was one

(Excuse me)
All the lonely people
(I'm sorry, excuse me)
Where do they all come from?
(that I can tell you in one word)
All the lonely people
Where do they all belong?

So let's take a look shall we
The highest statistics of child abuse in the EEC
And we say we're a Christian country
But we've lost contact with our history
See we used to worship God as a mother
We're sufferin from post traumatic stress disorder
Look at all our old men in the pubs
Look at all our young people on drugs
We used to worship God as a mother
Now look at what we're doing to each other
We've even made killers of ourselves
The most child-like trusting people in the Universe
And this is what's wrong with us
Our history books the parent figures lied to us

I see the Irish
As a race like a child
That got itself bashed in the face
And if there ever is gonna be healing
There has to be remembering

And then grieving
So that there then can be forgiving
There has to be knowledge and understanding

All the lonely people
Where do they all come from?
All the lonely people
Where do they all come from?

We stand on the brink of a great achievement
In this Ireland there is no solution
to be found to our disagreements
by shooting each other.

There is no real invader here
We are all Irish in all our
different kinds of ways
We must not, now or ever in the future,
show anything to each other
except tolerance, forbearance
and neighborly love
because of our tradition everyone here
knows how he is and what God expects him to do.

Half way through the song my throat constricted. My mind screamed and my soul was devoured by an evil I did not understand and could not see. I could hear Satan laughing at my ineptness. A Desperate Sorrow wallowed up within me. I did not know what to do. I could not speak and I could not think. I believe I wanted to die! My eyes finally filled with tears and I could not go on!

I pulled the car over to a stop. I did not have a reason I could express or explain. My blood boiled. My mind was screaming in Tongues. I could not understand a thing! I never felt so useless or unimagined. There was nothing left of me. The car coasted to a stop. I couldn't breathe. I couldn't feel. I couldn't stop crying!

It was like when the only reality that was allowed to live was one of Bereavement, Cessation and Departure! I summoned myself. I spoke to God to stop the Pain and Torture. In my weakness and humbleness I shamefully looked around me. Everybody in the car was weeping! Not crying, but howling and wailing. They shared my agony and affliction. Malady and convulsion became our paroxysm. Life became a misery. Obliteration obsessed us.

I tearfully share this inspiration with Irishmen Lost in Their Own Limbos;

Darkness Surrounds Us

Darkness surrounds us
All that we do
The Blackest of Magic
Darkest Voodoo!
Thunder and Lightening;
Powerful! Frightening!
Smiles and tears and
Deep Dark Fears!

With biases forming
When stars are all warning
The seas are all lost and
The deserts are storming.
Bad advice
And nothing's clear;
Behind those eyes hidin'
Deep Dark Fears!

Nothin's easy
But nothin's forever
Along the Way say
Never say Never!
Forget about the Darkness
We're all Friends here
So tell me about your
Deep Dark Fears!

I'm afraid too
I don't know what to do
I'm just concerned
And I'll listen to You.
Darkness surrounds Us
Look to the Light
Hear Better Angles
Fight the Good Fight!

Maybe tomorrow the
Sun will come out
Expose a few Truths and
Burn off some doubt.
Put on Your sun glasses
Hell have a beer and we'll
Share each Other's
Deep Dark Fears!

Nothin's easy
But nothin's forever
Along the Way say
Never say Never!
Forget about the Darkness
We're all Friends here

So tell me about those
Deep Dark Fears!

When nothin' makes sense;
Our minds burnt and bent
No time to predict
Too late to Repent!
Listen to the Wind
Whispers You hear
But You must be brave
When Shadows get near!

Scary words like
Real and Truth and
Age and pain and
Wasted Youth.
All come round
Like changin' gears
Look in the mirror
At Your Deep Dark Fears!

Nothin's easy
But nothin's forever
Along the Way say
Never say Never!
Forget about the Darkness
We're all Friends here
So tell me about those
Deep Dark Fears!

Close Your eyes
Shut the Darkness out
Cry if need be
Scream Baby Shout!
Battles get lost

Sometimes wars get won
Try one more time!
Put away the gun!

Darkness surrounds Us
All that we do
From Blackest of Magic
To Darkest voodoo!
Thunder and Lightening;
Powerful! Frightening!
Smiles and tears and
Deep Dark Fears!

I feel Your Pain Sinead.

Dick Irvin;

I was in Montreal in 1993 enjoying a memorable week with Kori and some Habitant Buddies. We all went to see the 'trois keler' at the Forum on Saturday night. Dell Delaney, Kori and I got there early in the morning for the guided tour of the fabled building. After the tour Kori went off on her own to further explore the historical Venue, while Dell and I watched 'les garcons pratiquent'. Kori meanwhile had arranged for her and I to sit in Don Cherry's and Ron Maclean's seats, in their tiny 'Coach's Corner' booth. The tiny stage was curved, and about the size of a park bench. I refused to sit in Maclean's chair, but I sat in Don's. The Studio workers told me that everything said on Coach's Corner, (remember that show Grapes had once?) was scripted. She then got us a *hitch* up in the 'Media's Lurch', high above the ice. She was taking pictures of me, as I was speaking on Red Fisher's phone to the Ghosts of Frank Selke.

That afternoon we ventured over to the Player's Bar across the street from the Forum, located at the corners of St. Catharines and Atwater Streets. Here is/was a lounge, with hundreds of pictures on the walls of distinguished Montreal players, through the ages. Some ex-players still made it there on winning game nights; C'est Montreal! Restricted chairs for distinguished players and management brass were off zone to buzzing and drooling fans. Guy La Flower had/has? a body-guard around Town. I took the cue and just paced myself; being cordial, and enduring the afternoon of etiquette, while sauntering about unnoticed in this Tavern of Legends!

And saunter I did up to the bar, and ordered drinks for me and my Lady. The wonderful, elderly lady behind the bar and I got to chit chatting. She introduced herself to me as was the Owner of the Tavern, Rita. She had been since the Fifties. I asked her many questions, and she was kind to converse with me for about three quarters of an hour. She told me to phone her after a game some time, and she would 'hook' me up with any player in the bar. Rita then stipulated to only do this after a win. She guaranteed that after a loss, no one talked.

Feeling good and informed, I then turned around to return to my table and *Boom!* I bumped right into Dick Irvin Jr. Mr. Irvin smiled and excused himself, to which I gladly accepted the blame for the bash. I thought to myself, "Say something interesting ... this is Dick!" I stumbled out,

"My name is John. It's my pleasure; I have followed your Father's three Stanley Cup victories in Montreal as Coach, and I've been enjoying your colour commentating since the early Sixties, though I realize you actually started in 1958. Your time commentating with Danny Gallivan was classic to us all."

He surmised, "Sounds like you've followed the Canadiens a long time".

I replied, "Like you, I've been on both sides of the fence."

Dick automatically understood the Toronto Maple Leaf reference, smiled, and said, "Let's have a beer and talk".

I got strangely polite, and assured him that I didn't want to take up his time, when he said to me,

"John, I've been with the Canadiens since 1940, when my Father became Coach. I'll tell you this; Floyd Curry died recently, and Jean Beliveau is retiring this year. Sometimes I just get lonely, and I would love to have a beer with you."

I was speechless.

We sat for an hour, drinking and conversing like old friends. Dick is very charismatic. As we conversed, he asked me where I lived. When I explained where my farm was in Ancaster, it turns out the one hundred and twenty year old farm which Kori and I lived at on Smith Road, off Book Road in Ancaster, (the ole Saloonatic Rehearsal House), was where Dick Irvin Sr. was born. I was flabbergasted when he told me this. Kori continued taking pictures of us having a warm time together. We finally had to go our own ways, as Dick needed to prepare for the HNIC broadcast coming up.

Dick asked me why I wasn't a Maple Leaf fan anymore, being from Ancaster, in Ontario. I told him my love of the Habs came through Le Gros Bill. He asked me if I would like to meet Jean, and have dinner with him before the game. I said I didn't wanna be a bother, still sauntering in my mind I guess. Dick then assured me that it was all in a day's work, as Jean was a Club de Montreal Ambassador, and he was only pleased to break bread with us simple adoring fans. I guaranteed him it would be my honour.

Upon meeting Mr. Beliveau an hour later, he shook my hand with grace, charm and said, "It's a pleasure to meet you John.

Dick says you know a lot about the Team." He then said, "Tell me something about yourself."

I answered, "Well, You saved my life once Mr. Beliveau."

He looked perplexed and said, "How did I do that?"

And I told him about Ormie and the Leafs, and my desertion to the Habs, leading to this conversion. He enjoyed the story. I guess it's true that 'it all comes round'.

Kori continued to flash her smile, and just before the Game ended, she got us an invitation down to the Montreal Locker Room. The game saw a disappointing Habitant loss to the New York Islanders. From the Locker Room, eventually we all flowed out onto Atwater Street, and we all stood there talking with the Players on the sidewalk. After about fifteen minutes Dick came out the door, and as he approached the Players where I was standing with Kori and Dell, he suddenly extended his arm and heartily shook my hand, saying, "Hi John. Good to see you again." Everybody looked at Dick, and then this shoulder-length-haired-creature, and shrugged.

Dick and I conversed over fifteen, twenty minutes. It was snowing. When the snow started coming down hard Dick said, "I'm parked a couple blocks away. I'd better high-tail it. It's been a pleasure." We shook hands, and I watched him depart down Atwater Street, with his brief case clutched in his gloved hand. I just stood and watched this frail man, bent over and leaning into the driving snow, in his trench coat, walking intently into the blizzard. Here's to you Dick. When the Stars are right, Montreal oozes with Class!

Cancun

I had been working for the last couple of years on different Crews at McMaster University. This was a strange and funny place to work. Hell, if Pierre Elliot Trudeau had of dropped by and witnessed this Crew, which was made up entirely of Europeans that acted like it was still 1942, he might have had second thoughts about his attempt to make Canada the most multicultural country in the world.

It was classic! The head guy was a large, muscular and authoritative German man. Second in charge was a small Italian man, who supported the boss man, but did not trust his methods. He believed that if they stood around and did nothing all day, then they would never run out of work contracts, thereby never becoming expendable. There was a Frenchman, who didn't trust either of them. There was a Polish man, a Ukrainian who spoke no English, a Hungarian man, and an Englishman who was polite, but always kept to himself in the distance. I suppose I filled in as the Irishman. We were neutral in 1942.

These guys were still living out the war, as they all grew up in Europe in the late 1930s and early forties. They brought their customs, beliefs, and prejudices of each other's nation, in the midst of the Cold War here in Canada. But none of them were actual Canadians, except me. None of them took out Canadian citizenship, so they could retire at their jobs here in Canada, and then immediately return to their homelands, thus collecting two pensions.

Who came up with this idea? Kudo's to them for a good scheme as such, but they collectively portrayed what it must have been like to live in Europe since WW2. I guess it's global where people work in foreign countries. I just never conceived, and still can't, of living, and working in a country for forty to fifty years without taking citizenship, not being allowed to vote, and in many cases, never learning the language at all!

Strange. And funny!

I told Kori to get a passport, as I wanted to travel to Costa Rica. She said she would buy the tickets on the way home from her work station in Hamilton. I asked her if she had her passport. She said no, but suggested that (back then) she wouldn't need a passport to get into Mexico. I told her I did not want to go to Mexico. She said ok, and came home the next day with tickets to Cancun. So for whatever reason, we went to Mexico.

When we got into Cancun, we went to our hotel room, and I suggested to Kori that she catch a wink or two as it had been a long day. When she lay down, I went out looking for some action. I found an authentic Mexican group playing like it was 1799! They were wild. They encouraged us for song requests. They laughed at me when I requested, "The Lonely Bull", and then played it.

Afterward the bass player came to my table and introduced himself as, "Juan."

We talked over a few beers and then he took me to some of his buddy's houses, outside of Cancun. We smoke, drank and snorted until it was light out. He gave me a big bud, his address, and told me to look him up the next afternoon.

I took Kori with me to Juan's the next day as planned. He had a gorgeous Mexican wife, and a cute son. He took Kori and I to all his buddy's places, and showed us an authentic Mexican time for the next week. It was grande! Kori probably thought I was nuts, but I refuse to take taxis when I travel to foreign countries. I always take the bus, to meet the people! And dig the grass roots cultures.

After a week, Kori had such a great time that Juan offered us a thirty year lease on a condominium, worth $12,555 for $5,000.

The price was right but I was still wary of crossing into Mexico for the next thirty years. Eventually I traded it for a bunch of hydroponic equipment to grow legal medical marijuana. Ha!

Our final night in town was splendid. Juan took us out once more to party with about a dozen of his friends, at an authentic Mexican bar with authentic Mexican marvelous entertainment. Here we were introduced to an interesting Mexican culture where, for every single beer each of us bought, we received an authentic plate of food. Six beers meant you suddenly had six delicious plates of food. It was a great time. As usual, Juan and I kept in touch for a couple years.

Kori and I travelled far and wisely in our times. From Vegas, to Venice Beach, the Sunset Strip, to Beverly Hills, the West Coast, San Francisco, Vancouver, Cancun, the Grand Canyon, and everywhere in between, we were there in a time that does not exist anymore. These were times of peace, prosperity, friendship, culture and simplicity. We went at a time when a passport was not even required. I sure wouldn't want to travel to most of these places today. They sure as hell aren't the same memories for tourists anymore. Time was on our side!

Chapter 25
Katrina

Katrina was different. Her mother was a mid-wife who married a Doctor. Her blood father was a retired policeman who had been seriously injured performing on duty. He was a full time invalid and a junkie when times were good.

The first time I saw Katrina was at a party in Burlington. I was by myself, and I took some notes. She told me she was from Ireland, and I was intrigued, of course. I asked what brought her to Burlington. She said that she would be back in Europe before long, but she was visiting her family. I laughed and joked that maybe I'd see her over there, since my brother was living in Dublin at that time.

I had just graduated from a Mechanical Drafting program that had dragged on for over two years. Half way through I realized that I didn't want to become a Drafts Person, but I felt compelled to complete the Program. Ironically, when I realized I didn't want to draw mechanical parts, or create items using Strength in Materials and read Engineering Magazines for a living, I decided to finish the Program as quickly and efficiently as I could.

I was indeed struggling with my *Strength in Materials* class. I averaged a bare pass of sixty percent, and even had to rewrite one test. Then one day the 'Cool Dude' in the class, Merle Maverick, asked me to step out for a joint... if I had one. I obliged, and while puffing I mentioned the last test was a mind scrambler, and how did he do on it? He puffed and told me he got his usual 100 percent.

I chuckled then said, "Yea. Seriously now?"

Merle said, "Yea seriously. I've got a 100 on every test so far."

I looked at the Dude and thought, "He doesn't seem any smarter than I am. What's going on?"

So from that moment on I spent ten to fourteen hours a day studying, creating, and modifying every aspect of my assignments. Merle and I took breaks at the Ripper Club, where every Ripper in the joint would scratch and claw to get to say hi to him first! I finished the Program five weeks ahead of time and my marks rose by twenty percent. Thanks Merle Maverick (and his distractions)!

Sometime later I saw Katrina at another party. My friend Phoenix had brought her, but we sat together talking most of the evening. I was telling her how I was basically through with Dundas by that time. Many of us were. In the Sixties we went to school there. The Seventies were one long party that we took on the road to many unsuspecting towns across Canada. There were three decades of *'Annual Ravine Bashes'*, which was one of my favorite annual Dundas events.

This *event* was held in late June from 1967 on until 1986. Every year the sponsors would supply five hundred large cases of beer, tons of drugs, and invited some bikers, freaks, drunks, kickers, and cowboys to a different open field each year, out in the country. There would be three to five hundred of us, getting drunk to the sounds of howls, yells, and laughter throughout the evening. When the daytime was starting to wane, we would call the cops, give them directions to where we were, and confess to them that we were drinking and drug taking in a public place. We would then challenge them to, "Come get us... if you got the balls!!"

Well, sure as hell they would show up! Those of us that didn't end up in jail joined in the annual riots at the Collins and the Last Chance Hotels. A fracas was guaranteed after each Bash, and we would be front and center in the newspaper the next day. It was a stone groove deluxe Baby! But, like with many fun things, there comes a time to leave the party… a time to go out on your own. Meet new people. But Kori didn't meet many new people at work all day, so we attended Dundas events that were great, but they were now 'been-there-done-that' events… Same ol', same ol'..

That is until we showed up at a party at Phoenix's farm, on the last day of festivities. He once again was with his friend Katrina. Katrina was thin with long brunette hair, long legs, and a wide smile that worked. We stayed together, chatting in the garden all day long. I didn't notice anybody else. No one else mattered. It was one of those things that only happened every so often, and it seemed we were both overdue! As everybody continued getting a buzz on throughout the day, Katrina and I talked about music, our histories, the funny guests getting drunker, Ireland, Dundas in the old days, and this new Dundas Circle that would be leaving soon…

About nine o'clock guests had started carefully stumbling their ways home. Phoenix collected Katrina and drove her home. She was staying at her sister's house until she returned home to Dublin. She slipped me a piece of paper with the address on it, just before they all disappeared. To start relaxing, and finish putting the raucous weekend behind myself, I decided to follow Katrina home and see what we might have missed discussing that day. Kori offered to accompany me. We soon arrived at Katrina's sister's house, where her sibling Sabrina was the only one home. She told us that Phoenix had taken Katrina over to our farmhouse. Ironic? Nope! We just dug being together. Everyone else was just frolicking scenery. Kori also perhaps, at that moment…

We returned to our farm but there was nobody there. There was a note on the door, however. It was from Katrina of course. It started off by saying, "Master. I seemed to have missed you. Here is my phone number. Call me!" Nobody had ever called me Master before. I can't even remember a Mister.

Now this was all going down right in front of Kori. But she didn't seem to mind. When I asked her how this was so, she explained that she could understand Katrina being a little struck with me. After all, she reminded me, we had spent six straight hours together all day in Phoenix's garden. I was intrigued when Kori basically gave me the *green light* for me to get to know Katrina better. As soon as she left for work in the morning, I took her up on it.

I called Katrina, and she invited me over to pick her up. She said her sister's car wouldn't start, and would I mind driving her to work. She said it was on the way back to my farm, sort of. So we headed over to the farm, got high, and continued getting to know one another...We watched 'Hard Day's Night' on my waterbed. After a while we got hungry. Katrina wondered aloud,

"Where can you get food out here?"

I said, "No problem", and proceeded to phone Kori at work.

I told her we were starving, and to bring us some food. She compared us to a couple of baby robins in a nest, waiting for their Mother to come home. We couldn't argue the point. She appeared an hour later with a pizza, and a curiosity to see what she might find.

We soon became three Close Friends. But it was really Katrina and me, with a pizza deliverer. Katrina and I would greet Kori at the farm after her day's work. We would wine and dine her and put her to bed, and then Take Off!

Katrina and I would leave the farm shortly before midnight most nights. We would Screammm into Burlington, and burst into the first Bar with entertainment that Rocked! But everywhere we went, Katrina and I soon became the entertainment. There's some Magic to walking in a bar around the midnight hour with a gal like Katrina. I mean every eye in the place turns. I'd be in my skins with my black leather hat I scored in Cancun. This was a period when I was working out five hours a day; working each muscle group, performing karate moves while stretching and running. My red hair was half way down my back. Katrina and I looked like we just came off a Beach Set.

We would raise hell, and after thirty minutes we would dash for the door, and go on to the next bar. We would repeat this five times in five Bars... Gator Ted's to Shoeless Joes, Anchor Bar to Jackson's Landing, until we docked ourselves at Honey Wests.

Other nights we might travel to Stoney Creek Bars for live entertainment. Sometimes we would do the Hamilton bar scene, ending up in the Hess Street Jungle of Blues Bars and parked cars. Hess Street had about twenty Bars in a row, on Hess and Queen Streets, and every establishment rocked to a different sound with fantastic live bands. When we used to visit *Hess Village*, as it was called, it was a guaranteed great time every night! When we arrived I would hush and stand on the corner, picking out which Bars were playing what kind of music, and zero in with a thirst. Crazy nights!

There were weekend parties that started at noon on Friday. Katrina liked the magic and the magic loved her. We rocked every Bar we visited, and at two a.m. we would travel up to Katrina's sister's house for a couple hours, and then I would make it back to the farm before Kori was up. It was a good life with no expectations or jealousies.

Then I became 'Ozzy' for a couple years. Katrina was there for that transformation. She insisted I take her to an Irish bar one evening, so I took her to the most rocking Irish Bar in the city at that time. This Bar was home of many fans who dug the Celtic bands of the Day. Celtic Music and Celtic Dancing were new inventions of the early Nineties. It actually had nothing to do with the Spirits of the Kelts, or Celts, which originated from 1600 to 1610. It was totally an invention of sound and borrowed culture that went over so huge that Celtic Bands became the rage. There were Celtic Dance contests all over the world.

The Kelts, were a branch of the Indo-European family of languages, including and especially Irish, Scottish Gaelic, Welsh, and Breton, and which survives now in Ireland, the Scottish Highlands, Wales, and Brittany.

On the way to the Bar, the radio D.J. man played 'Iron Man', and I was diggin' it totally. Which was a good thing, as Katrina was angry at me about something, so we were using Black Sabbath to *strangle the silence*. As we got out of the truck and walked towards the Noisy Bar, we walked by three young teens who were sitting on the cement curb of the paved city street. One nodded at me, and reflected to the other, "Ozzy!" Katrina smiled and followed me into the Bar. I was standing on the dance floor beside Katrina when the Lead Singer looked at me, grinned, talked to his Droogs for a sec, and then the Band broke into 'Paranoid' (Sabbath). Towards the end of the night they played another Tony Iommi song, and by that time, and a few beers, Katrina was talking to me again.

We boarded my pick-up and started off to her sister's house. On the way, radio Q107 played three Ozzy tunes in a row; 'Crazy Train, 'No More Tears' and 'Momma I'm Comin' Home'. I felt the presence of Ozzy taking me over as I listened to these songs. Katrina could see she had lost me. I wasn't Sal Paradise anymore. I was now Ozzy!

I live Up Town, I live Down Town, I live all around...

Katrina used to show up every year on Kori's birthday, and kidnap me for the day. She would attempt to get me home before it got too late. Once we went off to watch Angus Young and Keith Richards on stage, by themselves with their Bloody Blades!

One time Kori joined us on an adventure as we ventured to the Black Swan Bar in Burlington, where a drink becomes a contingency, and enough of them becomes *'a night out with the Moon Dog'*. One such night at the Swan, we were partying with the Dundas Crowd. About a *'baked-out-dozen'* of us were soakin' back the suds, downstairs, when Scary came back to the table and announced that there was a 'Poetry Reading' upstairs. People at the table started buying me beers to prepare me for my obvious impending recital. Now this was in the *'good ol' days'*, when you were free to drink as many beers in a Pub/Bar/Tavern as your freak flag could fly.

Well it was that kind of evening, as it unfolded. I had about eight or nine beers in me, and Kori and Katrina, Lenard, Boozy, Meister and Scary et-al were doing their best to get me upstairs, for an evening of culture... or whatever... I stated that when everybody at the table had bought me a beer, I would be ready for my recital.

Following a quick four or five beers I strutted up to the Stage, beer in hand with black leather hat protecting my head, and proceeded towards the microphone. The bar was loud. It was quite the crowd of poet lovers and haters. The Girls were excited. Scary was wary. Andy was ready. Scary's brother Phil, and his girlfriend, bought me another beer and handed it up to me. I drank it. I was ready. I grabbed the mic and growled,

"I live Up Town
I live Down Town
I live allllll around!"

263

I immediately dropped to the floor and withered around on my back. I flipped over on my stomach like a Lizard gone Charmed. The fellow that owned the nice new microphone freaked, and wanted to know what the hell I was doing on the floor like a snake?

I told him I was a "Horizontal Poet, and that I needed to recite horizontally."

He screamed, "Look, we're Vertical Poets up here man!"

I yelled, "Fuck you! Its Vertical Poets verses Horizontal Poets!"

A few more 'Vertical Poets' jumped up on stage, met by a few Horizontals. Pretty soon the place went wild. There were Poets punching and eye glasses flying everywhere. I think a good time was pretty much had by all by the end of our Evening of Culture.

Afternoons at the *Less than Level* bar in Burlington were a pre-cursor to its Midnight Magic. Katrina, Kori and I checked in one Sunday post meridian, with a wheel chair Sabrina had lent to Katrina. She had sprained her ankle, and found it more uncomplicated to wiz-along in this wheel chair, than bumping and grinding with Bar Room patrons. Katrina challenged me to, "spend an afternoon in her shoes"… or wheel chair as it were…

I took her up on it, and ambled along on my wheels up to a *gaggle of guys* that were catching a few brewskies on this stoic Sunday afternoon. Now here's this Dude in this wheel chair, with this black leather hat and leathers to match, with these two raucous Dead Heads who seemed to be lookin' for trouble. They asked Katrina what happened that I was in the wheel chair, and of course she told them I had my legs blown off in Viet Nam. Of course they could see my legs… I knew better, but I went for it anyway and played along. When Katrina and Kori went upstairs for a beer, I wistfully said, "I wish I could make it up there."

They carried me up the stairs in the wheel chair right away. Once up there, Katrina jumped on my lap as we rolled all around the room, spraying people with my Lager beer until there was a massive beer fight happening. When things got out of hand, the *Gaggle* picked me up and quickly escorted me out to their van. The Girls followed, jumped in, and asked, "Where are we going?" The lads said they had a nice boat with a couple 350's on the back, docked on the Burlington Bay. And it was filled with cold beer. Off we went!

It was a Stone Groove my Man! We rocked the waves and when it was time to return to the scene of the crime at the *Less than Level* bar, they needed to lift the wheelchair, with me in it, onto the dock. It was just too much for them. They couldn't lift me anymore. Katrina suddenly explained she was from a Family of Druids, and that if they took the wheel chair and placed it in the van, she would perform an ancient Ceremony which would allow me to walk as far as the van… They watched as I walked to the van, got in my wheel chair, and we drove back to the Bar. When we got there they carried me, still in the wheel chair, into the bar and up the stairs. They told everybody up there what a grand time we had on the Bay. What a Sunday afternoon. And the Lads got to see a Miracle!

Sometimes the Lights All Shinin' on Me!

The first Grateful Dead ticket I ever purchased was inscribed with the words; "There's nothing like a Grateful Dead Concert!" After the concert I perceived this was poignant and perfectly prosed. The Dead were all about seeing them live. I mean these weren't twenty minute Beatle concerts or Dylan playing in the Village to fifteen hundred Bob Heads. There really *was* nothing like a Dead concert.

St' Mary's was all about chasing them wherever they played. Oak and I chased after them through the Seventies down the West Coast, while Kori and I followed them from the Eighties until 1995. We saw them a few times at Wonderland in Toronto, two nights (in a row) in Copps-Coliseum in Hamilton (and the third night I took my daughter to a "New Kids on the Block concert, ouch) a few times in New York State, including some concerts at Ridge Stadium. I've been to too many concerts to remember them all, but I recall one concert at Ridge, when I typically said at the very last moment, "Let's go". So I stuck fifty joints behind my truck battery and motored down with Kori.

Within ten minutes there we saw about seventy-five buddies from Hamilton and surrounding area. I quickly bought some acid from some Heavenly Angels and gobbled it down with wine. Kori tracked down this twenty-six cube truck filled with tanks of nitrous oxide. I sat down and started suckin' off balloons and started hallucinating. I was sitting watching some dude in a Flintstone-like rock coffee shop. He ambled in looking somewhat hung over and quiet like. He was served a coffee. After the first coffee he feebly found the energy, and perhaps the courage, to order another. I began watching with a smirk on my face as he suddenly became a socialite and began gabbing to someone at the next table. He emphatically called for more caffeine and guzzled it down while discussing more tripe with fellow mud and blood brothers. I mean the *joe* was flowing!

He became livelier with every drop, soon snapping his fingers for the next cuppa java. Sitting at his stone table on his granite chair, he was ready to rock! The stone bistro suddenly seemed alive as this character, who I observed was wearing a sombrero, was conversing like he was rehearsing for a part in some *prime time* show for Fox Network. He talked and talked while doing the walk about the *Stone Café*, while calling over to the waiter for another hot brew, snapping his fingers and grinning like a fox.

Soon the waiter discreetly sidled up to him and declared "Excuse me sir, but I think you've had enough coffee." Like in an R. Crumb comic book, the next action square saw him sitting quietly back out in the stone alley, hands on chin and staring downwards, all dejected like… He just sat there with his head bent so I still could not see his face. I realized at this point that throughout his stint in the *hash house,* I had not noticed his face at all.

I got up and naturally walked towards this hallucination, and pressed forward to see his mug. I leaned forward and yelled, "Hey! Hey buddy! The figured slowly and stoically looked up at me and… It was Me!!

I went "Whoooooa." Freaked and frazzled I was jolted, and before I could come to any ratification on the matter of *discovering myself,* some dude floating about looked at me, and somewhat matter-of-factly exclaimed,

"Sting's over!"

I retorted, "OK".

He said "So Sting's over!"

I reiterated "Yea!" I then inquired "What does 'Sting's over' mean?"

He responded "Sting's over, and now it's time for the Dead!"

BOoM! I got off on the third hit of acid all at once and I tripped onto the field.

I was trippin' heartily as I noticed Kori was in front of me. I kinda sloppily gripped her for a while, when I noticed they were bouncing balloons through the crowd.

I let go of her long enough to tell everybody around me that it was an old-school Dead concert trick to bounce around nitrous oxide orbs for the crowd. One of the Equipment Managers grabbed one and went off to the forest of microphones and amplifiers to suck-er-back. I got hold of a balloon and half way through I ate the last tab of acid, thinking I would need it to stay fit for the drive home.

Kori and I eventually found ourselves backstage, quite unintentionally. It was no big thing. Jerry was willing to talk to anyone who actually had something to say. Once they got Rock Scully fired as Manager, Jerry was able to clear up from his five year addiction of Blow and Persian. A stroke left him with no ability to play his *Ax*. He had to teach himself to play again. Jerry lived a thousand lives in One!

A huge part of Grateful Dead Concerts were the legendary *Parking Lot Parties*. They were as entertaining as the acts on stage sometimes. Everything cool under the Sun from Frisco to Texas to New York were there for Dead Heads to cop. We were a Culture and World of Our Own! When Jerry died August ninth, 1995, the Spirits left us with memories that I personally could not have lived, or survived without...

Who was that Unmasked Man? He was part of the Trip!

Chapter 26
Me and Dell and
the Albino Bear

It was always strange going over to see Dell's buddy, Saul Bateman, who I called 'Batman'. Saul had a childhood chum named Alfred, so this nick-name was only natural to me. Saul lived in the City, so he was hangin' out all summer at a crony's country ranch on the brink of nowhere. His name was Joshua; he was about sixty-five, liked shot guns, had a wife, and a brother who was always there for a quick beer.

Joshua was a red-neck, and he seemed suspicious as hell of me. Which is why I always brought Kori with me...they could talk to her, and stare at her ampleness and sleek legs, while I would high-tail it back to the 'Shack' that Dell, Alfred, and Batman had erected a month before. But it was more of a decent small house; it was well built with running water and a shower. This made Joshua paranoid of the Town finding out it was there from the air. They built it with no legal permits. This was why it was built under the tall and spreading oak tree.

It was a warm May 24rth long weekend, and I was looking for somewhere to plant dozens of twenty-four inch high pots plants with great root systems. They needed to be planted ASAP. Dell and I had planted dozens already in every corn field within a short drive of my Farm, but I still had lots left to sow. He told me we could plant a dozen or so here, out-back, and Batman could keep an eye on them from the Shack. It was a done deal. But it sometimes took me thirty or forty minutes to drive past Josh's house, and onto the outback avenues and dirt country roads that eventually led to the Shack. Everyone would be waiting.

Upon finally arriving at the Shack (thanks Kori), we unloaded the car's trunk of plants, shovels, manure, jugs for water, and chicken wire to surround and cover the plants. I did the wire trip to protect the plants in the ground from rabbits, and other varmints that liked to get high. You might say we had it down pat. I had been doing it since I was a kid, until I started growing indoors. But my rented farmhouse could only hold so many plants, so I was always on the hunt for secluded and lonely spots that were out of sight, so out of mind. And this place was perfect. It had spacious patches of brush that were great for crawling into the middle of, and then eliminating enough of the center brushes to accommodate half a dozen or plants, or less. There were many brush-patches spread out over *the-out-back*. The day went on and the deed was done.

We partied hearty that night after planting, but the Harvest Party was always bigger, and better! The summer wore on and I visited every week; at first to look after fertilizing and watering, but soon just to curl up around the ferocious fire at night with some bottles, a few buds, and a breast or two. But who's counting?

Unfortunately, entering the laneway was always the cue for interrogation from Josh and his hillbilly family. I had the feeling he knew exactly what was going on, but I had Batman and Alfred keeping an eye on things. Trucking up the laneway, with Josh's eyes on us, must have been what it was like being examined by daunting eyes from the locals for the brave souls, who made the trek past Yasgur's Farm on the way to see Woodstock's Aquarian Exposition of Music and Peace. Josh looked like a hillbilly from the Ozarks. We looked like Freaks from Yorkville.

But that's always been such a big part of getting high for me; hiding like shadows in the dead of night, and always on the run to the next adventure... Meanwhile, fighting the odds of getting caught, like John Sinclair or some kind of strangeness in the bayou, we kept alert and on our toes! It made us band together, tighter each time. They watched over us like WW2 German Luftwaffe Fighters who were bombing citizens during the Blitz. Except we were getting bombed ourselves with no help from anybody.

When we were kids we were always hiding from Teachers, Cops, Parents, Narcs, Rednecks and Assholes. We drifted out into country communes, to be free from those who were running Society like criminals! It was cool being the Counter Culture to a Culture that frowned on Artists, getting high, getting laid, and being free from Authority Figures. That's what being Young is all about. It seems every generation had their Counter Cultural Heroes; from Jesus Christ to Oscar Wilde, Ghandi to Bill Burroughs, Picasso to Hemingway, Jack Kerouac to Ken Kesey, Allen Ginsberg to Ram Dass, and everyone else who was an Artist or Prophet that scared their Parents while changing the World!

One day in particular the Cultures must have clashed because as I drove in the laneway, Josh and his brother met me. I was expecting the usual 'go over', but they explained the 'City' had spotted the 'Shack' from the air, and sent Municipal Workers over to see it was dismantled. Losing their Shack, with comfortable beds and running water, Batman and Alfred went back to the City to do their dwellings. I figured this had to happen, one way or the other. Josh was somewhat uncomfortable seeing me drive back on his property all summer, and I certainly didn't blame him. Obviously he didn't need to endure our scene spilling out all over his back forty. And without Saul there, I had no visible function, or reason to be hangin' out there. But to be social we had a quick beer…

It was already late September, and we bid Josh a big 'thank you' for letting us party on his back forty all summer. We left on friendly '*Walmart vibes*' and I drove down the road, slowly, surveying out the best entrance to the pot plots after the Midnight Hour. There were a few houses off in the distance that offered no affront to my situation. There was a country store close by on the corner, with a laundry matt behind it, around the corner. The parking lot behind the Store was the only place to park my Pick-up when we would be harvesting the crops.

But before we harvested anything I had to have Dell pick me up at the Toronto Airport at midnight. I went to B.C. for a few weeks, to find and rent a house, and start a job at Langley Memorial Hospital. It was a busy couple weeks, but Leonardo et al helped me secure a house within walking distance of Leon's, and the Sumas U.S.A. border crossing. I bought a car (two as it turned out), met the Occupational Therapist who would refer clients to me as an OTA/PTA, and I enlisted at Fraser Valley College to be certified as a Fitness Instructor. With these titles I could work with Clients in a home or gym environment. I secured these job opportunities just before completing a two year Program at Humber College, in Toronto. Kori was nine months pregnant at this time. Dell, Kori and I were all moving out to B.C. together, and I was taming the Wild Frontier for their arrival.

So Dell, who had been staying with Kori and Katrina at the Farm, greeted me at Pearson Airport during the Midnight Hour. We drove straight to Joshua's ranch. I instructed him to park around the corner, and we scampered across the road, through the ditch, then across the fields until we arrived at the first plot of pot.

We slipped through the bushes and couldn't see the plants. We looked again. Just trees and leaves. Suddenly Dell gave a silent gasp. We both realised at the same time that these were not trees. It was the plants that we pampered all summer, with rotted manure, weekly watering with organic fertilizers, and tops topped to keep them low and out of sight.

I had instructed Dell to bring two saws, two flash lights, some rope, and x-large green garbage bags, which he indeed had. We tied these 'trees' together, and filled bag after bag with them. We then secured the bags with duct tape, and stashed the units in the ditch. We hustled off to get the truck, toss them in the back, cover them with a tarp, and drive home to see the Girls. The plan was set. It was around three a.m. (Devil's Hour).

With full bags patiently waiting in the ditch we started the short distance down the lonely road, towards the corner that the truck was hiding around. We were being quiet and deliberate. Suddenly Dell exclaimed, "Look at that!" I ignored him and continued down the empty road. Dell said again, much more excitedly this time, "John, Look!" He had my attention, and I swung around to look curiously. Suddenly I could see it! About seven hundred yards down the road, in the dark, running straight at us was about a four to five hundred pound beast of some sort. It was running very quickly towards us; I figured about twenty to thirty miles an hour. But it wasn't running at Dell. It seemed to have its sights directed straight at me! Dell yelled, "Run man!" And he booted it!

But I did not see this as the solution, for me at least, as the beast was bearing down towards me. I stared at the Creature, and realized it was an albino bear coming down the center line, with no breaks! We locked eyes, and I pondered my possibilities! I planted my feet on the pavement and unleashed a monolithic, "FUCK OFF!!" louder than I believe I had ever shouted before, or since. The albino bear suddenly, without breaking a stride, turned to its right and ran off the road and up a steep grassy hill, and out of sight. In a mega second this all went down. I yelled, to Dell,

"Hey, you can stop running. It's gone!"

Dell, insightfully as an Owl, screeched, "It might come back!"

I conceded to his conclusion and started running in overdrive.

We got to the truck, all spooked and spaced out, and hopped in. I told Dell to drive around the corner and along the ditch, as I threw the bags of plants in the back. I tied the tarp down and we hit the road. We drove carefully, as it was now a suspicious time of early morning to be cruising in a tarped truck, with our hearts racing and eyes like saucers!

We began to chill, and drove straight to the local corn fields to harvest the other crops. Arriving at the first field in the dark, Dell asked me how we would find the plants that we hadn't been to in months. We could barely even see. I told him that I had a trick up my sleeve, and I began to wade into the *Maise Menagerie* before us.

I signaled to a tree, and took a piece of paper out of my pocket. It had names of some of my favorite Montreal Canadien hockey players on it. Dell looked at it and queried a resounding, "Huh?" I explained the numbers of the players were how many rows to count in, to arrive at plants... seven rows in for Howie Morenz, and Yank! Four more rows in for Jean Beliveau; Yank! Five more rows for Boom Boom Geoffrion; Yank!, then nine more for Maurice Richard and Yank, Yank (there was two plants for the Rocket), ten more rows for Guy Lafleur; Yank!, Twelve more rows for Yvan Cournoyer and Dickie Moore; Yank!, Yank!, sixteen more rows in for Henri Richard; Yank!, eighteen for Serge Savard; Yank!, nineteen more in for Larry Robinson and Yank! Twenty two for John Ferguson; Yanked (the biggest one!), twenty-three for Bob Gainey; Yank!, another twenty-five rows for Jacques Lemaire; Yank!, and twenty-nine more rows for Ken Dryden brought us to the last plant in this field.

We drove off to other fields where I found my landmark trees, or posts, and counted the same pattern in for each field. We harvested every plant we planted. We got back to the Farm and immediately hung all the plants to dry, and then I woke up the Girls and enjoyed a Sweet Reunion.

Over the next five days, Dell and I loaded a rented twenty-six foot cube-truck with everything we owned. Then we finally embarked on our move Out West. Kori took a plane a week later to the Sumas, and moved into the rather empty house I had rented with Leon's assistance. She then needed to wait for us. She waited, and waited! Meanwhile Dell and I drove our rig unceremoniously until we got to 'Rogers Pass'; the steepest and most rickety stretch of road of the Canadian Rocky Mountains. Here our overloaded truck went through the brakes on the incredibly steep mountain roadways, which were more like paved trails.

I didn't tell Dell, but I was having a different problem at that moment. The last month of activities and travel was getting to me I guess, because I was seeing double as I was driving. I was about to enter a tunnel that went through the mountain, and I calmly asked, "Dell, which opening do I take?" Dell looked at me and asked what the hell I was talking about. I explained my conundrum, that there were two openings to enter the rock tunnel, and I couldn't tell which one to take.

Dell and I had been through a lot in the last ten days, but this was new to us; seeing double traversing Rogers Pass! I asked again, "Which opening do we take?" Dell ratified there was only one tunnel opening, so take it! I answered, "But is it the right opening, or the left?" I looked at Dell and realized I was truly on my own. I stared straight ahead and exclaimed, "Ok. I'm taking this one!" And at between seventy to eighty km's an hour, I drove into an oblivion. I shut my eyes, momentarily, and drove into what could be a blunt impact. I simply drove into what I presumed was the correct tunnel opening, and Whooosh!

I guess it was the right one because I'm telling the story today. Dell shook his head. He said that he had an epiphany that we were either in heaven, or hell. But actually we were still in the truck, and in one piece! We drove through the long lighted tunnel of otherwise darkness, and lumbered on.

I was now using the gears to descend the steep hills, jamming into lower gears to stay on the road. This went on for about twenty minutes of precipitous navigating, until Dell, who figured the worst must be behind us by now, calmly responded to my driving prowess that,

"This is kind of hard on the ol' gear box, didn't I think?"

I confided, "Dell, I wasn't gonna say anything, but we haven't had any brakes now for over twenty minutes!"

Seeing as I somehow chose the right tunnel, Dell decided to let me field this latest catastrophe. We were only half way down Rogers Pass and I could smell metal on metal burning. I was just waiting for the transmission to explode. Suddenly I saw a spot I could pull off the road on, with a tree at the far end for good measure.

I geared down one more steel scraping time, and veered off onto the small runway. We kept slowing down until we crept up to the tree at the end, and feebly stopped a couple inches before hitting it. I lit a joint, let the transmission and brakes cool off, and continued our western plight.

We made it to the house a couple days late. Kori figured we were dead. I wasn't sure she was wrong. Dell offered to unload some furniture and beds to make the situation more comfortable. I went out to the Pick-up and grabbed fifteen pot clones that I had perched on the dash board, to enjoy the sun on the trip out. We were all alive, the vehicles were ok, and the clones (named 'Elvis-clones') were doing just fine. I judged that the Trip had been a success, so I went over to Leonardo's to get real high.

The Bookmobile

Mrs. Griffiths was my inspiration to read more. When I was in grades four to seven, I read the Sports Section of the Hamilton Spector Newspaper daily, to follow Montreal hockey scores. They didn't televise Montreal games in Ontario, only Toronto's. I read the Canadian Magazine, and I scanned Hockey Magazines. Of course I read the comics. But Mrs. Griffiths demanded excellence and energy from her pupils, and excellence was obtained, she reasoned, through reading.

I read a new book every week or two from the Bookmobile. I don't know why I allowed her to mould me as she did. I guess I never really trusted anyone with my mind before Mrs. Griffiths.

I wonder if she touched anybody else the way she energised me. I was suddenly reading accounts of the British evacuating Dunkirk under the Nazi brow. I was reading National Geographic instead of comics, and not just for the pictures.

I would have missed so much of what I know as Life today without her. Cherish!

I've read in spurts much of my life. I took Native Studies in University English. We read thirty five books and stories about Native Life and Culture. I was intrigued to study the Human Beings. I always had interest in their music, and totems poles, and the Five Nations of the Iroquois, the Cree, Sitting Bull, Chief Dan George, their Artwork and carvings and their psyche. Leon once gave me a series of twenty-five inspiring Native paintings. Unfortunately, every Native story I read in my course opened with a basic theme of;

"I was born in this land. My parents were persecuted and their Native Language was beaten out of them. We were poor. We children were taken away from our parents to attend White Schools, and to learn the English language. I was an alcoholic at a young age, trying to cope with being a second class citizen in a White World. I became a whore for ten years in Vancouver. I sobered up one year, and started attending school. I achieved a degree in Sociology and another in Human Rights. I obtained a job teaching and wrote this book. I never saw my parents again, and I am working to make sure my children get the chances I didn't have."

Actually that's a good story. Many of them didn't have a 'happy' or 'fulfilled' ending. It was agonizing reading most of the texts. But I had to read through the sorrow to feel their Pain. I realized I needed to learn how lucky I'd been. I've been fortunate to know some Native Musicians. They are Strong Creatures and True Artists. Everything comes from pain. They are evolving, and turning their Pain into Art. Check out Musician Mark LaForme and His Rocks in Brantford!

During High School I was one of those dudes that always carried a novel in my pocket. Everybody I knew did, and some still do. The internet sucks, and is a blockage to the human experience of reading books that Artists/Authors spent years crafting into literary masterpieces! I've dug many contemporary Authors and Philosophers, including the *time tested volumes* of Voltaire, Locke, Emmerson, Engels, Einstein and of course I own a copy of 'Mein Kampf'. Nietzsche was a very popular read back then in the Age of searching for God, or finding out why we killed Him, or why He kills us.

Books that were essential to my being a young bibliophile in the Sixties, Seventies and Eighties were inspired by authors like Jacqueline Susann, Helen Gurly Brown, and Nelle Harper Lee, who helped bend the horizons for writers such as Ken Kesey, Thomas Wolfe, Tony Morison, Kurt Vonnegut, William Styron, Stephen King, Judith Krantz, Frederick Forsyth, E.L. Doctorow, Hunter S. Thompson, Judy Blume, Robert Pirsig (Zen and the Art of Motorcycle Maintenance), … let's just say all our pockets were always full of stimulating authors and adventures!

In Grade Nine I was captivated reading a book called 'The Magic of Myth and Legends. This handbook had us exploring the Adventures of Zeus, Hera, Poseidon, Demeter, Ares, Athena, Apollo, Artemis, Hephaestus, Aphrodite, Hermes, Dionysus, Hades, Hypnos, Nike, Janus, Nemesis, Iris, Hecate, and Tyche; aligning and alienating themselves from their own Creations. Many of these Gods I recognized mostly from movies and cartoons in my Youth. Of course many of these names have been given to cars; Native names like Chevrolet, Cheyenne, Apache, Impala, (dodge) Dakoda, (ford) Thunderbird, (Jeep) Cherokee and Comanche, Pontiac, Aztek and Winnebago. I find these scrounged names as offensive as Michael Jackson owning and using Beatle songs to sell shoes and such. Let him sell his own… I mean he was the greatest gift to unsung songs ever!

I inherited the complete selection of Hemingway, or should I say Kori did, but I read many of them. I still think he was over rated. But this led me to further explore the 'Lost Generation' authors that started the Twentieth Century off on a lost note. Thankyou Gertrude Stein!

These were books I could not read when I was young. My mind was not up to classics yet such as Ulysses, but I read Dubliners, The Dead, Finnegan's Wake and Exiles. I read The Portable James Joyce to examine what he was doing in 1968,

I read *J.J. Collected Poems* out of interest as I wrote poems before turning to writing books, and he the opposite. I read Ulysses when I was fifty eight. I had been writing every day for ten years and it prepared me for this modernist advent- garde technique from Dublin, as opposed to the Paris based books of much of the Lost Generation.

I was compelled to read The Great Gatsby because of my fixation for the 'Roaring Twenties'. Next I read 'Flappers and Philosophers'; then short fiction stories including 'Bernice Bobs Her Hair, The Ice Palace, Head and Shoulders, The Off Shore Pirate'... another Author who chose his War in Europe, as Hemingway and Orwell chose their Challenges in Spain. I read 'Tales of the Jazz Age' for insight into the topic, and I must admit, I read 'Tender is the Night' because I have used that line in poetry and prose and songs multiple times over the years. It is such a beautiful and insightful line to me. 'This Side of Paradise' offered me a key hole into the lives and morality after WW1. 'Babylon Revisited' gave a look into the end of the 'Jazz Age' and on into the Dirty Thirties; a time I find captivating due to my attraction for Woody Guthrie's stories of the Thirties in 'Bound for Glory' (which also inspired me to read 'This Land is Your Land',' House of Earth', 'Bling Bland' (which I read because of the cover), 'Seeds of Man' (his family trip in their Model T Ford from the Panhandle to Big Bend country in 1931), and the 'Woody Guthrie Songbook' I purchased in 2005.

Earnest Hemmingway forever captured my heart with his courage when he said about Scot Fitzgerald, "His talent was as natural as the pattern that was made by the dust on a butter-fly's wings."

T.S. Elliot was/is one of my favourite twentieth century poets (The Wasteland, The Hollow Men, The Love Song of J. Alfred Prufrock, Little Gidding). Ezra Pound (who Bob Dylan's 'Desolation Row' turned me on to), William Butler Yeats, Walt Whitman, Robert Frost, W.H. Auden, Andrew Lloyd Webber, E.E. Cummings, Emily Dickenson, Virginia Woolf (whose afraid?), Dylan Thomas, Sylvia Plath, Valarie Eliot, William Faulkner, etcetera… writers from different ages and galaxies!

Some of the most pleasant literary surprises I have been lucky enough to stumble upon was when purchasing paper backs in Bus Stations. There are always novels by Stephen King, Kurt Vonnegut, Salman Rushdie, Margaret Atwood Steve Stern or Terese Svoboda with her novels, stories, memoirs, biographies, poetry and even libretto! (check her out!).

One of my favourite 'surprises' came in the form of the Jerry Hopkins and Danny Sugerman's paperback 'No One Here Gets Out Alive'. Now I believe that the book is always almost embarrassingly superior to the movie (read 'The World According To Garp', and then suffer through Robbin Williams trying to portray John Irving's message through tinsel, glitter, Producers, Directors, and a battered Ego coming off Robert Altman's dud 'Popeye'). But Val Kilmer nailed this book-turned-script dead on ten years later! When I would be downtown at the Studio all day, or week, I would browse the Bus Station on Rebecca Street when driving by, for 'surprising or forgotten gems' on tacky steel book racks; something like searching the CD bins in Department Stores; exploiting the ending of a dead form of Art…

I was driving through Chicago with Oak once and I stopped into 'Myopic Books' on Milwaukee Avenue with pennies in my pockets and a couple books on my mind. But I quickly blew my budget on a hard copy version of Robert Kennedy's 'The Enemy Within'. This book inspired a few epic songs out of my creviced cranium, and sits perched beside my framed picture of RFK, with the caption, "Some men see things as they are, and ask why. I dream of things that never were, and ask why not?"…

Feeding my mantra of, 'I am not Worthy' every Christmas I received only books, and the odd pair of socks. I have received dozens of hard copied books on The Beatles, each with a crumble of something new for me, even though I was sure there was nothing about the Fab Four that I could not possibly know by then… but that's part of the 'Pleasant Surprises'!

My Aunt Kirk gave me every National Geographic from 1919 to 1979. The issues from 1919 to 1929 were bound in leather covers for each year.

Thank you Aunt Kirk!

A golden opportunity came along for me to devour a book a week when I was hired to feed and support some beautiful race horses, in the barns at Flamborough Downs Race Track. I found I could get all my chores done in the first three hours, which left me four hours of my eight hour shift to read. I was able to read over seventy books in just over a year.

I started off my perusal pleasures quite deliberately, with Hunter S. Thompson's 'Rum Diaries'. I read somewhere that this was one of his 'weaker' books and I immediately thought, "I'd love to read the rottenest thing Hunter ever wrote! I'd be my pleasure!" The movie with Johnny Depp was simply Artiste working with Artist. That means a lot more to me than labelling someone a 'genius'. Anyone can be a genus. But it's what you do with the earth, wind, and fire within is what counts!

I've been reading Hunter Thompson since 1971, as a Profit, Beelzebub, a Walking Contradiction, and a Problem when he's Stoned, (thanx Kris). His time spent at Rolling Stone was inspirational and brutal. But no one paid dues like this guy. He was shit kicked deluxe while in Cuba writing for the Newspaper, twice! A few years later the Hells Angels punched him out for royalties in his novel entitled 'Hells Angels'. But he wrote what he meant, and said what he thought, no matter what drug or incantation the thought originated from.

I tried to accomplish something on this spree I wanted to do for a while; to read every one of Thomas Wolfe's books. In my library

I built I have shelved around six hundred books. Kori bought a cross section of them for me through the years, knowing my train of thoughts and interests. I had at least a dozen of Wolfe's works tucked away in my bibliotheca. I started with his first and only fiction, 'Bonfire of the Vanities'. Who knew that sometimes fiction can be as good as fact... in the right hands! Next, I couldn't help it... I reread, for probably the twentieth time, my teenage bible; 'The Electric Kool-aide Acid Test'. I reread 'The Painted Word', as I did 'The Kandy-Kolored Tangerine-flake Streamlined Baby'. Next was 'From Bauhaus to our House', 'Radical Chick', 'I am Charlotte Simmons', 'The Pump House Gang', 'The Purple Decades', 'Mauve Gloves & Madmen, 'Clutter and Vine', 'The New Journalism', 'The Me Decade', 'Horse Carving', and 'Wood Spirits'. I deliberately left 'The Right Stuff' for last because I didn't think I'd like it!! But it was absolutely my favorite thing Wolfe ever wrote. Who would have thought! I never kept up to Tom in his volumes and volumes of 'carving codex's', which means I've probably still only read half of his books!

I read a variety of English and French philosophers during this spurt from Voltaire, Montesquieu, Jean-Jacques Rousseau, Denis Diderot, to John Locke, Thomas Reid, Daniel Raymond, K.L. Reinhold...

Reading takes me to Strange and Unknown Places. I always become part of the transcript I'm rendering... an unidentified character lost between the lines, but living out the plot on my own terms. I can be sitting on the couch scrutinizing a page, but there are winds blowing, leaves rustling, and Prophets and Druids behind every tree in my Erudite Mind. I'm Chuck Yeager searching for the seat ejection button, or Sammy Davis Junior grappling with the IRS...

Trouble is that I'm writing so much I don't have the time to read much these days. I sometimes don't have time enough to write either, so often when I want/need to, I have to make sacrifices.

Unfortunately I do not eschew enough reading because my clock has begun running backwards. Here's one for he Chart: 'I Need a New Sacrifice'!

Chapter 27
Goin' Home (but not
by helicopter)

Eventually the economy picked up after Reagan did his Voodoo Regan-omics thing in the White House. I'd been in different Colleges for most of the decade, and I went out West to Work for an Occupational Therapist I had hooked up with.

Dell was in love with B.C., and Kori started having babies. I had managed to save about fifty grand in my days of *Tricks and Treats*, and after my loving Aunty Gert left me a heart-felt inheritance, Bud phoned me and offered to sell me his Farm. Remember Bud?

I had tried to buy the field across the road from the Farm years earlier off Bud, only to find out I was a day late. Bud had sold it to Hunter Wagner (aka Killer) the day before. But this was even better. The farm had it all; a large brick house, barns, silos, tractors and *family memories*... hmmmmmmmm...

So anyway I quit my job and moved my expanding family east. I once again loaded up a rental twenty-four foot long cube truck with our possessions, and then I hitched up a four wheel trailer to tow my half ton pickup. I travelled through Rocky Mountain blizzards and flooded Canadian prairies in early April until I came to the Town of Iroquois, on the Precambrian Shield, in Northern Ontario. I had been travelling three days without many stops, and I figured I would make it back to Hamilton that night. Kori had rented a house in Hamilton where she would wait for me, and the purchase of Bud's Farm.

With 'Six days on the road and I'm gonna make it home Tonight' blaring on the speakers, I was pumped. As I ventured south on the Trans Canada, I was in a good mood. Suddenly I felt the truck sway unnaturally to the left, then dramatically to the right. I figured I must have had a double tire blowout because I swerved so uncontrollably.

I had a blowout back in the Rockies to compare this to; a blowout in the middle of absolutely nowhere. I pulled over in mountains amid the snowy remains of a winter that refused to leave. A quick glimpse out of my mirror revealed no traffic was behind me, and cell phones weren't the rage yet. I prepared myself that I was in the middle of nowhere, and it would be dark in two hours. I got out and surveyed the situation. The first thing I noticed, way out there, was a pay phone. Go figure! In an hour I was back on the road.

But that's another story. This was today's blowout. I became pissed when I thought of having two flat tires (at least) on one road trip in this Rented Monstrosity. This sucked hugely. I was thinking that the Rental Company was going to hear about this, and that I wasn't going home tonight. I looked out the window, once again looking for a phone booth.

Suddenly my head cleared and I thought out loud," The trailer!" I pulled over and jumped fearfully out of the truck. I was not looking for a flat tire, or two, I was looking for whoever the trailer had hit, and inevitably demolished! I was going out for a head count of smashed vehicles and broken bones! Again I thought out loud to myself, "Man! How many dead bodies could there be strewn on the hi-way!" I didn't want the Souls of those at Iroquois Falls to enter my mind the way the Indian Spirits did to Jim Morrison on that day he inadvertently became a Junior Shaman after witnessing the remnants of a car crash involving

Indian spirits out in the desert. Dead at twenty-seven! Lying in a bath tub bloated. Extinction! Was I going to jail? I figured it couldn't get any worse than this!

As I was running back I saw the pick-up truck and trailer were indeed gone! But further back I saw them harmlessly lying in the ditch. There were no fatalities.

I called the cops and directed them to the Scene. A tow truck pulled over and asked me if the truck in the ditch was mine. I affirmed it was, and he waded down for a closer look as the Police showed up. They assisted me to the cab where my rental papers were.

They wanted to know why the cab smelled like marijuana, and I suddenly remembered I had a big stash of pot stashed in the back of the cube truck. But it wasn't that pot that smelled. It was a tiny quarter ounce Leonardo had given me when I left Abbotsford to start this trip! I was not smoking it because with three consecutive days at the wheel, a joint would have burned me down... it would have knocked me out. The small pungent bag had been sitting in my coat pocket the whole time across the country. My coat was buried under a mound of clothes and supplies.

Now this was some boss Indica from Washington State. It smelled like a skunk, and so did the truck! He started searching immediately, but I suggested that maybe what we were actually smelling was the half dozen wine-tipped cigar butts that were sitting in the ashtray. After five futile minutes of searching he conceded that was probably the case. He crawled out of the cab and talked to the Tow Truck Driver, and left the scene.

The tow-truck driver asked me where I was headed, and I told him Hamilton. He suggested that the battered pick-up and trailer should be dropped off at the Truck Rental Office. I asked "Why take the demolished pick-up to the Rental Company?" He explained that the hitch had been broken when they rented the trailer to me. I asked him how he figured, and he showed me that where the fracture was, there was massive rust, verifying the old crack that had finally separated ... on my shift!

So I kept on truckin' on to the house in Hamilton Kori had rented. I phoned the small Rental Office called *'Gotta Move'* in Waterdown that rented me the truck to discuss the matter... In the meantime, I took the half hitches off the truck and the trailer to a Metallurgist, for an Expert's opinion, which would hopefully confirm my present claim that the hitch was cracked when they rented it to me. Prognosis Positive!

When I attended the meeting in Waterdown, they treated me shabbily and disrespectfully. Sort of confused, I said I could see I might as well leave, and I would have my Professional contact them about it. They smiled and drawled facetiously,

"O, so you're going to send a lawyer over?" she brayed sarcastically?

I answered, "No. A Metallurgist."

Every jaw in the garage dropped. "What's the name of the Metallurgist?" they demanded. When I told them which Metallurgist, they exclaimed that they were aware he was first rate. I answered, "I know. He says I could have been killed," and I proceeded towards the door. They called me back before I made it to the exit, and asked me to itemize every loss I had incurred, and to present them a total bill. They assured me I would be reimbursed for every cent. It's funny how things turn out when you use your head. Or, conversely, when you don't!

Later that night at my temporary lodgings I received a phone call from my brother-in-law Richard, who asked me how the trip was, and then got down to business telling me Bud had sold his farm to my cousin. I responded,

"So what am I doing here?"

Rich said, "I don't know."

When I phoned Bud, he quietly admitted it was true, and offered no explanation. I decided it was for the best, anyway. Too many memories and ghosts were attached to this farm. Like this latest one, and the one of my leaving this farm at fourteen years old, and Jack's departure, etcetera, etcetera...

Kori and I bought a spectacular couple of acres with a bungalow on it on the side of Bronte Creek, in Strabane. I gutted the house entirely, and rebuilt it using my imagination, and the code book. It kept me busy...

One busy day a relic from St. Mary's invited me to join the Dundas Chapter of the Odd Fellows. Food for thought, thought I.

The Independent Order of Odd Fellows (IOOF);

The Independent Order of Odd Fellows (IOOF) is a non-political and non-sectarian international fraternity order of Odd Fellowship. It was founded in 1819 by Thomas Wildery in Baltimore, Maryland, U.S. Evolving from the Order of Odd Fellows founded in England during the n1700s, the IOOF was originally charted by the Independent Order of Oddfellows Manchester Unity in England, but has operated as an independent organization since 1842, although it maintains an inter-fraternal relationship with the English Order. The order is also known as the Triple Link *Fraternity*, referring to the order's "Triple Links" symbol, alluding to its motto "Friendship, Love and Truth". The current organization of the Dundas Odd Fellows in the Valley City Lodge No 117, which received its official charter from the Grand Lodge of Ontario on July 10, 1873, has played a leading role in the community affairs ever since.

There were a core of sincere members of the Dundas Chapter, doing noteworthy-charity work and humanitarian causes. And there were those who enjoyed a cold beer with their Nineteenth Century Cultures. I must admit I fell into that latter category quickly. The Lodge was a fantastic building of Age and Customs. It had antique Pews and Pulpits, and rooms fashioned after Parliamentary Buildings in days of yore. It had the aura of an English Court House. But the most popular space used, after the formal weekly meeting, inevitably, was the Pub Room.

The Pub Room was like a ninetieth century Grog Shop. Everyone rolled comically out of the Hall late after a productive night. There was musical entertainment and frivolities most weeks. I met the President at that time, Phil Errup, who was a character, thank you! One night Phil was entertaining some Ladies and his alcohol Intake, at his apartment. When he found himself dry of liquidly ecstasies, he had the notion to walk a block over to the Hall, and use his key to enter. He intended to retrieve some stout he had left there earlier that day. And the genialness of his plan certainly held up, until he sat down for a moment to ponder his strategy outside the locked door. The next morning he was still sitting there, as he had fallen asleep. The alcohol in him kept him rosy over the freezing night. It was all good. I immediately thought to myself, "This is the fellow, I mean Odd Fellow I might want to get to know. I asked him, "Can you walk on water, too?" He grinned.

Cowboys and Superstars

I dazedly awoke one morning in 2009 to manually work on changing the septic beds in my back yard. While reconstructing my antiquated sewer system, I had to stop and write down another head full of ideas that were driving me insane. (Thankyou Mr. Zimmerman)! It was a poem I wrote to my favorite musical Artist ever, Gram Parsons! Gram was my Elvis. Everything evolved around his sound, for me. The Doors were my favorite group, and Dylan my favourite song writer, Jeff Beck was the greatest guitarist, but it was Gram that stirred my soul!

I went back to work digging when I was finished with my words. I chopped and chiselled the dirt from where it lay, and I was suddenly doing it to a beat. I went inside and sang the words I had written an hour before to the upbeat country style in my head. I suddenly realized I had written my first *Country* song. So here's to Gram;

Broken Wing

Got up to have my morning cry
And I had a coffee too
As the time it shortly came
I just sat and thought of you.
Though time and trouble were your only clue
That gift God gave named Emmy Lou
Kept you in tune to say good bye
I hear your voice when the desert winds cry.

In that hour of darkness that I see
The cowboy angel sings to me
Why couldn't you just smile and let it be
And join the circle around the Joshua Tree.

More time than I ever know what to do
Darkness seeps through my window pane
Sunrise peeking and daylight creeping
Today's country music is just profane!
Night smells of hickory in the wind
Got up in the morning to let the Hound Dog in
Singing soulful songs with that Waycross grin
While listening to Hank and drinkin' Southern gin.

In that hour of darkness that I see
The cowboy angel sings to me
Why couldn't you just smile and let it be
And join the circle around the Joshua Tree.

Soared high with Byrds singin' in the sky
On their way up saw you fly by
You warned us to never forget your lies
On your way through life you've found the time to die.
So take your Wheels and Do Right man
Farther Along they'll understand
We'll leave your soul in Sin City
And let you sleep in harmony.

This hour of daylight I can see
The cowboy angel sings to me
Seems now we've gotta let it be
Your time is your own under the Joshua Tree.

My buddy Stan came in and asked why he was the only one still digging. I sang him my new song but he was more into finishing the job. So we went back to workin' like dogs; digging and howling. Much later that night I went back to finishing up chapter three of my book I was doggedly writing.

The next morning Kori expressed that she would like to use the shower, and would I hurry up constructing the sewer system. She asked what the hold-up was. When I retorted that I needed a couple more days, as I had been writing 'at both ends of the candle', she said that was nice, but for me to knock-off writing until the sewer was completed, so she didn't have to shower at her mother's house again. I said that I couldn't help it that I was now writing songs.

I don't know if she took me seriously, but she reiterated to, "Get back on the shovel". She then stormed off to work. She *huffed* off, and I yelled to bid her adieu. She grumbled something and slammed the door behind her. I yelled, at nobody in particular at that point, "I'm an Artist for Freud sakes!" I immediately penned, 'Neon Blue':

I look in the light and see neon blue
Think back in time now without a clue
Good times ya I guess I had a few
I've seen better days but none of them are with You.

Don't matter what side of the bed that I rise
When you sleep in a one man cot
I think of the things that I should have done
You remind me of ones I did not.

Ya 20-20 ain't never one on one
But in a blaze I got burnt in the sun
Now if I never do get anything done
Gonna follow my heart gonna have some fun.

Paddling back up stream it's all clear now
Nothing you ever said but how
Those knock out years I never want a fight
No wonder cause I ain't never been right.

You say my problem is that log in your eye
I just take another toke and sigh
And feel something deep inside us both die
But you know I never did learn how to cry.

Ya 20-20 ain't never one on one
But in a blaze I got burnt in the sun
Now if I never do get anything done
Gonna follow my heart gonna have some fun.

So start up your engine and just amble along
And I'll just chalk it up in a song
In the end I guess that's where it belongs
Guess I should have wrote it when I was more young

I look in the light and see neon blue
Think back in time still without a clue
Good time ya I guess I've had a few
I've seen better days but none of them were with You!

I finished these daunting lyrics and put them down. Wow. What a lesson! I immediately realized everything said or done is absolute fuel for writing lyrics that don't go, "How much is that doggie in the Window?" I felt in my heart right away how the melody would go; burning and bitingly; southern rock style! I had written seven pages in my novella just hours before. I was going through a stage where the more I wrote the more ideas were coming out in every direction. For Beelzebub's sake, I took time off at two am to right down some stand-up comedy jokes and routines. Mozart must have been high as hash on natural gas!

Stan boxed in and grinned. He was a skilled entity; the type that excelled at all types of skilled labour, or Artistic challenge. I sang him my new composition. He dug it. Stan played acoustic guitar and I got him to teach my daughter, who today can play any instrument. Another natural! But I realized right then that I was a natural singer from the 'Yea, Yea, Yea' days of Ed Sullivan to this awakening moment. I substantiated that I should sing my own songs, and maybe put some time into finding a band.

But I didn't want a band of my talented buddies. I visited some Producers/Recorders who mostly efficiently worked out of their own houses effectively. Some were good. Most of the kids I went to High School with became musicians and were/ are a big part of the Hamilton Sound since the Seventies. Some friends wanted to record songs with me and I was thrilled they liked my songs! But when I got home, on a whim, I opened the Yellow Pages and looked under 'Recording Studios'. I looked up the number of Grant Avenue Studio and talked to Bob Doidge; Producer and Owner of the Studio on Grant Avenue, close to Downtown Hamilton. It was originally owned by Daniel Lanois as an extension of his basement, where it was getting crowded recording the likes of Raffi, Bruce Cockburn and many other Artists. Bob, originally from groups 'Tranquility Base' the 'Ian Thomas Band', Ray Materick and Shirley Eikard, took over ownership of *Grant Studio* in 1985.

I told Bob that at this point, I had completed about thirty songs, and I needed a Band, a Producer and a Studio. For some reason Bob sounded somewhat intrigued. He invited me down to see what I had going on. The next day I took a couple dozen songs and visited this rock icon. He appealed to me as an Irishman (he is actually half French on his mother's side, and part English, from Balliwick of Guernsey off Alderney of the Channel Islands) with a tale or twenty to tell. And he had the chance to tell them as often as he liked, owning a Studio that had attracted Artists to record such as Johnny Cash (he came in the Studio and the first thing he said was "Hello, I'm Johnny Cash") , Ani Difranco, U-2, Gordon Lightfoot, The Tea Party, Collective Soul, Finger Eleven, Theory of a Deadman, Default, Tom Wilson and many, many others.

Something that Bob said to me resounded as something rather interesting, which was, "Anyone can own recording equipment, even the finest and newest, but that doesn't mean he can record any good." I stood back and looked at the pictures on the wall of some of Rock & Roll's greatest Artists. I realized right there I was gonna be doin' some recording here on Grant Avenue.

Bob seemed to seem to think my songs were worth recording, and he offered to produce them. That was ok. But a disparity arose between what Bob wanted, and what I expected. Bob wanted to teach me 'ins and outs' of music, far more in depth from the habitual and conventional recording experience I expected. On our first visit together, he insisted I practice singing every song with a metronome because I was not a proficient enough musician, to his professional ear. Exacting the beats-per-minute (BPM) so the rhythms could be played accurately was our bridge to each other, at first.

Now when I got together with buddies who played my songs with me, either on piano or guitar, we relied on our simultaneous timing in reaction to my singing. That seemed to work better for me than worrying about being dead-on with a metronome. However Bob accurately insisted he needed it to understand where I was going with my rhythms and timing.

I figured I had sung along with the best of Ed Sullivan long enough to feel I had some *'natural timing'*. I could feel a song out *well enough* to express the chords for whoever I played with. I brought out a stack of metronome tunes at the Studio one day, and Bob patiently listened to them. Bob was a patient man, which was part of why he was a great producer. His horn playing is right out of the 40's (the golden age of Charlie Parker, Dizzy Gillespie, Thelonious Monk, Louis Armstrong, Glenn Miller)... He should have linked up with Gordon Lightfoot and become his bass player... but he did alright on his own path.

I was so sick of the boing-boing sound that I brought out some new songs. One started off;

When I look back without a sound
I see my footprints in the ground...

Bob really liked the start. He called it *genius,* something he would never admit to today, unless it became a Top Ten Hit of course. In today's Millennium, I guess there are just so many great singers, song writers and musicians that it's tough to be acknowledged. But I wasn't looking for complements (don't believe that) as much as I just wanted to start recording. Bob educated and waited on me to get it together musically. He insisted that I take my time, giving me examples of how some Artists rehearse and perform, like Golden Gord himself. I announced to a couple Musicians, who wanted to record with me, that it had been a couple months since I first entered Grant Avenue Studio, and I was thinking I was never gonna get anything recorded. That's when the phone rang.

Someone from Grant Studio named Amy King told me she had played a few of my songs I taped, and she "didn't know what the problem was"...She said she dug the songs, and saw no reason why we couldn't record them soon. She told me she had put some chords together on the bass guitar, and I should listen to them. She said if I liked the Sound, Bob could put the band together, and we could get some bed tracks down, and then we could take it from there... Now this was more my kind of language. No Master and Student scenario. Just, 'let's make some Music'!

I listened to a disc she made of four of my songs. I was knocked out. It was just what I was looking for. Or should I say, Amy was what/who I was looking for. I could feel a connection musically and intellectually between us immediately. She tuned into my Southern and Blues influences. I was as ready to rock as she was to roll.

That afternoon Kori led the kids and I into Tim Hortons. I overheard a couple of kids talking by the door. One of them expressed that she felt, "Like a Superstar!" As I walked through the door that one of the girls was holding open, I mused, "Yea but You can only be a Superstar so far!" I immediately started singing the line like a mantra. By the time we reached the counter I had half the song written in my head. It was so natural I knew it was finished in my head, and any time I wanted to retrieve it,

I could finish it. I realized that I could get a verse and a chorus in my head, and then I could move on to something else. After this little discovery I was able to write two, three songs a day. I had to put my first book on hold until I got these songs out of my system. But they didn't stop. And I started recording everything with Amy and my new Studio Band, which consisted of Stompin' Tom Connor's band members like drummer Danny Lockwood, the incredible Mark LaForme on harmonica, Bob on bass, Vince Rinaldo on Keyboards and such, Amy on piano and production (and every instrument available in the Studio), Frank Koran on guitars, as well as many professional Musicians from the area, as needed.

I filed into the Studio the next day with my usual four songs. Amy and I would transpose my audible notes into equivalent keys on the piano, and then transpose the keys on the frets. Once everyone knew the music and math in their minds, (it only takes about a minute) the bed-tracks could be quickly created. More times than not, it would be accomplished on the first run through. We would record four bed-tracks every morning. Afternoons were for over dubs and vocal tracks. We had a good system, and we were productive.

I had worked out the 'Superstar' song in my truck while waiting for the Band to show up one morning. I had dedicated the lyrics towards Sly Stone, who the radio had just announced was living in a trashed trailer after years of too much cocaine abuse, and not enough royalties from his crooked contract. They made it sound like he was truly undone. I scribbled out the last of the words as Amy appeared.

I followed her into the Studio where we doubled up at the Grand Piano. Bob and the other Lads picked up their instruments, and changed our keys into chords on their blades in no time. These guys were so in tune with each other musically that they simply played as One. They could finish a sneeze for each other; in the same beat of course.

Amy announced to the Lads that we would start with a song I had just written that morn. Everybody was primed and proper... this is what they did all their lives. Amy asked me to sing along on the first attempt. We were all so in synch we rarely ever did more than two tracks.

They started up and I sang;

You can only be a Superstar so far
You can only be a Superstar so far
Be a Superstar all your life that's fine
Long as in the end life leaves you a dime.

I love you for
Who you are
Shine on me you
Superstar.
Everybody's
Feelings getting stronger
Everyday people can't
Wait no longer.

You can only be a Superstar so far
You can only be a Superstar so far
Be a Superstar all your life that's fine
Long as in the end life leaves you a dime.

Stand tall
Using lines you know
Stood high in Vegas for
Every show.
Life on the ground finds
No need to come down

Keep smiling babe,
You used to blow that town.

You can only be a Superstar so far
You can only be a Superstar so far
Be a Superstar all your life that's fine
Long as in the end life leaves you a dime.

You got a sister
And a brother
Playing in harmony
With each other.
When you partied
You partied hearty
Next day always
Life got tardy.

You can only be a Superstar so far
You can only be a Superstar so far
Be a Superstar all your life that's fine
Long as in the end life leaves you a dime.

You can make it
If you try
I'm trying too but life
Seems to lie.
I don't know better
Neither did you
They took your royalties
And left you the blues.

You can only be a Superstar so far
You can only be a Superstar so far
Be a Superstar all your life that's fine
Long as in the end life leaves you a dime.

Those summer days
High, High, High
Shout when you want don't
Be so Sly.
Life is calling
It's your time put a
Smile on your face
Continue to shine.

You can only be a Superstar so far
You can only be a Superstar so far
Be a Superstar all your life that's fine
Long as in the end life leaves you a dime.

We finished the usual four bed tracks before lunch and then created over dubs for a couple hours. Bob was producing long after the Band left, with me by his side in the Control Room. It was a good session, and I wanted to do a vocal track for 'Superstar', which I thought was hot. Bob balked saying he was exhausted.

I countered, still full of energy, "Let me do a single vocal track; if it works fine, if not, c'est la vie." Bob nodded ok and I shuffled up to the mike and sang the song once, in a funky voice that simply worked. Behind the Board Bob announced, "Congratulations. You just recorded your song in one vocal track. Wonderful!"

I told Bob I wanted to sing it again, but he insisted it wasn't necessary. But I did sing it again, duplicating the first track the best I could. When finished, I suggested laying one track over the other for more sound and clarity. The result made it more powerful, though its delivery was still funky and laid back. Bob is a nifty producer, and the song took on a great sound. But something was still missing.

The next day Amy and I were alone in the Control Room, and I expressed to her that I felt something 'authentic' was missing on the track. She knew what I meant and made a call to a Black singing Artist she had heard of. The lady came over, and we played her the song as was. She said she liked it, so what did we want her to do with it? Only Amy could get away with the truth. She told her she wanted to make it sound, "More Black." The lady said she knew just what Amy meant, and she tore into it like a Southern Choir on fire! Amy layered her voice again and again until it sounded Black and Beautiful! It made the song into a whole new 'anthem'. I could see Amy understood my music and my beat. I had found my Studio Mentor! Thanks Amy!

Chapter 28
Johnny Depp

When I received Amy's phone call to record at Grant Studio, I was just about to purchase a new 'Screaming Eagle' motorcycle. But I had dozens of new songs driving me insane, so I took this new route and went into the Studio with a stack of more songs. She was a breath of fresh air. I needed an *inside Musician* that I could relate to. Bob provided a tight band and Amy became my Producer. All this was happening at a time when I had a sudden fascination with Johnny Depp. He was the inspiration, the trigger that provided musical images for a bunch of songs I wrote after watching some of his movies.

Having a beer, or twelve one night, and feeling, *'out on the range'*, I suddenly flipped on the tube, and in thirty five seconds my life would never be the same. The movie 'Blow' was playing. Johnny Depp, that is, George Jung, that is George Young in the movie, had just been admitted to Millbrook Penitentiary, where Gordon Liddy and his crew of NoGoodnicks were on hold.

George was in his shared cell, on the top bunk, battling with his cell mate Diego to let him sleep. In these thirty five seconds which I watched, Carlos had just confided to George that he was a Hombre con un sueno; a 'Dreamer with a Cause'. George was tired and tried to ignore Diego, until the Columbian asked him, "George, why are you in prison for trying to smuggle 660 pounds of pot into the basement of the Chicago Play Boy Club?" George said it was so because he got caught. Carlos explained to George that he got caught, "Because you had the wrong dream". George cocked his head and opened his eyes. Diego grinned and said "George... what do you know about cocaine?"

And there they suddenly were, oblivious that they were tired and lying on the dirty cement prison floor, discussing between them a plan... about George's single engine Cessna Plane (which he stole), and how much product it could carry, etcetera, etcetera... In the next frame, they were out of prison... putting into action their discussed dreams of transporting the greatest drug deals of manufactured cocaine, from the dirtiest Cartels in the Columbian Jungles, to the Concrete Jungles of Hollywood and America.

I checked the TVs program guide and saw this show was supplied by the Bell satellite, who replays movies the same night *ad nauseam*. So I switched the TV off and began to ponder. It took me back to days I hadn't thought about in years. Within the next three hours I located George Jung's book on-line, in which he wrote about his incredible adventures smuggling plane-loads of Columbian product. I then wrote a song, inspired by these thirty-five seconds of watching this Depp movie. Dozens of Depp inspirations followed quickly in the next weeks. (Some of these songs are on my website at: **go to YouTube & print in john-organ.rocks, and when the next page comes up, scroll down until you find John Organ - Topic, click on it & enjoy free songs!**)

What George and Diego were really about to do, unknown to them or an unsuspecting world, was to supply enough cocaine, in under a decade, to take out an entire American generation on dust. Not the kind from heaven, but the violent and disturbed slum-infested depths of hell, Columbia style. After watching *Blow* for thirty five seconds I turned off the TV and thought to myself, "Hell I knew people that were already doing this shit back in the early/mid Seventies. Our west coast clique was all freaked on the taste of Bolivian coke, and no other taste would do. I met people that would fly down to El Trompillo Airport and bring a consistent flow of Bolivian blow back; some to Ontario, and another to

B.C. Tourist passengers were allowed to bring back two bottles of wine each. That was the *catch*.

Now the only thing any of us ever stuck around grade twelve Chemistry Class for, was how to steal triple beam balance scales for a little dealing, and how to extract solids from liquids. An adequate education! So, emptied wine bottles were refilled with Bolivian water, and four ounces of Bolivian product each.

I knew different brave (or maybe stupid) people that made these trips for years. The first time I was introduced to this trip, a Columbian friend of mine who lived at Rochdale did it in 1972, just in time for the Stone's Exile on Main Street concert tour, which stopped for an evening at Maple Leaf Gardens. He hated the shitty blow sold at Rochdale College as much as I did. But that taste drove him to extremes, which included flights to violent third world countries for '*The Real Thing!*' Some friends of mine in B.C. knew people that did this trip also a couple years later. Would any of us ever even have dreamed of doing this before Beatle Ed set us straight?

I decided to tell the Freaks the Canadian story… just for the fact of the matter. The next day I went out and scored books on Carlo Escobar; Medellin el Padrino, George Jung; Smuggler, and Larry Lavin; who manically made three million a month dealing it out in greasy Philadelphia. I tied their biographies together with many personal stories from our own snow bleached days. For six weeks I researched these books, making notes and next I drafted a manuscript called, 'Important Exportin' Men'.

Coles Book Store said they would release it on consignment, so everything seemed to be going as should. But after a couple months of erudition, I suddenly wasn't just writing a book about the good ol' days. I started writing songs and melodies, basically inspired from the character(s) of Johnny Depp from his movies; Blow, Donnie Brasco, The Ninth Gate, The Rum Diary, Black Mass, and Dark Shadows'. Funny, considering how much Depp

affected my psyche with these movies, and made him my uncon-
tested favourite actor for twenty years,

I haven't liked any other Depp movies I've seen. But suddenly
I had written fifty songs ala J.D. and other galvanizing inspirations. And I was still writing my book every night. I decided I
needed a break somehow.

I realized I couldn't keep writing the book all night and
songs all day, so I phoned Grant Avenue Studio and told them I
needed a Producer, and a Band. And now here I was answering
this phone call from Producer Amy King, who would be part
of my band. Speed ahead to Now, and we have recorded over
two hundred and fifty songs together, with hundreds more tunes
ready to record (and hopefully sell). Thirty five seconds of Johnny
Depp led me to a new version of 'Vision and Adventure'!

I really should meet Johnny after a Hollywood Vampire
concert some dark shadowy night, and tell him I'm partly
His fault!

Chapter 29
Amy

Amy King is from The Rock, and she is living proof of the legend that Newfies are the result of one thousand years of breeding between the Irish, the Nordic Vikings, and every Rebel sailing on the rugged waves of the Atlantic! She doesn't wear an eye patch, but she walks with a swagger.

Amy and I have gone on rather incredible work sessions together at Grant Avenue Studio over the years. This includes recording fifty songs in twelve hours once in 2017. I sang for two days over and over to Amy's accompaniment on the Grand Piano. The next year we got together in May, and over three days we recorded sixty-three of me songs. In the early evening of the third day, I had nothing left, and I was falling asleep between songs. But Amy kept nudging me awake, and we kept recording. I was astounded that she could keep going herself, as well as keep me afloat. We finished off the fifty-odd songs I had rehearsed for months, and was prepared for. But Aim now asked me, "Didn't you say you had some more songs to record that you had just written before coming for this session, and shouldn't we record them?

I had been writing a lot after two months of rehearsing. I was inspired by Josh Homme of Queens of the Stone Age fame, as well as Eagles of Death Metal, Kyuss, Them Crooked Vultures, The Desert Sessions, Screaming Trees, Mondo Generator, Fififf Teeners, Masters of Reality, to name a few Projects. I've been in awe of Josh's Sound and Energy for fifteen years. I was devastated by the Islamic bombings in 2015 Paris, and the murders at the Bataclan Theatre, where the Eagles of Death Metal were playing before three Terrorists cowardly shot eighty-nine young fans. But we watched in awe as U-2 offered their Stage to Jesse and the Band three weeks later at Bercy Stadium. Jesse's interviews were stirring. They affectionately call him 'Cry Baby' and he has a 'Cry Baby' T-shirt. But Jesse was crying for the lost lives of his fans, his own lost trust in reality, and for the hope that his life, and everybody's involved in the tragedy, might ever be the same afterwards. Bono knew what to do to start the process by getting EODM back on stage before it became a stigma. Thanks Bono!

I felt particularly inspired by his interview he gave Paris TV before going on stage that night. I shared Jesse's grief with my own words of 'Cold Comfort';

Beyond Death
Fuck the thwart
I'm still alive
Cold Comfort.
Nothin' to Abort
Nothin' to snort
Devils High Court;
Rigors Mort.

Cold Comfort
Nothin' Hurts
Cold Comfort
Blood in Her Purse.
Cold Comfort
What's It mean?
Cold Comfort's
Just Obscene!

Night in Paris
Derailed
Somethin' fell Short

Ship Sailed.
Cowards; Fuck 'em
With guns
Never see
Another Sun!

Cold Comfort
I'm still Here!
Cold Comfort
Fuck the Fear!
Cold Comfort
My heart's Stranded!
Cold Comfort
The Eagle's Landed!

Where's the cops?
Fifteen Minutes!
Message in a Bottle
Fuckin' Spin It!
Get Down!
Get off the Stage!
Too Scared
To feel the Rage!

Cold Comfort
It's a Sin
Cold Comfort
Never Again!
Cold Comfort
I'm Alive
Cold Comfort
Moonlight Drive.

Call Bono-
In the Zone!

Call Again
Josh ain't Homme.
Best of Best
Night's a Mess!
Nos Amis
Everyone's Possessed!

Cold Comfort
So I'm told
Cold Comfort
Fuckers reload.
Cold Comfort
Wheat in the Wind
Cold Comfort
Revoke! Rescind!

Where's the cops?
Hit the Dirt!
Two Fuckin' Hours!
In the Desert!
Focus Pocus
Breath Jessie Breath!
Sky's Fallin'!
Time to Leave!

Cold Comfort
Cartridges Flyin'!
Cold Comfort
But there's still Five!
Eighty Nine
Hate that Number!
Cold Comfort
Eternal Slumber.

Them Crooked Vultures;
Means Something
Stone Age Queens
Still Erruptin'.
Night of Terror!
Black Arm Bands
Souls on Fire!
At the Bataclan.

Cold Comfort
For Us All
Cold Comfort
Rise to Fall.
Cold Comfort
All that's Left
Cold Comfort
Leaves us Bereft!

Take a Moment
To Remember
Hard Rock
In Black November.
Cold Comfort's
All we've Got
Mind's all Numb
Guts in a Knot!
Pourquoi ?

To Jessie, Dave, Julian, Eden, Matt & Baby Duck

Jessie Hughes BB 1200, MS 2000
Dave Catching Gibson Flying V Electric (Rancho de le Luna
Studio Joshua Tree)
Julian Dorio Drummer

311

Eden Galindo Guitar
Matt McJunkins Bassist
Baby Duck

Catch my CD of songs inspired by/to Josh Homme available
for free on my 'Just Bad News' web page at: go to YouTube &
type in address bar john-organ.rocks, & when next page comes,
scroll down until you find John Organ - Topic, click on it,
and enjoy!

Evil lurks in beautiful places!

The Studio can become a dark place filled with latitudes and
attitudes of Artists working out some Deep Psyches, Spiritualties,
or E'lan Vital within their souls. Some of the deepest lyrics are
lost in *'Punk Presentations'* and *'Rock Passions'* but the Artist knows
the pains and sufferings behind each vowel and the transitions of
every change-up. Then there's the insidious rewrites and *poignant* practicing until even the Artist is satisfied; for a moment! My
ticket to singing fifty, sixty songs in three days, as flawlessly as
possible, in a never ending effort to get on to the next tune, is to
rehearse ahead of time for five, six days a week for two to three
months (after two to three months of hard core redoes &rewrites).
I sing twenty songs a day, as many times as necessary, until it
becomes a flowing stream of vocal equity. Luckily Grant Avenue
is a masterful and affordable Studio.

When I was young, I heard an interview with Frank Sinatra
explaining that when he knew his vocal recording dates, he
went for three months without smoking, drinking, or dancing
the Hoochee-Coo before laying down tracks. I personally used
to think Bing Cosby had one of the best singing voices I'd ever
heard, Frank's probably just behind him. The thing is, Frank's
style imitates Bing's. But one day I heard Frank sing 'Old Man

River' on the tube and I was speechless. I figured if *abstinence* was Frank's recipe for his exotic crooned conjuring's, I'd give it a try!

I started puffing in 1969, so this year I am acknowledging my fiftieth anniversary, for the good and bad. So to stop smoking and drinking for months on end, while singing for hours every day, was a new form of existence, and torture, for me. But I need do it every time I have multi-day sessions with a 'ton-o-songs'. I can't imagine what Amy does to prepare herself for days and days of banging ivory keys to please. I know Piano Players that would need an eight ball to even conceive of playing through that much repetition and eventual pain. I guess Amy's still young and able to play through the cramping and discomfort.

I sure do appreciate her professionalism, dedication and Friendship.

We work together like gears in a finely tuned Swiss Watch. It's a labour of love for our craft, to say the least. I suggested to Amy in the Control Room during one long day of crafting, that I believed we worked together so well, and we knew where each other were coming from, because we understood each other's Darkness. She retorted, "I think I can hear a song coming out of this." I drove home thinking that we shared our Darkness the way the Moon shared it's Light while reflecting the Sun in sessions. I pulled over to reflect about her Light of Darkness, and wrote;

Light of Darkness

There isn't a living soul alive
Who hasn't found time to collide
With Darkness and its mystery
The Darkness even light can't see.
It's got nothing to do with hate
Nothing there to obfuscate
It could be your loving mate
But it's there...the Darkness!

John Leo Organ

You know where Darkness goes at night?
Into your eyes to rob your sight.
And when it's gone hold someone tight
Don't get lost inside your fright.
Darkness takes you by the hand
You can't see or understand
Nothing can be as you planned
But don't let go…in the Darkness!

It holds your fear
It'll find your tear
It's in your beer
The Darkness!
Don't be afraid
The darkness lays
Now at your feet. It's in the street.
The Darkness!

The Darkness there tries to expose
The Darkness covers least and most.
Darkness shows whenever you boast
Darkness reveals your closest ghost.
Time and place become the same
Darkness hides your face and shame
Darkness only feeds the flame
Be careful…of The Darkness!

You visit the Darkness most days
Get lost and stay in a haze
Stumble on your feet where Darkness lays
Darkness leaves you in a maze.
Life in the Dark always decays
Guided by distant alpha rays

Search out the light to which you pray
To hide you...from the Darkness!

It holds your fear
It'll find your tear
It's in your beer
The Darkness!
Don't be afraid
The Darkness lays
Now at your feet. It's in the street.
The Darkness!

Darkness guards the gates of hell
Down Lonely Street to Heart Break Hotel
Hope escapes with its hard sell
No way to run or to rebel.
Darkness covers up a thief
Darkness hides a new laid wreath
Darkness feeds on fear and grief
Don't trust...the Darkness!

In the night shadows can't hide
Nowhere to go nothing to guide
With nowhere left to confide
Just empty graves where no one dies.
Darkness comes to light the moon
Darkness always comes too soon.
Darkness in some eyes by noon
Darkness only plays one tune...Darkness!

It holds your fear
It'll find your tear
It's in your beer
The Darkness!
Don't be afraid

The darkness lays
Now at your feet. It's in the street.
The Darkness!

There isn't a living soul alive
Who hasn't found time to collide
With Darkness and its mystery
The Darkness even light can't see.
It's got nothing to do with hate
Nothing there to obfuscate
It could be your loving mate
But it's there...the Darkness!

I'm partially writing this book in response to so many people in my past and present, who have heard some of me good ol' Irish saloon-tales, and still tell me that I should write a book to share these antidotes, for a laugh. I never had really taken the notion seriously, until one day a successful female Artist at Grant Ave asked me to write a song about my life with her. I was taken back to think that anybody would care about a Canadian Loonie who jumps off bridges, or that followed a hippie Rock Band around for half my life. But I said, "Sure."

I ventured over the next day, but I pulled over on the way, on a lark, and wrote it before I went in. She liked some of the words and told me I might as well finish it myself. I got into the groove and I wrote three songs to cover my lunatic allegories. Amy and I recorded these ballads, revealing three different perspectives of the same scary story of the same Canadian Looney.

Song # 1 Mad Man Bad Man';

Chorus:
Nobody knows what it's like
To be the Mad Man
The Bad Man

Behind blues eyes.
Nobody knows what it's like
To be jaded
To be faded
To telling only lies.

Damn straight I'll tell ya
'Bout a life of pain
Of anger, frustration
Lost loyalties and shame.
Born on a cabbage farm
With cauliflower ears
Cloak of Satan to keep me warm
Livin' out my father's fears.
As every potato in the barn
Froze the night I was born
Guess my poppa should of
Been growin' corn.

Livin' under the kitchen table
With my dog named Jack
We co-existed amiably
We both had our own stash.
Pretty soon school
Tried to control my brain
But the joke was on them
Today I'm still the same.
Grade one was ok
Spent all my time in the hall
First cigarette
First time I showed my balls.
My teacher had a horse
She used to let in her kitchen
Spill a crumb at home

All that Irish bitchin'!
'Bout '64
My brain was wantin' more
Hadn't blown my mind
But there was nothin' to score.
Then I flipped on the tube
And caught the Fab Four
My mother scraped my brain
Off the livin' room floor.

Refrain:
Back in one piece
Livin' out on the street
'69 was high school
No exotic piece.
But life was always fun
Always on the run
We all ran together
And the decade was done.

Lookin' under a scab
Didn't go to rehab
Went to St. Catharine and Atwater
Catch a night with the Habs.
Rochdale College
Gave me front line education
Trips to Bogota
Gave us mass communication.
Every time I had two cents
I'd spend a nickel on the Lady
It's alright, it's cool
Up and up, nothin' shady.

Neil and Mouldy Johnny
Cruisin' down the Sunset Strip
Cotten to the core
But kinda on their own trip.
Me I'm still followin' Jerry
It's been a long strange trip
I've got a ex-Nam bud
Smugglin' Tai-weed on a ship.
Walkin' down Broadway
With my brief case in my hand
Suit and tie and free base
Only thing I understand.

Chorus:
When my fist clenches
Crack it open
Before I use it
And lose my cool.
If I smile
Tell me some bad news
Before I laugh
And look like a fool.

Caught Keith at the El Mocambo
In from the West Coast
Cards are stacked, everybody's cracked
Nation's floatin' like a ghost.
I'm hangin' out at Grant Street
Catch Doc Fingers in West Van
More wine bottles from Bolivia
Catch You catch Me if you can.
Attorney General pay cheques
And listenin' to Billy Jean

Cruisin' in my prime
Man I was a machine.

Refrain:
Women come, heartaches go
What do I got to show?
Different wife, different kids
Forget about the hoes.
Life ain't as much fun
Always on the run
We ran in different directions
And the decade was done.

Always time to move on
Join my brother in travellin'
In the next dimension
My life just keeps unravellin'.
Here the paper gets so chewed
Me survivin'; so amused
Writing all that I can
Just so I can be used.
Livin' life from day to day
Grant Avenue, what you say?
Doin' everythin' right or wrong
Well I do it my way.

Chorus:
And if I swallow anything evil
Put your fingers down my throat
If I shiver please give me a blanket
Keep me warm let me wear your coat!
Nobody knows what it's like
To be the Mad Man

To be the Bad Man
Behind blue eyes!

<u>Song # 2, I'm so Tired</u>

I'm so tired
Comin' into Frisco Airport
Feelin' cold
As a rock.
Head on fire
Jumpin' off the Peace Bridge
To see Tuna
That were Hot.

Cool that Desire
Swimmin' with Senioritis
Tryin'
Not to get shot.
Airport higher
Than jumping off Progreston Dam
Tryin' to land
On a spot.

Chorus:
Hess Village afternoon
With my long red hair
Recitin' Jim's poetry
On the floor on a dare.
Livin' Rochdale College
Room 609
Sex, drugs, rock & roll
Yea Times were fine.

Bogota line up
Just not movin'

Clillin' Sweatin'
Bullets of fire.
Airport blues
Tell ya anything ya want
Just don't call me
A liar.
Thinkin' 'bout Jerry
Playin' up in Portland
Catch 'em when I'm
Through.
Still in Frisco
Waitin' with the Lady
Feelin' blue Nothin' new.

Chorus:
Mind Escaping'
On the West Coast
See right through me
Feelin' like a ghost.
Catch Doc Fingers
When in West Van
Action out front
Back stage I'm The Man.

Headin' to Chicago
'59 Buick all night lightenin' storm
Blues and whites
Next mornin' feelin' like I wanna be reborn.
Back in Toronto
El Mocambo on Spadina keepin' it clean
Frisco Airport
Back again feelin' shabby and a little mean.

Off to Vegas
Desert marriage then it's off to the Coast
Sure thing
Back here in the city that I must love most.
Need a vacation
Flyin' every where's for the birds
Drive to Penticton
Rocky Mountain High that I deserve.

Chorus:
Starin' in the mirror
Never see myself
Leave it on the counter
And my mind on the shelf.
Travellin' through the city
With my brief case full of trouble
Hands on the sink
Always doin' double double.

Seein' green
Live in Dublin next America's obscene
See my family
Been there before the famine tell me what they've seen.
In the Now
Writin' music all night struggle through the day
Doin' it My Way
Gettin' lost in the jungle I just can't stay.

The River Flows
I follow to the source follow where it goes
Like Tom Sawyer
Paths I followed weren't always ones I chose.
Here I go
Following new trails in space and time

Lucky me
I'm ironic and a paradigm.

Chorus:
Thinkin' 'bout the Future
Forget the Past
Whatever's happenin' Now
Ain't gonna last.
Keep my passport valid
And my focus unparted
I'm so tired
Hell I've barely even started.

I'm so tired
Comin' into Frisco Airport
Feelin' cold
As a rock.
Head on fire
Jumpin' off the Peace Bridge
To see Tuna
That were Hot.

Cool that Desire
Swimmin' with Senioritis
Tryin'
Not to get shot.
Airport higher
Than jumping off Progreston Dam
Tryin' to land
On a spot.

Chorus:
Hess Village afternoon
With my long red hair
Recitin' Jim's poetry

On the floor on a dare.
Livin' Rochdale College
Room 609
Sex, drugs, rock & roll
Yea Times were fine.

I'm so tired
I'm so tired
I'm so tired
I'm so tired

Song # 3, Here's a Rocker! ... Johnny O;

I wasn't born standin' up!
And never talkin' back
My blue jeans are fadin'
Lord I ain't the Man in Black.
My name is Johnny O
Partied in Vegas way back
Everyone I owe is gone
I'm still holdin' the Black Jack.

Chorus:

Times are hard ...
But I'm still stakin' out my claim
Cards are bent and chipped
And the Dealer has no shame.

Raised on God and gospel
Hit and run by rock n roll
Lips dried and cracked
And eyes black as coals.
I stand like a flamingo
With one leg on the ledge

Life is like a knife
And I'midin' on the edge.

Chorus:
Cry me a river
But you know that I can't swim
Leave me on the shore
Where I'll sing to Him.

Times of memory and loss
I leave at the back door
Through time and trouble and toil
I don't know now what they're for.
Searchin' and hopin'
And lookin' for things to find
I'm searchin' standin' up
Think it's hidin' in my mind.

Chorus:
I've never looked for trouble
If ya chase me I'm gonna run
I don't take no orders
Ain't holdin' no smokin' gun.

Don't wanna start a rumble
And I don't mess around
Just look into my face
Tell me what ya found.
My daddy was a farmer
Harvested misery
I'm only flesh and blood
So don't you mess around with me.

Chorus:
Evil is as evil does

Evil You stay away from me
Was born God and gospel
I won't mess with You so don't you mess with Me!

I wasn't born standin' up!
And never talkin' back
My blue jeans are faded
Lord I ain't the Man in Black.
My name is Johnny O
Partied in Vegas way back
Everyone I owe is gone
I'm still holdin' the Black Jack!!

Thoughts and Songs

I moved North in 2016 to a secluded cottage on Kinesis Lake, in Haliburton County. I was moving into Winter Seclusion, and I was ready for some serious writing. In my aloof, isolated detachment, I've recorded some two hundred songs with Amy at Grant since 2017. But this rustic romantic recluse soon needed money to keep recording and I secured a job at the local Golf Course on the Greens Crew.

The nature of working on a golf course is that everything needs to be prepared and ready for the first tee-off at 7 am. That meant that from seven am until two pm, I needed to keep myself busy. Which is funny ya know, because I'm real good at that! About eight o'clock a.m. I would grab a Cart and motor about, grinning at the Young Beauties, while searching out an inspiration for my first song of the day.

I've written songs to the motorized Cold Golf Beer Cart damsels, songs about Maids who liked to puff by the Pool... Hell I wrote a song about the lady who served me my meal in the lounge one afternoon. I wrote songs inspired by almost every lady there. The ladies seemed to enjoy my daily offerings. O well. I got the odd cold beer...

There was one fella that joined our Crew after a while. He wasn't really any good at machinery, not that working on a golf-course Maintenance Crew would hint at needing to be... but he puttered about and the guys left him on his own. But he knew every woman on the premises so I figured, well, we all have our talents! We were jawin' at Break Time and he mentioned that Glen Campbell died during the past night. Everybody knew I would write a song about it. I've written my rock-eulogies to many Artists who had just passed on, and some Musicians at

John Leo Organ

Grant told me not to write songs about them until they were already gone, for their safety. Someone made a joke that I must check the Obituary to write my ballads. At least I think it was a joke.

A buddy on the Crew drove me around all day while I scribbled down lines to the 'Wichita Linesman'. Man, Glen Campbell was big around 1968. He had the 'Glen Campbell Good Time Hour' TV show, where he got Johnny Cash, Willie Nelson, Kris Kristofferson, and, unfortunately for Glen as it turned out, Mason Williams, who is remembered for his guitar riff on his chartered song, 'Classical Gas'. Mason wowed everybody with his Ax, but when Glen tried to emulate the riffs, he flubbed it, and eventually gave up on it, on international T.V.!

It was one of those things that you had to be there to know about it, or remember it. But at school the next day, everyone was talking about how Glen Campbell wasn't really that big a deal, and how disappointed we all were at his lame effort the night before as a guitarist. Even at the moment Glen flubbed it my brother Paul exclaimed, "Wow! He screwed it up!"

It really became a big deal! And his Show was cancelled the next year. In a couple years he was down to about one hundred and twenty pounds, playing with the *lady* with buddies like Sly Stone. When he released his comeback album at the start of the Seventies, his wife protested that he would become a joke if he released the song 'Like a Rhinestone Cowboy' on the radio. They argued about it, and she said she would leave him if it was released. When it was released it and it became a Top-10 hit, she left him! Here's to the Rhinestone Country Boy...

Laid Back Gentle on My Mind;

The Wichita Lineman
Lays Gentle on My Mind
Hand rocks the Cradle

330

Be a little kind.
Upbeat breeze in Galveston
Southern Nights hurt a bit
But it's only Make Believe and
In dreams it's all True Grit.

With Rhinestones in his eyes
The Southern Country Boy
Took the act on the road as
A Brian Wilson decoy.
Turn around, look at me
Before something goes wrong
Try some Classical Gas then
Try Sly's newest freest bong.

Chorus: Gather round the Good Time Hour
Johnny, Willie comin' round
Then catch you up in Phoenix
Tryin' out some new sound.
Try a Little Kindness
When passin' round the hat
Cause even Rhinestone Cowboys
Can't begin when all's begat.

A good woman's hard to find
When everything's gone wrong
Leave ya for the strangest reason
Even writin' the wrong song!
Dreams of an Everyday Housewife
With night mares in the back
She's Gone Gone Gone
And the table deals the jack.

Wet your lips in the desert
Visit the Joshua Tree

John Leo Organ

When you're done with Frank and Elvis
Come grow old with me.
Natures Elusive Butterfly
With everything a man could need
When life and breath have moved on
You just bleed and bleed.

Chorus:
Gather round the Good Time Hour
Johnny, Willie comin' round
Then catch you up in Phoenix
Tryin' out some new sound.
Try a Little Kindness
When passin' round the hat
Cause even Rhinestone Cowboys
Can't begin when all's begat.

It's time to take a small vacation
Visit Bonaparte's Retreat
Pink limo to the airport
Draggin' those dusty feet.
But I want You I don't need You
And I need You more right now
Earth Wind Fire
Bring you Homeward Bound.

When Nature shows what you find
Simplest things can leave ya blind
Things that you must leave behind
Leaves You Gentle on My Mind.
So Adios my sweet friend;
Poet, singer, traveler, Glen
When I think of You, I'll be kind
Laid Back Gentle on my Mind.

<u>Polly;</u>

I never dreamed 'Polly' was anything but a Classic Kurt Cobain song. Kind of a shuffle to the beat, back and forth and nothing too much about anything really... Polly wants a cracker. Ok...

"It isn't me
We have some seed
Let me clip
Your dirty wings"

...soooooooooo... 'let me take a ride, Don't cut yourself, I want some help, To please myself'... How many times did I listen to this? Well I owned the CD and I played it constantly... every day.............. HOW MANY TIMES DID I HEAR THIS? I can't imagine... Often! It was catchy, different. Very Kurtish!

And then one day my Fragile Existence was Shattered! The radio was playing the album in its entirety, giving background information on each cut ahead of time.

The DJ explained that Polly was a kidnapped girl who was tortured, and eventually the bastard murdered her! And then he played the F*C@ING song:
"Polly wants a cracker
Maybe she would like some food
She asks me to untie her
A chase would be nice for a few".

I was broken!!! I felt like I had been hit in the stomach with a baseball bat. My soul was hemorrhaging. I was disgusted. And then I got angry. I was enraged that Kurt put me through this. I trusted him; a West Coast Lad! This was brutal!

I probably had listened to that song hundreds, maybe thousands of times going do-do-do along with it mindlessly. Now I was hurting. All I could sense was Darkness and Evil. I needed to cleanse my Psyche and Soul so I scribbled this down and recorded it with a vengeance, and tears.

Until I Heard;

Polly
I thought you were a lover
Under the covers
I wanna be smothered!
O Sister!
O brother!
I swear I thought it was
Something Other!

I thought the blow torch
Was your passion flame
Thought it was a kinky act,
Never been south of Blain.
Thought I was following the Act
As a song I didn't care
She says untie me
Assumed she was the right kind of bare.

Chorus:
It isn't me
What does it mean?
Got some rope
I thought for green.
We all want help
Been there myself
Light me on fire
For my mental health!

To me some rope
Was Robin Williams
One for the road
There was no villain.
Taking a ride
Enjoying the slide
Clippin' the wings off
Frankenstein's Bride.

Set myself up
On my way down
Don't cut yourself
I'll do it myself.
Polly wants a cracker
O.k. She ain't a bird
Everything was just so
Until I fuckin' heard!

Chorus:
It isn't me
What does it mean?
Got some rope
I thought for green.
We all want help
Been there myself
Light me on fire
For my mental health!

The North West can be cold
Fog haunts ya to the bone
Winds off the ocean
Sounds like a frantic moan.
Promises by lunatics?
Is a daily occurance

Putting out the blow torch
Merely tests your endurance.

Caught me off myguard
Well to say the least
Boredom, pain, and instinct
Help to please the Beast.
I know the world is fucked
Copyright BMG
Caught me off my guard
It still amazes me.

Chorus: It isn't me
What does it mean?
Got some rope
I thought for green.
We all want help
Been there myself
Light me on fire
For my mental health.

Don't wanna stop
My penance goes on and on
I missed the life of Polly
'Till I heard it in a song.
Satan did his work;
Made me feel like I belonged
Thought I had a clue
How could I be so god damned wrong?

The ending is the beginning
The start's not worth a glance
The body is just some seed
The Truth is just a rant.
The peace you search for Polly

Will never leave my mind
Wind and rain, heaven and hell
May the next world be more kind.

Kurt was deeper than Dirt!

Amy left the Grand piano to awake me again to resume recording. I learned to sleep sitting upright in the Studio. We had recorded sixty songs and she was ready for more! I couldn't believe that she was up to this work load. Amy gets up early every morn and walks her big German Shepard named Windsor. Windsor has become a Regular at the Studio. Fellow Artists and Guitar Collectors on Grant Avenue come over multiple times daily to walk him. When he's not there we all notice quickly.

I had written material and rehearsed it for the last four months and then recorded with Amy for three straight days. I had been falling asleep between almost every song for the last hour. But if Amy was up to it, than so was I! She called me from the Piano, asking what the next song would be. I said 'Overwhelmed'. She asked if I wanted to stop. I countered, "What do you mean stop?" She rebutted that I was the one who claimed to be 'Overwhelmed'. I started laughing heartily (manically?) and explained that 'Overwhelmed' was the name of the song. She rolled her eyes. I ranted:

Overwhelmed!
My mind is trippin'
World won't stop bitchin'
Overwhelmed!
My eyes are cryin'
All my friends are dyin'
Overwhelmed!
Half the world's got no food
I'm in need of a lude

Overwhelmed!
Try not to look in most eyes
Fucker's just filled with lies
Overwhelmed!
I don't know what to do
You look fucked up too
Overwhelmed!
Waitin' to start feelin' better
Depressin' cold winter weather
Overwhelmed!!

Chorus: I'm just
meltin' in the sun
the wind don't
help me.
Only
answer is if you've
got the balls to
tell me.
I'm scared
don't have a clue
how to
fix things.
I'm lost
and life just seems
to wanna
kill me.

Cause I'm…
Overwhelmed!
When life drowns in blood
As it becomes a flood
Overwhelmed!
When warm justice calls

Down cold marble halls
Overwhelmed!
When I just don't know
On killer blow
Overwhelmed!
When pain calls on me
To see what it sees
Overwhelmed!
When I can't breath
To sleep is to grieve
Overwhelmed!
When the world hates me
And my sanity's the fee
Overwhelmed!
When I don't understand
When gifts are commands
Overwhelmed!!

Chorus:
I'm just
runnin'on the spot;
goin'
nowhere.
can't stop
I'm hurt
takin' the wrong pills
rape me.
angry
and I've lost my way
all my words
cut me.
I'm used
mistrusted, confused

have a drink
fuck it.

Cough it up…

Overwhelmed!
Go to fuckin' hell
Everything's hard sell
Overwhelmed!
No one left to trust
Truth to me is dust
Overwhelmed!
No on fuckin' cares
Every deed's a dare
Overwhelmed!
Straight and narrow's a bend
Nothin' left to defend
Overwhelmed!
Reality's a trap
Honesty has the clap
Overwhelmed!
Everything good has yeast
I wanna kill a priest
Overwhelmed!
Like Mars needs a Rover
When it's over it's over
Overwhelmed!!

I started working on the songs from the Internet with some help from Phil Eurrup on the Lake. We got Cosmic on this song with echoes from my head, revere made absurd and an assortment of sounds… and the plot thickened!

I awoke one morning in June of 2019 and ambled to the table with a coffee. As soon as I sat down I could feel that I was going to start writing something. I sat back and started scribbling. It suddenly became a race between the words and my pen. I was swamped with visions and images of mountains, deserts, the sky, and how I fit in to these Entities. I realized that all these factions are part of what makes me who I am. Meanwhile, the pen went into overdrive, and began taking responsibility for who I believed I was, and who I aimed to be. I started walking around the cottage, writing decidedly and deliberately. Within thirty minutes or less, I put the paper on the table in front of me and read the words that seemed to be prompting me to read them. It was like I had no idea what I had written until I read it. So I read on;

That's What I Am

I'd rather touch the surface
For the reasons of my memory
Far past the melting Waste Land
And the treasons of the desert
That watch me from the mountains...
And protect me from my dreams
Then wander to the unexpected;
That's who I am this morning!

The sun it seems to simmer
On the crests of waves of passion
The rocks and birds and menstrual
Sing their cries to open skies
But I refuse to be libel...
I search behind the scenes
Where bitter lies are better dreams
That's who I am this moment.

I huddle to the masses
That cling to the fringes

Of the truth as we know it
The secrets in the soil
That clothe my naked lies...
The leaves dance in memories
As they fall from certain safeties
That's who I'll be tomorrow.

The sunlight filters gently through
The sorrows of fleeting moments;
The faces of the young
Blend the azure skies of autumn
Then sparkle in their silence...
Eyes of morning seem to soften
The pains of distant shores
That's who I stake my claim to.

The spirits whisper endlessly mimicking
Mysterious mortal magic
Belonging to their constant rituals
And healed with ceremonies
And blackness hides its virtues...
Clouds can't hide their lightning
When running with the thunder
That's who I'll dance with at midnight.

Knowledge holds the foundations for
Mosses and mellow meadows
Winding rivers tickling valleys
Rainbows measure nature's sorrows
And the snow caps the mountains...
Time hides waiting for us all to
Take us past unborn memories
That's who I'll always be!

I e-mailed the words to Amy and she responded right away, "Wow. When are you coming down to record?" But writing eight to twelve hours a day leaves an Artist honest, and hungry, and broke. I expressed to Amy that I had been rehearsing another forty to fifty songs, and that I was ready to record right Then and There! But I was waiting on a new job… so shall we start recording and let me pay off my tab in a couple weeks, or months, or decades… Amy resounded that she was glad that we were friends and that I had the confidence to make the request, and that she would be happy to do so.

Now how many Professionals would be inclined to make such a deal? But Amy is different. She trusts me, and vice versa. And she likes those work days of twenty songs each. Amy is diminutive in size, but is blessed with huge talent and a Celtic Spirit work ethic. Everybody round the globe wants to work with her, and I feel lucky to be her Friend. I will not record with anyone else. She has no ego, but she does have a heart of gold. I wrote this beer ballad in a bar one evening when the Bartender shouted, "Last Call! Any Dead Soldiers?" I wrote <u>Another Dead Soldier;</u>

Just another dead soldier
Lyin' on the beach
And hidin' in the weeds;
For ten cents out of reach.
Just another drained and tamed
Empty mercenary with no shame
First in war, first in peace
First in victory first in pain.

One for the road, one in the ditch
One for the war in Spain
One for the ones who never came home
Half full's half empty again.
Blotted and battled labels

Best days now a blur
Another unknown in the back ground;
Another dead soldier.

Chorus:
Morning sun
On golden hops
Smooth and cold and
The world stops.
Another dead soldier
Around the bend
Dented and dead and
A refund to spend.

Barbed and wired, retired
With a story to tell
'Bout goin' over the edge
And landin' square in hell.
Dead soldiers in the water frock
Once robust younger and bolder
Claim to fame in this game
Tastes better and wetter when colder.

Legions of yesterday's bravest
Sadly stored now away
Dust and gloom in Satan's back room
Wait for souls that need spare change.
Scrambling in the bramble
Refuel and be back by noon
Just another dead soldier
Floating in the lagoon.

Chorus:
Morning sun
On golden hops

Smooth and cold and
The world stops.
Another dead soldier
Around the bend
Dented and dead and
A refund to spend.

One for the road, one in the ditch
One for the war in Spain
One for the ones who never came home
Half full's half empty again.
Blotted and battled labels
Best days now a blur
Another unknown in the back ground;
Another dead soldier.

Just another dead soldier
Lyin' on the beach
And hidin' in the weeds
For ten cents out of reach.

An Aside;

My greatest disappointment in Life was that I never met David
Geffen in the early Seventies, when I was rambling up and down
the West Coast writing lines down and dreaming up melodies
that I never recorded. And just forgot. I used to listen to songs
as a teen and I would always say geeze, Morrison shouldn't have
said, "Take a long holiday" he should have sang, "Take hey-long
Harley Days." Or I would joust with Mick and sing, "I'm a two
bit fisted Monkey" to start Monkey Man instead of his, "I'm a
flea bit peanut monkey"...I would start writing my versions up,
and melodies came too easily.

But I could never sing these things to my Musical Muses. I figured it was cheating if my inspiration came off the back of another's... Then one day I was listening to Beatle Paul on the tube, and he said that he had never written a song in his life that didn't come from somewhere; a part of someone's song he had heard subconsciously, or whatever. He sighted that something as huge as ,"Yea, Yea, Yea" came from Little Richard going, "Whoo, Whoo, Whoo!" But by the time I was crooning comfortably, David was too rich for somebody that banked Romantic Notions and not Best Sellers, like me...

Somehow it wasn't meant to be, David.

Merle;

Back in the Millennium up here, I was writing and rehearsing every day. Amy's become my Recording Rock; my Interpreter, my Mentor. I think she was the only one who really took my work seriously. I got complements from each one of the Musicians on different songs, but they had their own careers, and they didn't give a hoot. I made my first Rock Video with Kori and the Kids. I chose 'The Climate's Changin' Again' where Bob Doidge impressed me in with his bass lines. He puts out a very commanding sound, yet his first attempt sounded like a Stevey Ray Vaughan riff. I said we needed to make it more original. I was very pleased with the result.

We put a few different days of filming into the video, in different locations, in different towns. I was stoked that we did it ourselves for next to nothing. I wrote a script that related to the lyrics. So many video themes are lost on me. But they were on M-TV, not me. So here's to the Actors and Artists of my first Video;

The Climates Changing Again;

When I look back
Without a sound
I see my footprints
In the ground.
Every stage of life
I've come to know
I'm a man in a cave
And I come out to show.

The climates changing again
The climates changing again
Every man, woman, child
Committing their sins
Look out man
The climates changing again!

The Ice Age gouged a deep
Impression in me
Filled it with my tears
Made the Dead Sea!
Homo Sapiens passed Erectus
No time to meet when
God said get up
And walk on two feet.

Next thing I know seas
Thawing below ground
We're walking everywhere
And we're making new sounds
Journey out of Africa
Travel bug has bitten
The next chapter of life
Is still to be written!

Now skies above my head
Ground below my feet
Two million years later there's
There's a party on the beach
Earth plates moving mountains
Between me and you
Evolution continues
To make me feel blue!

The climates changing again
The climates changing again
Every man, woman, child
Committing their sins
Look out man
The weather's changing again!
Every man, woman, child
Committing their sins
Look out man
The climate's changing again!

We were filming under a waterfall in one segment of the video, and I stubbed my toe, which somehow became infected. I cursed that I had to spend my time in the Hospital to see a Specialist, but I figured if I really needed a Specialist, then maybe I had better go. I knew the game of the slow evolutions and non-motions of Emergency Wards, so I took along a book Keith Richards wrote; Life. It was fascinating and very well written, of course. Keith was expressing himself eloquently in one passage, when he alluded that one series of his actions left him 'high and lonesome'.

Well you only get so many gifts in life, and this definitely served up as one. Like other writers/song writers, I rarely can make it through reading a chapter in a book without being inspired to write my own concept on a notion or two. I relished the image of being 'High and lonesome'. This takes me any way and everywhere I choose to go. I rushed up and asked the Nurse at the counter for a pen, as I had left mine in my truck. She was fascinated with the ability to write songs. I told her I was fascinated with those who possessed pens. It worked; I got a pen, and a smile. So I could now relax and let my fingers amuse themselves. Pens are like baby-sitters for the mind. If I'm writing something I'm never bored, and I rarely get into trouble.

I felt somehow honoured that I was writing a ditty for Keith. He really is the Dark Horse of Rhythm and Blues. I started writing a book (that I haven't finished) bout the careers put in arrears recording with Keith... Poppa John Philips, Gram Parsons, John Hyatt, et al... Artists who met Keith at the Studio for their 'big break' and who just ended up doing jolts and ending up lost. Poppa John talked in an interview once about such an experience, when he and Keith were so high, they ended up tuning their guitars for eight hours... Trouble is that most shit doesn't get done on good shit. Getting high is not recommended for an expensive day working with X-Pensive Artists. Keith puts everything in proper perspective:

When he's told some information
that's supposed to fire his imagination,
he just can't get no...
Satisfaction!

This one's on you Keith;

<u>High and Lonesome</u>

Out of a bright sky
Nothing there to hide
The truth always hurts
Guess I should have lied.
Clouds line the peripheral
Coming to an eclipse

You're thinking that I'm evil
I'm thinking of your lips.

Rain is coming down
Washes off your frown
Times are hard now baby
Let me be your clown.
Tomorrow's just another day
Tomorrow's all you ever say
My heart beats on borrowed time
Your soul's broken, just take mine.

Tell me it's OK
Let me hear your lies
Say that you don't love me
I see it in your eyes.
Winds blow off the showers
Waited underground for hours
Your touch makes me lonely
Yes you hold the power.

Rain is coming down
Washes off your frown
Times are hard now baby
Let me be your clown.
Tomorrow's just another day
Tomorrow's all you ever say
My heart beats on borrowed time
Your soul's broken, just take mine.

Another day I'd take it home
Enjoy the pain in my bones
Today the sky is so bright
Leave the darkness for the night.
Time goes by now slowly

Takes me by the hand
Your shadow goes by daily
Makes me understand.

Rain is coming down
Washes off your frown
Times are hard now baby
Let me be your clown.
Tomorrow's just another day
Tomorrow's all you ever say
My heart beats on borrowed time
Your soul's broken, just take mine.

Keith is an inspiration on his worst day. I believe his worst days might indeed be his most inspirational.

It was November 21rst and I was booked into the Studio for the next couple of days. I had narrowed my selections of *tunes to take* to about ten songs. I could get the Band to do bed tracks for eight and Amy and I could do a couple during lunch. After a rather full day it was fifteen minutes before midnight. I suddenly decided to write one to the Kennedys for the November 22nd assassination. I would write it, record it and do the vocal track all on the 22nd. Seconds beat down to midnight and I began.

I was stoked as I began. This was an antiquated fantasy of John Lennon's; to write and record a song in one day. Of course he would have had to wrestle with Paul for precious studio time, ignore George when he argued about being a Third World Artist (pardon the pun) when it came to recognition of his songs, escape a family trying to capture a moment of John's precious time, while attempting to transpose a sound that could not be rushed or duplicated. I just had to try and get my Band interested in playing with the right song. Every song seemed to work for someone, so that created the Edge necessary when performing with each other. Playing while sliding down that Edge is what keeps things bloody fresh and inspired.

On this day everybody was Irish, and the fact that it was November twenty-second made me realize that so many hard things have historically happened in November;

Escape from September
To Endless November;
Sun's always Black
Life accepts no new Members.
April's the Hardest
Sleeping Forests so Mild
Sleep my Dears, have no fears
Lay down with Decembers Child.

There were the murders in November 2015 in Paris by Islamic terrorists from Iraq. The Allied Powers brought World War 1 to an end in November 1918. The Tehran Conference in November 1943. Gatling invented the machine gun for mass killings in November 1862. The Berlin Wall torn down in November 1989.

Tojo was executed for war crimes in November 1948. And in November 1963 the first Irish President was assassinated. It was the start of Evil as we know it to this very day. I tried to rationalize one single segment of a month that begins with cold and ends in so many tragedies. I was stoked for JFK that day;

Kennedys Don't Cry;

A fresh new bear with loving stare
Given a career of smoothing arrears,
A Brave New Age they liked to say
He called it the New Frontier.
With brother near it became clear
Gave innocence a whole new look;

The Enemy Within, institutional sins
We read it in his books.

Chorus:
I wept through my pain
And then asked Why?
The only answer I heard
Was Kennedys don't cry.
I thought through the years
While America got high
What can I do for my country
If Kennedys don't cry?

And those who could beside them stood
Hickory Hill was a family place
Edgar J, the CIA,
He gave them no pretense.
And through the years they brought their fears
With no one on the fence
The brothers two, inter racial coupe;
A man's blood is his race!

Chorus:
I wept through my pain
And then asked Why?
The only answer I heard
Was Kennedys don't cry.
I thought through the years
While America got high
What can I do for my country
If Kennedys don't cry?

They gathered round Havana Town
Warmest spot in the Cold War
Dominoes for fun, it had begun

But he knew they had tumbled before.
The Mob, Southern foe, Edgar Allen Poe
All the same before the Bench
And all of Space became a race;
Viet Nam became a trench.

Chorus:
I wept through my pain
And then asked Why?
The only answer I heard
Was Kennedys don't cry.
I thought through the years
While America got high
What can I do for my country
If Kennedys don't cry?

Justice tuned, the young hearts swooned
It was the Coming Year
But one heart's mend was another one's end
He left us with our fears.
The fears went fast, the tears they passed
They melted into years
What could they say, in just one day
They buried the New Frontier.

Chorus:
I wept through my pain
And then asked Why?
The only answer I heard
Was Kennedys don't cry.
I thought through the years
While America got high
What can I do for my country
If Kennedys don't cry?

Kennedys don't cry!
Kennedys don't cry!

I was cruising downtown Hamilton, listening to Q107 one morning, and the news at noon announced their congratulations to Merle Haggard for his birthday. Like a reflex I said to myself; Merle's seventy-nine today. Far Out! The next line from the DJ, was that he was indeed seventy-nine, and he was dead.

Now Merle was always Beyond Special. He influenced everyone. The Grateful Dead played his songs, and Jed Clampett thought the world of him as he removed his hat and put his hand on his heart every time his name was mentioned. I pulled over immediately, and within ten minutes I wrote my ode to Merle.

I phoned Amy and asked her to record it within an hour, and could she come up with a great Telecaster guitar player. Amy arranged things, like the professional she is, and we recorded my song in its entirety within a couple hours. I had a video made by suppertime and posted it all within the same day. Merle was Beyond Special and these words are for his genius;

Merle;

There was Willie and Johnny,
Conway and Earle;
But there's only one country boy
And His name was Merle.
Merle Haggard.
Sang how his Momma tried.
Merle Haggard;
Testified!

Born a Oildale Rebel
Took the short cut to hell
Now he's singing back home in heaven
With another tale to tell.

Saint Merle
Bob Willis, Lefty and Hank's there too;
Crafted the Bakersfield Sound
With help from some Strangers too.

A good ol' Muskogee boy
He let his freak flag unfurl
On his seventy-ninth birthday today
Let's all light a joint for Merle.
Merle Ronald Haggard
Frozen freight cars, hitch hike 'till blue
Like daddy James Francis before him
He was Bound for Glory too!

On the run from a life time
While searchin' for something true
One thing you found for sure:
San Quintin hates you too!
Brother Merle
Wives and kids and Come backs too
Jed Clampett loved you
But there's a fightin' side of ya too!

Branded Lonesome Fugitive
My favorite country outlaw dude
Remembering Bonnie and Clyde
With a Lone Star and a 'lude.
Father Merle
Preached that don't judge me kind of cause
Same train different time
Lord he took pride in who he was!

That Blue Ridge Mountain air
Tastes like one ninety proof
With Bar Room buddies like Clint

Living hard and bullet proof!
Hey there Merle
Your Telecaster took me far
Man I'm gonna get me a Martin's
Merle Haggard Limited Edition (00)0-28 acoustic guitar!

Oklahoma's south of the Mason
As Bakersfield's all sun shine
New York has the Factory
California has Yesterday's Wine.
Good night Merle
Cruisin' Merle Haggard Drive
I'll change your flat tire Merle
Your legend's in over drive!

Johnny Cash told Merle to quit hiding it, and to pronounce the time he spent in San Quinton with the same pride that Johnny had playing there for him. Merle is the Standard for country quality, and a feeling that's the same for your grandparents as it is for Millennials. He was one of a kind. His 'We don't smoke marijuana in Muskogee' is one of the greatest played and celebrated Freak songs of all time! His legend's in over drive!

What?

I was driving downtown Hamilton one morning to a job where I did nothing but write songs all day. This was not my job, but the attractive blond Boss liked me, and treated me Special. She used to kneel and tie my shoes for me to start my shift. I cannot tie my shoe laces; apparently neither could Einstein. The comparisons stop there. Everybody dug my songs, and it was a very nourishing environment for me to write hundreds of songs. Grant Avenue Studio was a small walk away. I enjoyed my time there at work.

It was a little like High School; always goofing off and doing only whatever came natural.

Driving on Plains Road towards the Urban Culture again one morning, I quickly put my joint out as there were police on the roadway stopping traffic. I prepared to communicate with Officers as necessary, but none approached my Pick-up.

I sat for five minutes with no indication of what the holdup was for. Eventually Officers started directing traffic into one lane, and then directed the one lane to drive on towards the Metropolitan. As I inched forward on the bridge, over the Hamilton Bay, traffic suddenly picked up, and my speed increased back to speed limit again. The radio said it was 10 a.m. Oh well, late again…

I was driving towards the middle of the high steel and cement bridge structure when I suddenly turned my head towards the bay, and briefly caught a glimpse of a man, in his twenties, standing on the railing in an obvious attempt to jump to a sure death. I had to keep driving, and in seconds I was out of sight of the event. There were Police all around him, and the sky was gray on this rainy July morning. I asked myself, "Why is this man jumping off the bridge at ten o'clock?"

I got to work, where I wrote down my question. I told my buddy that came in about the impending ordeal that I *almost* witnessed. He inquired if I was writing a song about it yet. I told him I had a question written down, but that I couldn't finish the lyrics yet. He asked if that meant I was actually going to do some work that day. I laughed that off and reciprocated, "I didn't know if he jumped or not… I gotta phone the cops and see what happened." Which I did, but I decided to leave it to the listener to decide what happened in;

<u>What?</u>

Why is this man jumping
Off the bridge at ten o'clock?

Is it something in the stars?
Tattoos a back covered in scars?
Rain dripping off his chin
Lights reflecting all his sins,
Life on the outside
Standing sideways, looking thin.

Traffic inches forward
Life is frozen still,
Time in fragments showing
The balance of two wills.
Death still just an option
Of two separate worlds,
Life calls on us when we fail;
Square nails and tattered sails.

Talking sure and slow
Like he's not guessing anymore,
Gull glides gracefully
As it lands upon the shore.
Every word ever spoken
He can't hear them anymore,
But they just don't stop
And he's searching for the door.

Traffic inches forward
Life is frozen still,
Time in fragments showing
The balance of two wills.
Death still just an option
Of two separate worlds,
Life calls on us when we fail;
Square nails and tattered sails.

Waves are getting rough
As the wind slaps the land,
One more time no one listens;
This time he takes a stand!
What is there to say
When you're standing on the ledge,
Is there something that he missed?
Something to give that edge?

Traffic inches forward
Life is frozen still,
Time in fragments showing
The balance of two wills.
Death still just an option
Of two separate worlds,
Life calls on us when we fail;
Square nails and tattered sails.

The wind is more a breeze now
The whipping leaves the eyes,
With the commotion dying down
There's less now to despise.
Give this man back his place
Back up, give him space!
Give him time to ponder, surely,
That his life is not a race.

Traffic inches forward
Life is frozen still,
Time in fragments showing
The balance of two wills.
Death still just an option
Of two separate worlds,

Life calls on us when we fail;
Square nails and tattered sails.

Why is this man jumping
Off the bridge at ten o'clock?
Is it something in them stars?
Tattoos, a back covered in scars?
Rain dripping off his chin
Lights reflecting all his sins,
Life on the outside
Standing sideways looking thin.

Traffic inches forward
Life is frozen still
Time in fragments showing
The balance of two wills.
Death still just an option
Of two separate worlds
Life calls on us when we fail;
Square nails and tattered sails.

Talking sure and slow
Like he's not guessing anymore
Gull glides gracefully
As it lands upon the shore.
Every word ever spoken
He can't hear them anymore
But they just don't stop
And he's searching for the door.

Traffic inches forward
Life is frozen still
Time in fragments showing
The balance of two wills.
Death still just an option

Of two separate worlds
Life calls on us when we fail;
Square nails and tattered sails.

There are many singing voices that you either love, or scratch your head at... Dylan, Mick, Geddy Lee, Me and Gord Downey. The latter sometimes makes me wonder. I was still at the Golf Course driving around all day looking for inspirations and subject relations when I heard of Gord's demise.

I wasn't much of a Tragically Hipster; I owned none of their music and many songs were not my cuppa java. But saying that, I really dug the song, 'New Orleans is Sinkin', back in '87. *'Fifty Mission Cap'* was simply a Classic. The first time I heard it I revealed that the lyrics were off the back of the Bill Barilko hockey card, which I had owned. I had over two thousand hockey cards by the beginning of the Seventies. I had so many rookie Bobby Orr cards that I traded one for Norm Ulman, because he was the only Toronto M.L. player I didn't have. I had Phil Esposito's cards in a Chicago jersey. But when I took off in 1972 for Vancouver, Regina threw all my cards and my personal books of poetry out... to even the Universe out somehow I guess.

'Poets' was poignant Downey, and 'Courage' was brave. In an interview, Downey said the reference to 'Bobcaygeon' was because it rhymed with constellation. Ha! "Could have been the Willy Nelson...Could have been the wine"... does it get any better than that? In 1997 I was truckin' across country and 'Ahead by a Century' started coming on the radio. It quickly became my main-stay for the trip, even though I delayed starting my cross country voyage for a couple hours, so I could buy the first Kenny Wayne Sheppard CD, for Rocky Mountain Groovin'! But this was the song I perked up to every time I heard it. So I guess this is some pretty high praise for six songs from me when

I started by stating that I didn't dig their Sound...So here's to you Gord;

<u>Blues From Bobcaygeon</u>

Darkness tells the tale
'Bout a Soul who continues to Shine
Whom the Constellations revealed Themselves
One star at a time!
Filled with Courage Completely
And blessed with Grace, Too
In a World Possessed by the Human Mind
Transformed by the Morning Moon.

What on Earth makes Spirits Scared?
Three Pistols or Boots or Hearts?
Lonely End of the Rink lookin' to happen
Tears Spirits apart.
Ancient race found a place
Gathered at the Hundredth Meridian
Past Fiddler's Green and Wheat Kings Dreams
Meet them At the Transformation.

Chorus:
Man Machine Poem
Spirit did the bro-hymn
Prophet, Singer, Giver of Sight;
In Violet Light!
Kick Road Apples, Twist my Arm
Yer Not the Ocean, just it's Charm
It's a Good Life if You Don't Weaken
Blues from Bobcaygeon, off the deep end!

Silver Jet straight through my heart
What life looks like in reproach

Tragically absorbed in that too
Life's Too Short for awkward approach.
Trouble in the Henhouse
Night in Toronto You said What Blue
Line between Us only made it better
What drove You drives me too.

What happened to Plan A;
Great Soul, Hot Mic, Ocean Next
Day for Night We are the Same
It's all just Tragically Hip.
Yer Favourites at Café Metro
Here in the Dark have a beer
Spirits of Chicago '91
Yea They're all drinkin' Here.

Chorus:
Man Machine Poem
Spirit did the bro-hymn
Prophet, Singer, Giver of Sight
In Violet Light.
Kick Road Apples, Twist my Arm
Yer Not the Ocean, just it's Charm
It's a Good Life if You Don't Weaken
Blues from Bobcaygeon, off the deep end!

Great Soul – Almost Rubber
Flower of Light gives a reprise
Cauza Southern Lights, Because Your Eyes
Fly Away I Still Believe.
Battle of Nudes and Conquering the Sun
Better times had come
Introduced to the Great Tragic Mend
Off the Deep end!

Darkness tells the tale
'Bout a Soul who continues to Shine
Whom the Constellations revealed Themselves
One star at a time!
Filled with Courage Completely
And blessed with Grace, Too
In a World Possessed by the Human Mind
Transformed by the Morning Moon.

Chorus:
Man Machine Poem
Spirit did the bro-hymn
Prophet, Singer, Giver of Sight;
In Violet Light!
Kick Road Apples, Twist my Arm
Yer Not the Ocean, just it's Charm
It's a Good Life if You Don't Weaken
Blues from Bobcaygeon, off the deep end!
It's a Good Life if You Don't Weaken
Blues from Bobcaygeon, off the deep end!

Another year goes by, and there is more proof offered that perhaps Lincoln's death was one of the greatest losses for the American Black race since the 'Hunter-Gatherer' Caucasians learned how to sail. It seems every week there is an inhumane act perpetrated by the Police against the Black Race. Cops shootin' blacks for target practice, it would seem. Shootings across the United States are now daily Global News with the Internet filling our every space. These murders used to get censored, for the Government's convenience and better TV ratings.

President Lyndon Baines Johnson offered the most Civil Rights Reforms in American history and then blew his own mind with Viet Nam atrocities. In the end he refused to accept a nomination to repeat as President elect. This allowed Nixon to get in, which set the whole human race back a century, but affected Blacks even worse with segregated Employment Programs, an Economy that basically excluded them, and violence to keep them in line while imprisoning Black Panthers.

A hundred years passed between Lincoln and Kennedy, and two hundred years, so it seems, between Johnson and Trump. People are confused and scared by shootings and murders they see on TV. And it never seems to stop. 'Black Lives Matter' is an example of how prejudice and hatred are used to discredit valid causes and attempts to expose the continuing plight of the demo grated Black Race. And white kids bringing guns to school seem to make random Black shootings less imperative or vital. There is such affluent violence, and so many living in the streets, that times are getting scarier every day. I have no power, so I do what I can to expose the Roots of Evil that work at eroding at Society's foundations, while keeping Human Rights just for Whites. Here's how I see it;

Black & White;

Yea those cars in black and white
Always lookin' for a fight
Only thing left to say
Is that you can all bite
Me on my purple head
Beat me leave me for dead
Try to hide behind your badges
And change what's been said.

Tin soldiers on the way
And the bull shit keeps a-comin'
They use our heads to keep
Bangin' out their drummin'.
Those boys in blue
Yea the stories keep a-comin'

Don't know all the words
But injustice keeps a hummin'.

Here we go
Yea we're hearin' it again
Same ol' lies
Same Original Sin.
Don't give up
Take a stand across the land
Take those guns and badges
Flush 'em down the fuckin' can.

I ain't lookin' to be no
Billy the Kid
Though his story's ace
I mean I dug what he did.
Seems I'm searchin' for
What can't be found
Another black ass shot
By another copper clown.

Why can't we have coppers
Think in the norm
Ya know the kind women love
To see in uniform?
Man try to remember
Why you became a cop
If ya can't remember boy
Then I think it's time to stop

Hear we go
Yea we're hearin' it again
Same ol' lies
Same Original Sin.
Don't give up

Take a stand across the land
Take those guns and badges
Flush 'em down the fuckin' can.

Some days I wake up
Angrier than others
Best thing for me
Just stay under the covers.
But they'll be comin' round
Hear what I gotta say
Justice is a game
Fill your quotas day by day.

I don't wanna say things
Just to be mean
Just warnin' my fellow man
Of the damage that I've seen.
The tears on the cheeks
Of a mother with a child
Whose a victim of the game
Of a copper gone wild.

Here we go
Yea we're hearin' it again
Same ol' lies
Same Original Sin.
Don't give up
Take a stand across the land
Take those guns and badges
Flush 'em down the fuckin' can.

Here's one more verse
A little more perverse
It has black children
Lyin' in a Hearst.

Look out your window
At what's goin' on
Maybe someone will listen
If I put it in a song.

It's a funny world
Out here in the street
Gets even funnier
If you're on the wrong cop's beat.
Sleep with one eye open
Don't show your pain
When they come with their guns
Get their numbers and names.

Hear we go
Yea we're hearin' it again
Same ol' lies
Same Original Sin.
Don't give up
Take a stand across the land
Take those guns and badges
Flush 'em down the fuckin' can.

Don't give up
Take a stand across the land
Take those guns and badges
Flush 'em down the fuckin' can.

It only takes one crazy cop to take a black life.
And get away with it!

I was talking to Phil Eurrup on the phone in the Spring of 2018, about a dream I had where I was at Bud's Farm with a bunch of Eagles of Death Metal fans. We were all sitting on the back porch waiting for Josh Homme to show up. It was taking a while, and we broke off into many conversations that stretched from U-2's concert at the Bercy Arena in Paris, to a 'Queens of the Stone Age' concert we all wanted to attend. I told Phil I had just written 'Cold Comfort' about the murders at the Bataclan in 2015, and about other songs I was writing in an album inspired by Josh. He commented that his girlfriend was going to be in Paris, and he alluded to hoping the bombings were over. I told him in the end, I just wanted to worthy of my own death. I excused myself and immediately wrote;

No Rehearsals;

I just;

Wanna be worthy
Of My own Death
Fuck second chances
Fuck ecstasy, meth.
Just a Ghost to guide
Somethin' like Macbeth
Gimme My Black Soul
Give the Devil My breath.

No Rehearsals
No second guesses
No adrenaline
No bloody messes.
No fake halos
Or guilty blesses
Nothin' left
No soft caresses.

Take My face
Burn it to ashes
Stick it where

Keith won't smoke my ashes.
Call it one of
Satan's dirty stashes
Bury it where
Next life hatches.

I just;
Wanna be worthy
Don't wanna be late
Wanna be part
Of My own fate.
Wanna blow in the wind
Not stuck in a crate
Wanna be somewhere near
The Ninth Gate.

No rehearsals
No variations
No cold and empty
No castrations.
No promises
No damnations
No ravaged night mares
No fake cessations.

All the fear
Fuck the dread
All My heroes
Are fuckin' dead.
Panic and pain
Are every day feelin's
Meet the Grim Reaper
Get's My heart reelin'.

Cause I just;

Wanna be worthy
Of My own Death
Make it a true trip
Get shit off My chest.
Don't distort My story
Or babble shibboleth
I wanna be proud
Of My own Death.

No fuckin' feed back
No eulogy
No Reaper Angels
God won't help Me.
No time or space
No more pain
No bullshit baby
Or bein' vain.

Honour to Thanatos;
Son of Sleep
Don't bring Me back
I'm dead too deep.
Turn off the light
Forever Midnight
Tunnel's forever
No wrong or right.

I just;

Wanna be worthy
Of My own Death
Fuck second chances
Fuck ecstasy, meth.
Just a Ghost to guide
Somethin' like Macbeth

Give Me My Black Soul
And the Devil My Breath!

Chapter 30
Lonely Scared
Frightened

Brian Wilson is at least a few books by himself. Or whoever he is on the day his name comes up. There are many stories of his brilliant song writing, and all his well-documented mental breakdowns that plagued him, probably to this very day to some extent. He was a patient of Therapist Eugene Landry from 1975, until he was fired. In 1982 Landry was re-employed to tend to Brian, subsequently becoming his business manager, co-signer, executive producer as well as Brian's business manager. The Wilsons did not interfere with this one sided relationship.

Landry accompanied Brian to shop for a car one day in 1986, where Brian met his present wife Melinda Ledbetter. Melinda was a former model, and then a car salesperson. She was talking to Brian when he suddenly whisked her into a new model car, and began conversing, while trusting her in short order. Eventually Landry stopped their conversation, but Brian offered to buy the car, if she handled the deal personally. The deal was sealed. Brian and Landry left, saying they would be back the next day. As Brian was leaving, he secretly shoved a piece of paper into her hand that read, 'Lonely Scared Frightened.'

Melinda sold Brian the car, and began dating him. The note he pressed into her hand made Melinda investigate Brian's stature and status in his relationship with Landry. In time she had Brian revealing what a domineering and disruptive force Landry had been in his life. She saw that he was inappropriately intimidating Brian into writing and recording music that he had no heart in.

But Brian had been ruled by Landry for so long that he found it almost impossible to find the courage to sever the relationship.

Melinda helped instigate Brian's eventual court-ordered separation from Landry. In time they were married, and she is still his mate and manager today. Brian's family was classically defunct; from his bully father Murray, to his delusional brother Dennis, who hung with the Mansion Tribe until he got too scared. Band member and cousin Mike Love was jealous of Brian, and criticized him on 'Pet Sounds'. His mother eventually divorced Murray, and there was nobody to protect Brian from his family, until Landry. Melinda became Brian's protection from Landry. Brian and Melinda live happy and productive lives together today, and Brian has released music with her as his manager. So is this a story that has a happy ending? I believe it is more of a story of being,

'Lonely, Scared and Frightened';

Voices in my head
Leave me far behind
Lord knows I can't keep up
And I sure can't unwind.
It's not like in my youth:
All caught up – all enlightened,
If you must know behind my eyes I'm
Lonely scared frightened.

Separated from my art
I need my screws tightened
Lost in the Dark Zone
On stage with my face whitened.
Watch this fool rush in
Want and need both now enlightened
But who can I trust all
Lonely scared frightened.

Things I can't remember
Maybe tryin' to forget
Places in my mind
I haven't been to yet.
All the dank, dark corners
That leave me unenlightened
Leave me bent, leave me tense,
Leave me lonely scared frightened.

Winter in my mind;
All the leaves have fallen
There is no trace of life
No flowers, no spring pollen.
My empty head aches
On bruised knees I'm a crawlin'
On my mothers' grave still
Lonely scared frightened fallen.

Tarzan, chickens and monkey semen
Flash at once upon the screen
Seems everything I say
Is selfish or obscene.
I'm hard as rock
With no time to ripen
Rain in my eyes and I'm
Lonely scared frightened.

Things I can't remember
Maybe tryin' to forget
Places in my mind
I haven't been to yet.
All the dank, dark corners
That leave me unenlightened

Leave me bent, leave me tense,
Leave me lonely scared frightened.

Where am I to go?
And do what when I get there?
I don't really know
And no one seems to care.
I've fallen on the rocks
Lost on the Crooked Path
Where I've searched all my life
To find Hell and Pain and Wrath.

I look to the Spirits
As I hide from the Brute
Hungry and tired, all I find
Is Strange Fruit.
No where is peace
Nothing is Good or Enlightened
I'm under a rock feelin'
Lonely scared frightened.

Things I can't remember
Maybe tryin' to forget
Places in my mind
I haven't been to yet.
All the dank, dark corners
That leave me unenlightened
Leave me bent, leave me tense,
Leave me lonely scared frightened.

Voices in my head
I don't understand a word
Life's blowin' in the breeze
Wind's gettin' more absurd.
Feel like I've been here before

On a day just like this
First time for every thing
Even the things I missed.

Those voices now a mumble
I survive in the jungle
Never look in people's eyes
On every crack I stumble.
Just tryin' to keep up
Tryin' not to pretend
Tryin' to make it through the night
Lonely scared frightened.

Things I can't remember
Maybe tryin' to forget
Places in my mind
I haven't been to yet.
All the dank, dark corners
That leave me unenlightened
Leave me bent, leave me tense,
Leave me lonely scared frightened.
Leave me bent, leave me tense,
Leave me lonely scared frightened!

First

Elvis was the First Punk. There were Rippers, Rapers and
Rasputin before him, but Elvis was the First Punk. Brando was
a Rebel. James Dean actually had a cause. Little Richard was
Rock and Roll, Tom Jones was sex, and Chuck Berry would deck
ya if you called him a Punk. Mick, Keith, Kurt, the Moondog,
Jim and John Joseph Lydon came later. So on the thirtieth of
July in 1954, when this skinny nineteen-year-old kid from Tupelo

Mississippi climbed aboard the Stage at the Overton Park Orchestra Shell in Memphis Tennessee and started to croon, the whole world swooned in tune.

It surely was one of those moments that passed when the Galaxy, as we know it, was never the same again. Elvis became a bigger star than the one that led the three Wise Men to Bethlehem. He was the first 'One-Namer' I can remember... Elvis! There was just nothing left to say. Elvis was third on the bill that day at Overton Park. To me, that means that the last singer of the past and antiquated world was Slim Whitman, who Elvis followed. Can you imagine hearing good ol' Slim yodelling along, and then suddenly seeing Satan, with his hair slicked black, and a cheek that tweaked to the beat in his eyes.

I was exposed to Elvis early with three older sisters. But I was never 'hypnotised' by him. Love me Tender was Classic, Hound Dog rocked, and Heartbreak Hotel was the coolest song with the coolest first line of all time. What was cooler than:

Ever since my Baby left me
I found a new place to dwell
It's down at the End of Lonely Street at
Heartbreak Hotel!!!

I loved Elvis more than his music. He was 'It'. But I was first anesthetized by 'Blowin' in the Wind' and I rocked to 'Twist and Shout'. Like everyone, I recognized early that his movies were lame, but you watched them because it was Elvis! In every Interview for ten years (maybe fifty) all the Artists said they started playing guitar, or whatever, because they were inspired by Elvis.

But after Sergeant Peppers and the Summer of Love were over, this was the period of Elvis that was the greatest to me... specifically the televised 'Come Back Show' in '68! It was masterful! He came on down-low in black leathers, playin' acoustic guitar with the Boys. They started with an instrumental. Brilliant! It was a Boy becoming a Man On-Stage. His sex appeal, after a Summer of Strangeness, could finally be taken for granted. Women weren't as easily shocked or intimidated at this point of time. Woman's Lib was gaining meaning with the 'Pill', and Janis Joplin put them more in control of their own lives than their Mothers could even imagine. Hard to believe there still hasn't been a Female President yet…oh right…

In 1969 Elvis released 'Suspicious Minds'! Truly one of the Top Five songs of the Decade! The song makes me tremble!…"We're caught in a Trap!" This was the Second Phase of *'Elvis the Black Leather Punk'*. And to close out the Decade that everyone says was represented by Andy Warhol, Wood Stock and The Beatles, Elvis went to Los Vegas to gig at the International Hotel and Casino. Soon you could not say Vegas without saying Elvis. Vegas got thick after a while, but it was a substitute for those damn puppy dog movies!

Following the successful TV 'Come Back Show', Elvis rewarded his fans for taking him back with some of the best songs of his career. His songs became 'Americana' in image and sound. *'In the Ghetto'* transformed him into singing about civil rights, poverty, pain, and being *current and real* about Society at that time. When RFK was assassinated he sang,

"There must be lights burning brighter somewhere,
Trapped in a cloud with too much rain."

Elvis, for a short time here, was not living up to his Image. He was living up to Real Life. He intoned 'Burning Love', though he hated singing it. Priscilla was on her way towards *the door* by then, and he had to lose massive weight before performing for over a billion fans in 1973 on Satellite. The story goes how he manically couldn't sleep and got hooked on sleeping pills, which escalated him to a prescription drug addict junkie.

Thus began Elvis' third phase of Punk; *'Fat and Drugged-Out Vegas Punk Elvis'*. With his hopes of touring globally much behind him now, and Colonel Tom Parker tragically keeping him America bound with nothing new to do, and now with no Pricilla, Mother long gone, and a monkey on his back full time, Elvis sank lower than the mud in Tupelo Mississippi. There was no living up to any Image by the end. He looked bloated, like Gram Parsons, for his last five years. Was it for the money or the fame? Like a True Punk, it was for both.

I was in Penticton visiting some Dundas Relics when I heard Elvis had died on August 17th, 1977. The second the radio announcement was over every woman in the room broke down crying. It was just part of the script. Remorse over fallen Gods has every Mother and Lover in Aphrodite's Hell. Pricilla once commented Punk Elvis was always asking, "Why Me?" from the death of his twin brother at birth, to God's compensating him with fame, and then taking away his Mother at his height.

Elvis was a Good Man, a Proud Man, a Singer, a Poet, a Picker, a Soldier, a Family Man, a Star, a God, a Resident of Graceland, an Entertainer, a Prophet, an Actor, a Son, an Icon, a Standard, a Human Being , an Original, a Re-inventor, a Hound Dog, and the First Punk!

I was watching a re-run of the train with RFK's body being taken to Section 45 of Arlington National Cemetery in Arlington, Virginia. When interviewed at the time Elvis advised a crippled nation, "I want you to understand me, because this is a moment in Time when we will need to understand each other." I thought then, as much as I do now, that this is profound and true. I then was inclined to write a song about what I imagined a conversation between God and Elvis would sound like, on his,

Long Road back to Salvation;

Headin' down the hiway
One more time thanks doin' it my way
Sit back, relax, leanin' on my sword
Starin' at the stars and talkin' to the Lord.
Asked em if He still remembered me
And if I'm ever on His mind
And if He'd like to puff a reefer
Before I go rap with the Grim Reaper.

We talked 'bout dreams that fell by the way
Discussed what it takes to make another day
Cried 'bout all we leave behind
Rollin' in Your Shrine between the pines.
We laughed 'bout riddles in space and time
And why I fought for what was never mine
Then I thought of myself as His Creation
And the long way back to Salvation.

Chorus: Cruisin' on in over drive
Tryin' to keep my soul alive
Full out with no hesitation
The long road back to Salvation.
No sun glasses just eye to eye
Only time we talk's when think I gonna die
Down an ol' stone road listenin' to the country station
On the long road back to Salvation.

My feet are worn my tires are too
Thought by now You'd give me a clue
Where I am and where I'm goin'
What I got hidden and what's showin'.
Talkin' to the Lord and starin' at the sky
Feelin' Spiritual, just a little high

Said Lord if you're everywhere yer in my beer
In everythin' I love and everything I fear.

My car breaks down I phone CAA
Like askin' the doctor for another day
Lucky for me I drive a Ford
In the glove box got the number of the Lord.
Headin' down the hi way once again
Passin' life with all it's sins
When the day's done pull in the station
And start the long road back to Salvation.

Chorus:
Cruisin' on in over drive
Tryin' to keep my soul alive
Full out with no hesitation
The long road back to Salvation.
No sun glasses just eye to eye
Only time we talk's when I think gonna die
Down an ol' stone road listenin' to the country station
On the long road back to Salvation.

Ford radio's blarin' out ol' Merle
Sky is cloudy as a pearl
Bible sits closed too strange to read
Get same message with head fulla weed.
The Good Life is hard to live
In the end knows what you did
Run forever if ya like try to hide
Trust me Lord knows I've tried.

Talkin' again you'd think I've had enough
But's good to talk to someone ya trust
Sit back, relax, leanin' on my sword
Starin' at the stars and talkin' to the Lord.

Eyes on the road hands on the wheel
Round the next corner's part of the deal
Runnin' low gotta find the next station
On the long road back to Salvation.

Chorus:
Cruisin' on in over drive
Tryin' to keep my soul alive
Full out with no hesitation
The long road back to Salvation.
No sun glasses just eye to eye
Only time we talk's when I think gonna die
Down an ol' stone road listenin' to the country station
On the long road back to Salvation.

I know I've talked about and quoted Frank (another One-Namer) throughout my journal, but in reality, I never was in time or tune to listen to his music. That is until a friend of mine came over to my house with one of his CDs in 1990. I had to go through almost thirty years of Jerry Garcia before I could hear anything else, but one day I did hear Frank.

Frank was like Paul McCartney with connections... or Michael Jackson without Bubbles; and a true Pop God for the Ladies! Frank was another soldier that re-invented himself, every decade, until he played with 'em all. I wrote this song for Frank to sing, with a melody he would have been a natural to sing;

Can't find a Reason;

Can't find a reason
If that's all it takes
Night time's the right time
Hate daybreak.
Cruisin' along
Runnin' from your heartache

You're dealin' the cards
I can't catch a break.

S'like I'm on a diet
And You're cheese cake
I'm getting' hotter
And You're a snow flake.
One of a kind
My only mistake
What can I say
I can't catch a break.

Chorus:
We're at the finish line
We're past a hand shake
I'm playin' with the Devil
But You taste like Angel Cake.
All the tributaries
That make You a Lake
But I sprung a leak cause
I can't catch a break!

Today's now tomorrow
Gives a new take
Line in the sand
Becomes an earth quake.
Good times are memories
When ya used to slake
But You can't remember
And I can't catch a break.

Forever and ever
These are just words
When ya think about 'em
They're just absurd.

Play your last hand
My little sweep stakes
I know I can't win
I can't catch a break.

Chorus:
Game of chess with Debbie
See Marilyn for a line
Breakfast at Tiffiny's
Gigi on Broadway doin' fine.
From Here to Eternity
And back for Liz's sake
Leaves no time for Shirley
Lord I can't catch a break!

Friday night at the Copa
Gotta be late
Purple Room Supper Club
Enjoy a rack then a steak.
Jet set to Ciro's
Coconut Grove before dawn
Scream at Park Plaza
Madame Wong and we're gone.

Good times and bad
Are a roll of the dice
Rollin' along
Pink Rolls done up nice.
One for the road
To keep me awake
Flashin' red lights
I can't catch a break.

Chorus:
Sammy's torchin' the Sands

Dino's toastin' Gini
Aloof from Pete and Pat
How is your martini?
Can't find a reason
If that's all it takes
I'm doin' it My Way
I can't catch a break!

Frank, you was the Rat in the Pack!

Sid and Nancy

Like probably most writers, I tend to write while driving. I've had to pull over so many times to write things down its no wonder I don't go out much. I'm afraid my cheap Panasonic Zoom Mic burner would melt if I left it in the truck on a warm day. You don't leave children, pets or electrical devices in vehicles with the windows up. You can end up out of tunes, or in jail. On my way into work one warm July, I had to pull over repeatedly as I was writing two songs at once, as it turned out.

I was ignoring a loathsome radio commercial while travelling the winding roads that hug the lakes, when I turned the noise off and enjoyed the morning sun and the sounds of Nothingness. I mumbled to myself;

Thank you, Silence

Thank You, Silence
Truly My only friend
With no, callous sounds
Tellin' me it's the End.
Hello, Loneliness
Crumpled on the floor Ha

And you thought you'd make it
Least to the nearest door!

Use me, Torment
To please your needs
I'll make, you Stronger
You'll just have me bleed.
Free me, Spirits
To search out my soul
And assemble, the broken parts
That make me whole.

Chorus:
You don't know what fear is
Till it haunts you at its fancy
Tales told in nightmares like when Bonnie and
Clyde meet Sid and Nancy.
Things you can't imagine
Lost in the forest
Unknown Soldiers with dead flowers
For me the Unknown Guest.

Hiding in, my circumstance
Bless me father I have sinned
Give me pennants, chants that rhyme
Crap that leaves me less chagrined
Take me, to the river
Define my space and time
Not waste myself, in Paradoxes
Least survive my own Paradigm.

Hello, Patience
When is truth not a lie
Someone, is on to me
And the hunt has gone awry

Sorry, 'bout the unexplained
And probably what's comin' next
I'll take a chance, throw it out there
See just what it'll fetch.

Chorus:
You don't know what fear is
Till it haunts you at it's fancy
Tales told in nightmares like when Bonnie and
Clyde meet Sid and Nancy.
Things you can't imagine
Lost in the forest
Unknown Soldiers with dead flowers
For me the Unknown Guest.

Save me, Again
From myself who else?
Tell me, Secrets
Quickly before my mind melts.
Steer me, gently
Away from the Abyss
Help me, don't let me
Lose my way to reminisce.

Brandin', each Other
With distortion and dirty words
Learnin', the values
Of volume and vivacious words.
Thank You, Silence
Truly My only friend
With no, callous sounds
Tellin' me that it's the end.

Chorus:
You don't know what fear is

Till it haunts you at its fancy
Tales told in nightmares like when Bonnie and
Clyde meet Sid and Nancy.
Things you can't imagine
Lost in the forest
Unknown Soldiers with dead flowers
For me the Unknown Guest.

Thank you, Silence
Truly My only Friend
With no, callous sounds
Tellin' me that it's the End!

Ten kilometres into my drive I had pulled over numerous times. Finally I found a choice spot on a lake, and decided to finish the second song. I phoned work and said I'd be late. It didn't matter to anyone if I adjusted my hours, which made this job plausible. In a couple minutes, I went from a calm, intense song of talking to the Stars, to this 'Ragin' Rocker'! It's all from stayin' up too late and too much pizza! Feelin' Zombified I rattled out;

Zombie land;

Take yourself out of Nurseryland
Life on the road's never like you planned
Nothin' to do with fairness ya understand
Just we're all Orphans here in Zombieland.
Something's gone astray in the Heartland
Sun's gone south of the Promised Land
Life's fallen to the palm of the Dark Hand
Cause we're all Orphans here in Zombieland.

Chorus:
Back on the road lookin' for a remand

Hope sinkin' fast like hearts in quick sand
Everything's been said, all that's left got banned
Damn we're all Orphans here in Zombieland.

On your hands and knees searchin' every strand
Doin' what ya gotta for a break in the sand
Don't look behind ya, nothin' looks grand
Man we're all Orphans here in Zombieland.
No olive no martini, nothin' at hand
Nothin' left to salvage from Dreamland
Light a candle wear a black arm band
'Member we're all Orphans here in Zombieland.

Chorus:
Nothin' new same ol' story at the news stand
All ya own's on your back no supply or demand
Forget about the love lost in the Lowlands
Lord we're all Orphans here in Zombieland.

They keep your mind in a trunk with no room to expand
Kick 'em down the stairs man it's all I can stand
Nothing left in the grasslands or the fryin' pan
Fuck we're all Orphans here in Zombieland.
Those who toast at the top – jackals in command
Left hand sides to the equations, wrong sides of the back hand
Hope resonates in bottles of jug bands
Help! We're all Orphans here in Zombieland.

Chorus: Road getting narrow as we approach the Rand
No room to breathe on the mainland
Continue muckin' through the Wasteland
Shit we're all Orphans here in Zombieland.

Perform incantations in the woodlands
Meditate with sage in the back of a van

What happened to sticks from Thai Land
When we're all Orphans here in Zombieland.
Lookin' for compensation, not reprimand
Not lookin' for anything second hand
Life goes on with Death in command
Look out we're all Orphans here in Zombieland.
Chorus:
Back on the road lookin' for a remand
Hope sinkin' fast like hearts in quick sand
Everything's been said, all that's left got banned
Damn we're all Orphans here in Zombieland.

Somethin's gone astray in the Heartland
Now we're all Orphans here in Zombieland!!!

I used to have a Sunday night card game every week when I lived at my rented house inside the gates of Dundurn Park. I was hosting a game for all the Dundas dudes and dudettes that I grew up with, and drank with every day at the Last Chance Hotel. I didn't get a chance to play often. I was always going somewhere for some drug deal, or partying with some new friends. My poker guests were a rather tame bunch, which was good, because I was always going out to Rochdale or meeting up with B Cautious, Serge, or Heinz Berlin's biker droogs. I am celebrating my Golden Anniversary this year for smoking Golden Buds. So before Grow-Ops, I was compulsively busy buying and dealing drugs eight days a week.

I should have been playing cards but the Jack of Spades is for keepin' up your sleeve, not your nose.

Leonardo staged a Sunday night poker game three thousand miles away also. When it came time to flee to B.C., I was there for most poker nights. One blizzardly night nobody showed up, so Leon and I amused ourselves with some poems I always had stashed in my back pocket. Leon appreciated my way with words, and he was always telling me I would regret not writing a book, or recording them as songs.

We smoked some stinky exotic Indica and he told me to write a 'Poker Poem' to hang on the wall for the next week's game. Before I got started some of Leon's clients dropped in, and we started a new session. We got loaded and I never bothered. But I always intended to, but ya know how that goes...but...but...

Leonardo was a master games player. Sessions of the game Risk would transpire for days and days before that became the norm. I taught Leon to play chess. For years our games were legendary. Like with Serge, Leon and I bet on every game for something; usually drugs. I have never met another game player like Leon.

Leonardo died almost fifteen years ago, and there is not a day goes by that I do not think of him, for one comical or crazy reason. Recently I was puffing a Biggee and I realized I never wrote his 'Poker Song'. So I made up for lost time and wrote words to the Sky while I was High. This one's for You Leon;

<u>Corners of my Mind;</u>

There's a card game goin' on
In the corners of my mind
One more round I'll figure out 'yactly
What I'm tryin' to find.-
Hidden up my sleeve
Arranged there by design
Cards against humanity
And other games left undefned.

Queen of Diamonds Jack of Hearts
Now they're all left behind
Desperate and vicious
Line of credit's been declined.
What don't make sense leaves ya bent

All the rest leaves ya inclined
There's clouds buildin' shrouds
In the corners of my mind.

Chorus:
Deals goin' nowhere nothin' found
Eyes straight front no lookin' round
Devil cards keep comin' round
Kings and Queens polish their crowns.
Loaded dice and bad advise
Top of the mountain west end ice
Pillage plunder pay the price
With the corners of my mind.

Bettin' on a bluff
Hopin' my red face don't flush
In the west corner of my skull
Bad beat says it's had enough.
Probability tellin' me
House of cards ready to fold
Hand I'm holdin' ain't real
And I'm dreamin' of fool's gold.

There's a darkness in the corner
Where cards hide that are wild-
A darkness laced with mold
Mixed with the innocence of a child.
Luck of the draw
Says there's one hand left to play
Win or lose sanguineous
My mind's playin' games again today.

Chorus: Deals goin' nowhere nothin' found
Eyes straight front no lookin' round
Devil cards keep comin' round

Kings and Queens polish their crowns.
Loaded dice and bad advise
Top of the mountain west end ice
Pillage plunder pay the price
With the corners of my mind.

There's a card game goin' on
In the corners of my mind
One more round I'll figure out 'yactly
What I'm tryin' to find.
Hidden up my sleeve
Arranged there by design
Cards against humanity
And other games left undefined.

Queen of Diamonds Jack of Hearts
Now they're all left behind
Desperate and vicious
Line of credit's been declined.
What don't make sense leaves ya bent
All the rest leaves ya inclined
There's clouds buildin' shrouds
In the corners of my mind.

Chorus:
Deals goin' nowhere nothin' found
Eyes straight front no lookin' round
Devil cards keep comin' round
Kings and Queens polish their crowns.
Loaded dice and bad advise
Top of the mountain west end ice
Pillage plunder pay the price
With the corners of my mind.

There's a card game goin' on in the corner of my mind.

Chapter 31
No False Gods no
Johnny Depp

Paul McCartney wrote Helter Skelter in response to reading an article in Crawdaddy Magazine, where Robert Plant said that, "Zeppelin was writing the wildest songs in Rock" at that time. Paul immediately took him up on the challenge! The next day the Four Lads went to an Amusement Park for ideas and inspirations.

Paul encountered a massive slide called *Helter Skelter*. The name affected him; maybe not the same as it affected Charlie Manson, but he was intrigued by the words. Before they left Paul scribbled down some very simple words to describe the Slide, lest he forget. The words and images he wrote were simply;

When I get to the bottom
I go back to the top of the Slide
Where I stop and I turn and I go for a ride
Till I get to the bottom and I see you again.
Helter Shelter!!

Who would believe that such simple verses with innocent instructions would become one of the darkest tunes ever written by the Fabs. I wonder if Plant has ever performed that Satanic Verse in his repertoire. The melody is a natural for him. Maybe like Lennon, he just didn't wanna go there…

Zeppelin were Sonic Explosions! As I mentioned earlier, I was into the West Coast Sound since 1970, so I couldn't afford Zeppelin vinyls. Kori gave me a copy of the paperback, 'Hammers of the Gods' by Stephen Davis. The Village Voice weren't just whistlin' Dixie when they dubbed it, "Incredible!" For me, it was an incredible Adventure! It was an accurate account of their saga, and I relished it lavishly.

Each Chapter covered a period of time representing the mosaic of events around each album. I enjoyed reading about their endeavors so dearly, that when I came to the end of a chapter, I would play the album the book had just covered for ten days before starting to read the next chapter. It was a whirlwind of stories I had heard about over the years, but reliving them was majestic. I can't remember loving a book that much since devouring 'Twenty Years with the Grateful Dead' by Rock Scully. 'The Right Stuff' was close.

I deliberately did not write a song about Zeppelin until I was finished the book, as I did not want to take away from my reading and enjoyment time. I dragged the compendium of chapters out for two months, while going through every album/CD as I progressed. When the sad day came that I finished the paperback, I smiled with a tale to tell myself. My aphorism for Zeppelin is one of a 'passing'.

I thought in the Tree of Life, they are 'Wayward Pines' not allowing themselves to be left behind. With early morning meadows and leprechauns in mind, I wrote about the Wayward Zeppelins...<u>Hammer of the Gods / Wayward Pines;</u>

Sweet and gentle golden fields
Rays creep until they're real
Waves help the rocks to shine
As Wayward Pines get left behind.
Sun burns out the lonely sky
Charcoal colours burnt and black
Wayward Pines line the track
There really ain't no turning back.

Chorus:
Mountains crumble to the sea
Promises stumble their ways to me
The truth to me's another way of lyin'
Hear those Wayward Pines a – cryin'.
Stars expose the darkest night
Moon beams expose romance
Wayward Pines lost in the forest
Looking for just one more chance.

Gentle breath on my neck
Brings on a summer breeze
Wayward Pines in the back of my mind
So real yet such a tease.
Needles crackle under weight
Of nature, pain and time
The Path I take's not only mine
As Wayward Pines get left behind.

Chorus:
Mountains crumble to the sea
Promises stumble their ways to me
The truth to Me's another way of lyin'
Hear those Wayward Pines a – cryin'.
Stars expose the darkest night
Moon beams expose romance
Wayward Pines lost in the forest
Looking for just one more chance.

Flowers hide my state of mind
Sun through clouds still leave me blind
Stop and check just one more time;
Now Wayward Pines lag far behind.
Jagged rocks reach for the sky

Heave and crack until they die
Then start again until they're high
Never ask Nature why.

Chorus:
Mountains crumble to the sea
Promises stumble their ways to me
The truth to me's another way of lyin'
Hear those Wayward Pines a – cryin'.
Stars expose the darkest night
Moon beams expose romance
Wayward Pines lost in the forest
Looking for just one more chance.

Foggy skies and mystic trails
Rest your wings let your mind sail
Rain turns to rock and falls as hale
Laughing winds begin to wail.
Show it one more time to me
Together we will search and find
Chanting words that seem to rhyme
As Wayward Pines are left behind.

Chorus:
Mountains crumble to the sea
Promises stumble their ways to me
The truth to me's another way of lyin'
Hear those Wayward Pines a – cryin'.
Stars expose the darkest night
Moon beams expose romance
Wayward Pines lost in the forest
Looking for just one more chance.

Ride the stars fight the good fight
Through the darkness find the light

Close your eyes increase your sight
And wish the Wayward Pines good night.
Midnights come and Heartaches go
Battle Gods of the Ice and Cold
Across the skies they sing and dance
Give Wayward Pines just one more chance.

I sang this song for weeks before I decided how to use my voice. Because it's the epic it Is, I tended to 'over-do it' in my steal and zeal. Amy talked to me of 'toning down' my voice to tell the story like a Woodsman in the Pines. This made sense in the end, and we began building layer after layer of Irish and Celtic sounds until Andrew finally encompassed the tune with what he called an 'Irish Flute'. It was a masterful ending to a good effort. I have a vision for a video for this where an English family is standing on the back of the caboose watching the Pine Forests disappear behind them at days end. When they travel round the bend the Wayward Pines come alive and play their instruments wildly as the four Zulu Members! Rock lives on! Zeppelin rules!

Summer can be the hardest when you get sun in your eyes and lose your way.

I was walking with the wind to my back as I wrote two songs one day. I figured they were good enough to sing for a friend in town. Upon singing them and groovin' and puffin'for a while, I made my way back to the Lake. I had a new idea of a melody for one, and I liked it. I searched out and found the song entitled 'Black Roses for Jerry,' but search as I did, I could not find the other song, which went to its demise without a name. My remorse was mortifying. I lost one of my creations! Motherless Child blowin' in the wind!

I was veeped. I looked for it later in the day throughout the house, the truck, my files, and finally I gave up and sat vexed. I texted my Artist Friend, but it was not there. I sat brooding with furrowed brow. That was when I decided that I had no one to blame but myself. And it came to me; I would write another song about having no one to blame for the catastrophe, but myself.

I Lost My Song:

I have no one to blame
Except for myself
No false gods no Johnny Depp
And there ain't no one else.
Change everything
It doesn't really matter
Forget your face drop your name
Become the Madd Hatter.

I'll start at the bottom
Till I fall off the top
Nothin's real I can't feel
And I'm never gonna stop.
Look in my eyes
The wind rustles the leaves
I'll do anything you say
You'll do what you please.

Chorus: Life is death there is no rest
Wind makes us all so lame
Everything hurts then it's gone
But I have no one to blame.

Life hurts on the shore line
The sky bleeds overhead
But life is so sacred I should
Stop wishing I was dead.
Someone tell me somethin'
That doesn't sound the same

I have no recourse
I have no one to blame.

Please stop the pain
Let me cry,let me try
Let me talk to the corpses
That were allowed to die.
Take me on a journey
That will make me feel ashamed
Life goes on no excuses
I have no one to blame.

Chorus:
Lost and found on battle grounds
I am not fit to tame
I search my soul for what to say
But I have no one to blame.

Nothing is sacred
And I know judgment sucks
Our rate of flow exchanges
Into radiant flux.-
No explanations
I'll rehearse for you
I've been there before and
This ai't deja vu.

Disciples wanna follow
I'm here by myself
I ain't blamin' no one
It's all on myself.
We all have a passion
We keep on the shelf
We shake 'em and we break 'em
I only blame myself.

Please stop the pain
Let me cry let me try
Let me talk to the corpses
That were allowed to die.
Take me on a journey
That will make me feel ashamed
Life goes on no excuses
I have no one to blame.

I have no one to blame
I have no one to blame
I have no one to blame,
But myself..................

Amy said she liked this hopeless, self-abusing pitiful psalm the best of the forty songs I recorded in that two day session. I could tell as she seemed swept away on the Grand grandly. It starts softly for every verse then builds into a crescendo of grief and self-loathing. Obviously you need to hear it to see my affliction and anguish. Enjoy!

The song I didn't lose was a long overdue ode to Jerry Garcia. The Dead were a troop, but it was always about Jerry. If Bob Weir put out a brilliant album, it was always on the back of Jerry. He once took six months off and put together, and then edited the illustrious Grateful Dead movie. He was teaching Bob to play guitar in 1965. He decided at one point to fire Bob and Pig Pen in '69, because with their lack of progress, Jerry figured they were holding the Band back. Garcia was the connection for all the others, from Cassidy, Kesey, Tom Wolfe, Owsley, the Haight, 710 Ashbury Street crowd, Mountain Girl, Hell's Angles and the Other Side of this Life.

Jerry was the back-drop of my time in St. Mary's and the Seventies. By the Time the Eighties came along, you could catch him playing in three different bands; Old and in the Way, NRSPs, and the Garcia and Howard Wales Band. After playing in Egypt, he was just trying to keep himself in good Blow and Persian. It's true what they say, "Life IS a bitch, and then ya die." Jerry died on August ninth, 1995. I was released. I started writing more on my own until it became a syndrome. Sorry it took so long Jerrrrr…

American Song Bird;

American Songbird
Leader of the Pack
Somethin' almost Holy
And nothin's gonna bring Him back!
Seems like a Storm
From the Great North West
Pickin' and Tickin' and
Tested and Blessed!

Unbroken Chain
Up and down the Coast
Gods give the Least to
Those They love the most.
California Jug Bands
On Paths seldom used
Lost in the Forest
Intrepidly Amused!

Chorus:
Delta Blues and Blue Shoes
Lightning Bolt Skulls with a Cherry
Three Hundred Mics becomes Planetary
Offering Black Roses for Jerry.
Riders became New Riders
Three Continents became the Primary

Impulsively caprice, Ultimately Arbitrary
I Gratefully offer Black Roses for Jerry.

Conquistador
High Noon in the Haight
Anthem of the Sun
Eulogies soundin' Great.
It's either Right or Left
On Columbia Street
Tower of Technology
Freaks Olympic Athlete!

Seven Hundred
And ten Plaid Iguanas
Viola Le like Crazy
Like a Bantu Bechuana.
Workin' for a Livin'
Takin' what the Devil's givin'
Talkin' singin' the Blues
With Death so Unforgivin'.

Chorus:
Delta Blues and Blue Shoes
Lightning Bolt Skulls with a Cherry
Three Hundred Mics becomes Planetary
Offering Black Roses for Jerry.
Riders became New Riders
Three Continents became the Primary
Impulsively caprice, Ultimately Arbitrary
I Gratefully offer Black Roses for Jerry.

Runnin' down the Tracks
Flippin' out that Jack
Spinnin' that Sledge Hammer
And He ain't comin' back.

Shadow hidin' from the Sun
Grace the Stage like Hit and Run
Father of a Mind Set
Mother Nature's Favourite Son!

Touch of Grey's now Bone White;
You got Your Chips Cashed In
Gotta New Game goin'
Aces High to Win.
American Songbird
Leader of the Pack
Somethin' almost Holy
Nothin's gonna bring Hin Back!

Moose Head Beer

I was coming out of the Beer Store one day with a case of Moose Head Beer; the best head on my favorite beer. I had just finished a couple days at Grant and my head began to fill up again. This was the type of song, for me, that after the first lines, it was basically finished… there was only one way to write it. I worked out the melody for the chorus the next day. I was thinking that all songs should be that easy.

But sing it over and over again as I did I could not sing this tune adequately at all. I took it down to 'Grant' a couple months later… no go again! I eventually got Amy to sing it. Perfect! I don't understand whether Amy understands, or believes this, but she has an eloquent voice. So quiescent, it overcomes the male! Every time I talk her into singing one of my songs, it automatically becomes my favorite.

And everybody agrees! It's true that she is not a forceful lead singer, but she sings delicately and pleasingly. I've got a large vocal range, but in the past three years I have settled into a baritone that dips in the neighbourhood of the Man in Black's; or so I've been told. Putting my name in any sentence with the name Johnny Cash is exciting and an honour and makes my knees quake.

But it was Amy who sailed with the wind on this one. So thanks again Amy...

<u>Been Looking;</u>

Been looking for
So long
Through clouds and
My songs
Which way did You go?
Where are You now?
Time passes slow
Cry if You know how.

Wind chases the
Dark Sky
Sun's gone no
Good byes
So what was why for?
Roses on the floor
Feelings galore
And left wanting more.

Chorus:
Bank of the River beginning of Time
Synch My heart with one that rhymes
Search life calling on distant shores
Find out what I've been looking for!

Birds serenade
The moor

Rich and poor
Endure
Counting the stars
So near yet so far
Was that Gods breeze?
Or just My guitar?

Sun meets the
Horizon
Each doin' their
Own Zen
Space waits to absorb
Us all off this Orb
Erase Us in Time
Each in our own Warp.

Waves roll up and capture the Shore
Thrash and crash on age shut doors
Time and Space in a different Age
Let Me go I'm turnin' the page.

Starin' up at
The Trees
Sharin' secrets
With Me
Ceremoniously close
My favorite Ghost
Leaves My heart sage'd
Whispering adios. –

World full of
Secrets
Sincerest and
Rejects
Which way do I turn

Should I be concerned?
Was there somethin' to learn?
Am I gonna burn?

Chorus:
Bank of the River beginning of Time
Synch My heart with one that rhymes
Search out life calling on distant shores
Find out what I've been looking for!

Been looking for
So long
Through clouds and
My songs
Which way did You go?
Where are You now?
Time passes slow
Cry if You know how.

Wind chases the
Dark Sky
Sun's gone no
Good byes
So what was why for
Roses on the floor
Feelings galore
And left wanting more…

Chapter 32
Thank Galileo
for My Sight

We've all stared at the Stars before. We've witnessed comets soaring through Constellations and Galaxies too far away! I used to have access to a 200 x's telescope to stare at wondrous sights, and marvel at my insignificance. I can pick out the constellations of the Zodiac on clear nights, when staring up at the Galaxies of Celestial Spheres, Universes and Planets. The prophecy of the Stars is for us to uncover as we stare up at the Gods.

But one night I caught the self-luminous Heavenly Bodies staring back at me!

I swear the Stars twinkled in my eyes, and the Moon smiled toothlessly in my direction! Polaris was posing and Capricorn was calling! I could feel under my skin that I was about to merge with the Universal Cosmos. I was the Microcosm of Their Macrocosm. I recognized the solar systems within us all. I spoke to the Wholeness and awaited our answer together. In my elated state, I wrote down everything that went on. It was Divinity on Demand. I was interpreting for the Gods when I wrote:

Search Out the Darkness;

I have loved the, Stars so blindly
Thank Galileo for my sight!
Cut Him out in, tiny pieces
And throw Him against the night.
I search out, the Darkness
Gather strength for Artemis to fight

Feeling out iniquities, to find Black Holes
That guard me from the Light.

O save me, from the Orion
Give me to my frights
Searching blindly, forevermore
Hide my cunning eyes all too contrite.
Too many, truths to hide
Newton confused by orbits of Uranus
Allowed Neptune, to be found
Making lonely skies more luminous.

Chorus: The Gods are aligning with Apollo
I want to return all their toys
Even the one I stole
But not the ones that I enjoy.
Wake up the Olympians
Dionysus crush the grape
Search the Heavens; insist to Hades
There's a place He can escape.

Wickedness and, desolation
Fills my blacked out mind
Shadows of shade, and obscurity
Leave dark despair behind.
Sucked into, the Abyss
Where obfuscation understands
Lights so bright, obscuring the sight
Of Gods and Mortal Man.

O save me, Caliginous Skies
Of black pallor and swarthiness
Where Heavenly Bodies, obscured the life
Orpheus begged to have exist.
Reflecting cosmic, refraction

Raining in my eyes
Look above, for glory
Sharing truth with lies.

Chorus:
The Gods are aligning with Apollo
I want to return all their toys
Even the one I stole
But not the ones that I enjoy!
Wake up the Olympians
Dionysus crush the grape
Search the Heavens; insist to Hades
There's a place He can escape.

Opaque Clouds, displease and disguise
Transparent skies blurred by the mist
Sirius, Vegas, the Gammas and Majoris
And others are soon missed.
The Betas, Deltas, Gamma Draconis,
Jupiter 2 searches Alpha Centauri,
Pollux, Hamal, Gruis, Alcor,
All part of the Cosmic Glory.

O save time, to talk to Bellatrix
Polaris customizes your ride
Alphecca; the broken rings of stars
Reposed, takes a moon for a bride.
Aphrodite, gave birth to Cupid
Her vanity was the Trojan War
When gazing the stars she worshiped too far
And complied with the waves on the shore.

Chorus:
The Gods are aligning with Apollo
I want to return all their toys

Even the one I stole
But not the ones that I enjoy!
Wake up the Olympians
Dionysus crush the grape
Search the Heavens; insist to Hades
There's a place He can escape.

O Starry, Starry, Night, Mr. Van Gogh!

Alice

Who doesn't like Alice Cooper? Alice is an Icon of Black Leather Punks and bored House Wives. But not like Elvis. Alice is more like Beelzebub Himself.

Alice goes where he is needed across the Galaxy. They were hisssssssssssssed out of L.A. after recording their first album, 'Pretties for You', which was produced by Zappa. So the Band decided they would set up at the first City that actually cheered for them. Obviously, the Motor City was the Corner to hide on until they were discovered.

With Groups like MC-5, Wayne County and Iggy Pop, they fit right in! Their break came at the Toronto Rock and Roll Revival in 1969, when Manager Shep Gordon gave the Concert Producers the last lump of cash they had to let them be the band that went on directly before John Lennon and his Plastic Ono Band. That is where they threw a chicken onstage, and when Alice threw it back, they tore it apart! Ozzy had bats and Alice had a chicken. Karma for them both!

What was cooler as a teenager than getting high and seeing Alice's head get guillotined off into a basket? And then plucked out by the hair for a hungry audience to spiritually devour?! Those were the days! Just ask Mary Hopkins... 'Pretties for You' was my fave album, but Alice Cooper's Trip was introduced in the epic; ' Ballad of Dwight Fry'.

That song is full of every image related to the first stage of Alice;

Mommy, when is Daddy coming home…
He's been gone so long
Do you think he'll ever come home?...

I made friends with a lot of people
In the Danger Zone!...

Sleeping don't come very easy
In a straight white vest!...

See my lonely life unfold
I see it every day
See my lonely mind explode
When I've gone insane!...

I, I want to get out of here
I, I want to get out of here

Ya got to let me out of here
Let me out of here
I gotta get out of here
I gotta get out of here
I gotta get out of here
I gotta get out of here
I gotta get out of here
I gotta get out of here' …

Said to myself this is very strange
I'm glad it wasn't me
But now I hear those sirens callin'
And so I am not free …

I didn't want to be
I didn't want to be
I didn't want to be ...

See my lonely life unfold
(Leave me alone)
(I didn't want to be)
(Don't touch me)
See my lonely mind explode
When I've gone insane!!

As a young Teen, that had about the same effect on me as the first time I heard 'Smells like Teenage Spirit'... it took my mind and blew it up and gave it back in pieces .... And I begged for more!

But after 'Dwight Fry' the 'shock-rock reputation' softened, perhaps after the song 'I'm Eighteen'. 'Billion Dollar Babies' had the edge in Vince's voice, but it did not cut me. By the time he was in the space of Salvador Dali, and doing the Muppet Show, he was more image than sound. The 'Welcome to my Nightmare' separation album was great, but the edge after Dwight was already ridden, and a bandage was not needed. Mothers take young children to Alice concerts in the last twenty years to emphasize that it was a new age of Family Entertainment (Kori with our kids included).

But I still love Alice, and I have written him into many songs and stories in my last twenty years. He is Devious and Eloquent; Scary and Surreal, and still hugely in demand! Today he performs his shtick with the Hollywood Vampires, rising from the Dead with Johnny Depp, Duff McKagan, Matt Sorem, Robert DeLeo, Joe Perry, and guests from David Grohl to Paul McCartney. The name comes from a celebrity Drinking Club that Alice formed in the Seventies that included John Lennon,

Ringo Starr, Keith Moon, Mickey Dolenz, Joe Walsh and other gentlemen who liked to bend their elbows behind closed doors.

This is one of my Alice songs that I recorded with Amy last year…

<u>Looking for Vince:</u>

Far away Alice is
Looking for Vince
All His nightmares
And the Chicken.
Vince was into Earwigs
Even more Spiders
Call him Alice
He's already inside Her.

Detroit loves
L.A. winners
L.A. only likes
Freaks and Sinners.
Frank loves anything that
Vincent hurls
Vince loved Frank and all
The GTO Girls!

A Villain Woman Killer
In tattered skirt and make-up
Pretties For You come
In a C-Cup.
Alice drove a stake
Through Love's Flower
Came to there was fun
Sex, Death, Power.

Chorus:
Mommy, where's Daddy?
He's been gone so long!
Do you think
He'll ever come home?
Daddy Looks like an Artist,
Sounds like a Hun,
Shits like an Animal;
Licks his lips when done.

Success breeds contempt
Alice lost his head
He loved his third album
'Till it was dead.
Alice learned to Climax
In his Electric Chair
Villainous Androgyny
Bratty machismo dares.

School's Out
Billion Babies high
Alice tells us
No More Mister Nice Guy!
Muscle Of Love spent
Teenage Lament
Life Of Alice Cooper'
Twisted, burnt and bent.

He 'jaculated in the morn
Glam Rock was born
His son Dee Snider
And Johnny Rotten mourned.
Just another victim
Road Kill on the rage

Society mourned
So Alice turned the page.

Chorus:
Mommy, where's Daddy?
He's been gone so long!
Do you think
He'll ever come home?
Daddy Looks like an Artist,
Sounds like a Hun,
Shits like an Animal;
Licks his lips when done.

Invited to His Nightmare
Only Women Bleed
Umbilical cord cut
Planted his new seed.
Alice went To Hell
Dressed in Whiskey and Lace
He Never Cried
Though his sanity's chased.

Once outside
Made the Muppet Show
Black Out albums
Bought the Letter O.
Divorcing all
Like Warner on the run
Alice now a free man
First since it begun.

Constricted yet distorted
Alice says, "I'm Back"
Raised his fist Yelled Like Hell
David Blunkett gave attack.

John Leo Organ

On A Bed of Nails
His Life and Crimes
Found their way to Wayne's World;
King for a day, hell all time!

Chorus:
Mommy, where's Daddy?
He's been gone so long!
Do you think
He'll ever come home?
Daddy Looks like an Artist,
Sounds like a Hun,
Shits like an Animal;
Licks his lips when done.

Now a Hollywood Vampire
Alice flies town to town
With more dark clouds
Than any circus clown.
Alcohol, guillotines
All hooks in the glory
Alice is looking for Vince
To tell him all his stories!

With a smile
Drove Mothers wild
Now he's America's
Darkest child.
Like a raven
He can't be bored
Story of Alice
Evermore!

Far away Alice is
Looking for Vince

All His night mares
And the chicken.
Vince was into Earwigs
Even more Spiders
Call him Alice
He's already inside Her.

Chorus:
Mommy, where's Daddy?
He's been gone so long!
Do you think
He'll ever come home?
Daddy Looks like an Artist,
Sounds like a Hun,
Shits like an Animal;
Licks his lips when done.

Back to Mono

Back to Mono was a box set compilation of Phil Spector's recorded works in the Sixties, starting from his time performing with group, The Teddy Bears, in 1958. ABKCO released the compilation in 1991. By then Spector was long gone from producing and recording, but he was remembered because of his successful work and his original 'Wall of Sound'.

Spector was also remembered as a gun carrying lunatic who would threaten girlfriends and wives with his weapons, as well as many Recording Artists, according to many of them. He married Veronica Bennett, by then known as Ronny Spector, who claims he threatened her with guns repeatedly until she left him. Shades of Hunter S.!

By 1975 Spector had produced eighteen top ten hits on the US Top Ten Chart for many Artists, including the Beatles. Phil actually produced Harrison's 'My Sweet Lord'!!! In 1989 he was inducted into the Rock and Roll Hall of Fame, and in 1997 he was inducted into the Songwriters Hall of Fame. In 1994, Rolling Stone Mag ranked Spector number sixty-three on their list of the hundred Greatest Artists of all time. According to IBM, the song Spector produced, 'You've Lost that Loving Feeling', is the song that received the most US airplay in the Twentieth Century.

But Spector is not remembered for any of these grand accomplishments. In 2003 actress wanna-be Lana Clarkson was reported to have shot herself in Phil's house, but Phil was charged with her 'murder'. I do not believe he did it, because first he had no reason whatsoever to do it. Second, he had almost virtually no blood on him or his white suit afterward. Third, Phil Spector was just a despised man, and his public image had much to do with his brutal sentencing in 2009. He has served ten of a nineteen year sentence, and can be out on parole in 2025.

The Justice System did not allow his lawyer to enact a shooting in the Court Room. That would definitely have shown he could not have performed shooting Lana in her mouth without being virtually painted with her blood. Why?

Well... Why did O.J. get off when he was so obviously guilty? Snoop Dog was acquitted from Philip Woldemariam's shooting. R. Kelly's child pornography case was overturned despite overwhelming evidence against him. Du Pont family fortune heir, Robert H. Richards 1V, was sentenced to a mere fourth degree rape plea for allegedly repeatedly raping his five year daughter. Kobe Bryant was acquitted for an alleged violent rape in 2003, in which he was allowed to pay her off. In 2001, Robert Blake was acquitted for the charge of *possibly* having his wife shot to death while she was waiting in their car. Despite fourteen counts of child molestation, Michael Jackson, twice in ten years, walked. It cost him millions to stay free, despite showing *'pornographs'* to young boys who claimed Jackson had drugged and molested them, several times.

Now it seems that for some reason, Spector's money was no good for a corrupt Justice System with too many strange acquittals for rich celebrities to list here. He was just a very unpopular human being. Phil's case showed volumes of doubt towards his guilt compared to any of these examples I listed off the top of my head. Phil Spector was a Jew from the Bronx. Was that a factor? Who knows? Spector's case is enough to make me want to scream, "Bring Phil Spector back from hell!!!"

<u>Back to Mono;</u>

Back to Mono
One of a Kind
Past is Modern
Hear what ya find.
Twist and Shout
Heart Break Hotel
Bring Phil Spector
Back from hell.

Walls to climb
Rubble on the floor
Bring a 45
Studios a war.
Mono to Mono
Blue on Blue
Man here comes
The Wrecking Crew.

Chorus:
American Producer
Lana Clarkson's seducer
Long and Winding Road

Ronny Spector's Loser.
Fab Five Fraught
A Sonic Sound Machine
Dubbed by Tom Wolfe
First Tycoon of Teen.

Brute from the Bronx
Just a Teddy Bear
To Know Him is to Love Him
When you're not too scared.
That Loving Feeling lost
Another Ronette tossed
Wagnerian Wizard
At such a cost!

Power to the People
Movin' on
Ladies' Man's Dead next
Killed Cohen's songs.
Dee Ramone
Another hostage
Another session
Another bandage.

Chorus:
Phil Harvey broke the Crystals
Dark smiles with polished pistols
Lucky 13 Black Pearl
Super hits seem superficial.
Let it Be, Instant Karma
My Sweet Lord belated Dharma
In the end All Things Must Pass
Troubles double now en masse.

Silence is easy
But not for Phil
Hired and fired
Come backs and pills.
When ya defend
Dudes like Ike
Be My Baby don't
Fit in so nice.

Kiss the gun
And make her cry
Superior Court;
All bout lies.
We'll never know
Who what or why
It's too River Deep
Mountain High.

Chorus:

American Producer
Lana Clarkson's seducer
Long and Winding Road
Ronny Spector's Loser.
Fab Five Fraught
A Sonic Sound Machine
Dubbed by Tom Wolfe
First Tycoon of Teen.

Back to Mono
One of a Kind
Past is Modern
Hear what ya find.
Twist and Shout
Heart Break Hotel

Bring Phil Spector
Back from hell!!!

Spit Out My Seed

I was having a conversation with a lady on the beach one day, whom I knew had just left her husband of over ten years. She was telling me the story of her separation, and I reminded her at least that they had no children, so that made it possible to start over much easier than if it had of been otherwise. She agreed, and in her anger and disgust, she claimed she was glad to have 'spit out his unholy seed'. I gave her a look of some kind of recognition, and she immediately exclaimed, "You're gonna write a song about this, aren't you?"

I answered her that the phrase, "Spit out his seed" was a classic, and I could not resist. I immediately started scribbling lines down, and after she came out of the water, she was interested in what I had written. She seemed confused that I had changed things around where I was saying to 'spit out my seed', as opposed to her approach of 'spitting out his seed'. We both laughed when we considered her *confusion*. I told her I was sympathetic for her pains, but when a line like this presented itself, I had to react.

I sang it to her and she started strumming along on her guitar diligently. A week later I recorded it with Amy. When we sat down at the Grand Piano together I sang much of the song to her. She grinned but did not ask any questions about the obviously obtuse lyrics. Amy is a professional, and she never gets in the way of my beguiling bullets. I told her it was just tongue-in-cheek, and we recorded ...

Spit Out My Seed;

Feed my illusions
With your selfie love
Laugh as I crawl
Perched from up above.
Rip my ego
Make me bleed
Take me now
Spit out my seed.

Empty my universe
Turn off the T.V.
Throw me at the sky
Stomp me if I plea.
Starve my illusions
Gimme your blood
Bury me deep
Beneath your Avon Mud.

Chorus:
I don't care
If I shrivel and die
I don't give a fuck
Who ya crucify.
Rip my ego
Make me bleed
Take me now
Spit out my seed.

Distort everything
That I do and say
No one likes the truth
Anyway.
Swingin' that ax

Crossin' that line
Careful what ya wish for
Might be what you find.

Kick me while I'm down
Keep yourself amused
Everything I have's
Creepy, old and used.
So predictable
Time for a change
Don't analyze
I know I'm strange.

Chorus:
I don't care
If I shrivel and die
I don't give a fuck
Who ya crucify.
Rip my ego
Make me bleed
Take me now
Spit out my seed.

Chain me to the sun
Watch me peel and flame
Like another day in hell
'Cept I got no shame.
Feed the hungry
'fore I eat 'em all
Army the unlaid
All goin' awol.

Feed my illusions
With cement, clay and glass
Don't forget dessert

Sautéed in high test gas.
Reality's
Far away
So what's the fuckin' norm
When we're all on display.

Chorus: I don't care
If I shrivel and die
I don't give a fuck
Who ya crucify.
Rip my ego
Make me bleed
Take me now
Spit out my seed.

Make me hurt
Watch my pain
When ya get bored
Do it again.
Chokin' on the ashes
Spittin' out the rain
Drownin' on the sidewalk
Floatin' down the drain.

Feed my illusions
Dark carnal knowledge
Not the blue collar crap
Crammed down your throats in college.
Shiverin' in the night
Waitin' to be saved
Waitin' patiently in line
Eyes glazed over so depraved.

Chorus:
I don't care

John Leo Organ

If I shrivel and die
I don't give a fuck
Who ya crucify.
Rip my ego
Make me bleed
Take me now
Spit out my seed.

Rip my ego
Make me bleed
Take me now
Spit out my seed.

Take me now
Spit out my seed.

Chapter 33
Living On the
Lake in 2020

Well, I just woke up to 2020, After Death. The Lake is frozen yet the birds fly way up high regardless. God we humans are so fragile! Yet we ski down mountains, and travel far beyond the speed of sound and light visiting distant universes in the Milky Way, while still planning to go Beyond. How do we do it?

All I can reason is that the atoms and molecules, drifting in Space of the Cosmos, all floated together at the same time as the planets aligned, and an Astronomical Phenomenon of Interest became involved with, and interacted upon, Celestial Objects, triggering Cyclical Phases of the Moon, Solar and Lunar Eclipses, Transits and Occultations, Planetary Oppositions and Conjunctions, Meteor Showers, Comet Flybys… and Man!! Today, on the first of January, the Moon is in Pisces Trine Mars in Scorpio, at 6:43 Post Meridiem. And the wind howls up from the numb lake to chill my windowpane…!

I wrote like mad last year; perhaps writing about my madness. Living on the Lake gives a perspective of being in the front row of the best Picture playing in Town. There's a black Momma Bear with two Cubs just down the rocky forest from my Cabin. A curve beyond that, following the Lake, is a large rafter of turkeys. I see them every time I go out.

A few lake bends further there is a herd of Odocoileus Virginianus; aka white tailed Deer. They have an area staked out where they cross the road early every morning, to have their morning drink on the Lake. There are usually a dozen of them hiding around the curve, but no one has ever collided with them. It's an understood thing; they will be there every day, because like us, they drink every day, at the same early time. Maybe they brush their teeth, for a refreshed attitude and an enlightened prospect of a new day. Perhaps this has been going on since the Dawn of the First Light, or at least before this intrusion of an inroad arose, surely.

I'm intrigued, and absorbed, at what obligations and under-takings the Gods have ready for me in this coming decade. Maybe I am here purifying my soul while preparing for my last *one night stand*. I'll soon be heading to Grant Studio for my next recording session. I hope the Gods and Amy are as intrigued and absorbed as I am with my assembly of songs for our next magical, maniacal, musical call of duty. I've got to start giggin' more, and I will! I've got to get a new Band.

It's January and I hear there is a new corona virus emanating from China. Let's hope our western egos don't get in the way of nipping this in the bud...

I have no New Year's Resolutions, other than to just keep on keeping on. Maybe read more R. Crumb comic books. OK I resolve to do more boating this summer. But alas, whenever I get near the water, it opens the damn dams in my mind, and I resort to writing most of my time upon the reservoir. I will visit a new Friend in Perry Sound, when the ice and snow retreat. I love Perry Sound. I used to attend the West Parry Sound District Museum, on Tower Hill, when I was being trained to operate Ontario Museums by the OMA. Tower Hill is where Bobby Orr came from; that is, his parents lived on 'The Tower' until Bobby bought them a new house.

Bobby signed a 'C' Form with the Boston Bruins, which at the time meant he was a Bruin for life. My Bro Paul used to work at the Loblaw Store in the Sound, where Bobby's brother worked also. Paul says he was invited up to the house a couple times. There was a stream that went through their kitchen, every thaw. Apparently Paul offered to fix it, but Bobby's father, Doug said,

"Ah, it's always been that way ... no need to fix it ... it'll fix itself in a week." Like a true profit!

But I digress. This is about Life on the Lake, 2020 style. Living in the North turns the clock and calendar back to where ever ya want to go. And when done, you can come back to 2020 for a quick hot meal, and the game at seven on satellite. It's all good!

I'm headin' down to the Lake right now, with a joint for the journey and a few swigs of Forty Creek to keep me warm. Until I get back, I'll leave you with this thought I jotted down last time I was basking in the Basin. See ya later! Be Water!

<u>Living with the Lake</u>

No matter how many souls
You try to save,
Remember there's two sides
To every wave.
Those long lazy clouds,
Seem so Southern, seem so proud,
Skies of blue with eyes equipped
To misbehave!

Chorus:
Life exposed on the shore,
Creativity in every pore,
Rocks battle sand to becme
What was before!
Driftwood adorns the beach,
Guarding memories out of reach,
Boats sail by and wonder
What it all is for.

But long lazy clouds,
Sometimes loud behind it's shroud,
Brings out the storm the sky
Lingers to absorb.
A sky black and blue with strife
Cuts through seasons like a knife,
Reflect the faces of lunar
Passing orbs.

Chorus:
Life exposed on the shore,
Creativity in every pore,
Rocks battle sand to become
What was before!
Driftwood adorns the beach,
Guarding memories out of reach,
Boats sail by and wonder
What it all is for.

Those stories that go on
In poetry or songs,
They write about themselves
But it's really me.
Every blues every fight
They all come out at night,
'Bout ego and pussy but
'member 'bout bein' free?

Chorus:
Life exposed on the shore,
Creativity in every pore,
Rocks battle sand to become
What was before!
Driftwood adorns the beach,

Guarding memories out of reach,
Boats sail by and wonder
What it all is for.

Count your pennies, count your strife
Count 'em all with a switch blade knife,
When you're done do it again
The next day.
Don't be passive, plan an attack
Hell ya can't even afford some crack,
Start with the first step
Read Lao Zeus 'The Way.'

Chorus:
Life exposed on the shore,
Creativity in every pore,
Rocks battle sand to become
What was before!
Driftwood adorns the beach,
Guarding memories out of reach,
Boats sail by and wonder
What it all is for.

Choose a Path you'll be fine
Don't rent out your mind,
How's that goin'
You've been there before.
You've slept on the shore
In the end it's just a bore,
Third world countries know
You're just a hoar.

Chorus:
Life exposed on the shore,
Creativity in every pore,

Rocks battle sand to become
What was before!
Driftwood adorns the beach,
Guarding memories out of reach,
Boats sail by and wonder
What it all is for.

No matter how many souls
You try to save,
Remember there's two sides
To every wave.
Those long lazy clouds
Seem so Southern, seem so proud,
Skies of blue with eyes equipped
To misbehave ...

Printed in Canada